FLY FISHING STRATEGY

BOOKS BY DOUG SWISHER AND CARL RICHARDS

Selective Trout
Fly Fishing Strategy

FLY FISHING STRATEGY

DOUG SWISHER AND CARL RICHARDS

Illustrated by Dave Whitlock

NLB

NICK LYONS BOOKS

WINCHESTER PRESS

We are particularly grateful to René Harrop, the superb flytier from St. Anthony, Idaho, for supplying the flies representing the stillborn duns, the Double-wing No-Hackle, and other patterns, and to Mike Lawson and Bob Marvin for supplying other valuable patterns illustrated and described in this book.

A portion of this book appeared first in *Fly Fisherman* magazine.

Published and distributed by
WINCHESTER PRESS
New Century Publishers
220 Old New Brunswick Road
Piscataway, New Jersey 08854

Produced by
NICK LYONS BOOKS
31 West 21st Street
New York, New York 10010

PRINTED IN THE UNITED STATES OF AMERICA
10 9 8 7 6 5 4 3 2

Designed by Deborah Daly

Library of Congress Cataloging in Publication Data

Swisher, Doug.
   Fly fishing strategy.

Included index.
   1. Fly fishing.   I. Richards, Carl, 1933-
joint author.   II. Title.
SH456.S9   799.1'2   84-063022
ISBN: 0-8329-0379-5

CONTENTS

FLY FISHING STRATEGY

INTRODUCTION

WE ONCE MADE THIS STATEMENT: "The single most overriding problem the fly fisherman must deal with is procuring an artificial fly that will gull the trout into thinking it is a natural insect." Much later we discovered this statement to be only half true. For once the fly fisherman procures the right fly at the right time, he must also be able to present it properly—that is, in the same way a natural insect would act in a natural environment. Apparently this is not so easy to accomplish as we once assumed. At the time we took this very important part of fly fishing for granted. We both had been fly fishing for over thirty years and, mostly by trial and error and long experience, proper tactics and presentation had become almost instinctive.

Our first study, a search for truly effective patterns, was extraordinarily well received. Many of the patterns, tying techniques, and materials recommended in *Selective Trout* have been written about, used, and sold by mail-order houses and tackle companies. Some of these people changed the names of our patterns a little but since imitation is the sincerest form of flattery, we have no real complaint.

Since the flies do work extremely well, we merely assumed that all we needed to do was inform any angler which fly to use at a certain time and that person literally could not help but take fish. Unfortunately, it did not work out quite that way. One particular fishing trip in 1969 is a perfect illustration of what can happen when an angler

1

has exactly the right fly but does not know what to do with it. It all began some years ago when the president of a large Chicago corporation wrote and offered us a large fee if we would fish with him and teach him our methods. Since we were not in the guiding business, we declined the fee but we did invite him to join us when we would be on the river anyway. He accepted, met us in Grand Rapids, and we all drove to the legendary Au Sable River where we had booked rooms at the famous Au Sable Lodge.

It was late July and the peak of the *Tricorythodes* hatch was in progress. Every morning without fail, trout by the hundreds fed on tiny #28 duns and spinners. Arising at first light, we proceeded to "Louie's Landing" on the main stream, an area prolific in the micro duns of *Tricorythodes*. We then outfitted this very likeable millionaire with correct patterns and leaders for the rise and permitted him to fish ahead of us so he got first crack at the feeding fish.

This man was not a beginner; he had fished all over the world and seemed to cast fairly well, at least for short distances. Frankly, we were trying to prove to him how effective our #28 White Black Hen Spinners were during this rise and we fully expected him to do very well indeed. Even though he was casting for two hours over hundreds of eagerly rising fish, he caught no trout, period! Obviously, neither he nor we would have believed such a thing could have happened. At the very least, we thought he would land six or seven good fish. He never even got a strike. This was a real shocker. It proved that something else was needed besides an effective pattern. That something else turned out to be presentation.

Presentation can encompass many things. Even though wading is part of presentation, basically it boils down to good casting, especially some form of pinpoint slack-line casting to prevent drag. In the course of conducting fly fishing schools during the next few years, we learned that very few anglers were really good casters. Almost none had a mastery of curve casts. A well-rounded fly caster *must* be able to cast both wide and tight loops on command, and be able to cast a considerable distance, 70 to 80 feet, with very little effort. The ability to cast right- and left-hand curves and other types of slack-line casts, is essential. The angler who is incapable of presenting a fly correctly in any and all situations will take fewer fish than he might otherwise.

That was our corporation president's problem. He did not have pinpoint accuracy nor could he prevent drag; he just could not present the fly well. Presentation and technique are clearly as important as effective patterns. One will not work without the other and a mastery of both is essential to be a truly effective fly fisherman. In the past few seasons we have, time and time again, proved to ourselves that the best pattern in the world won't work if you can't cast, nor will the most delicate, pinpoint curve be effective if the flies are not realistic. To be a complete fly fisherman, one must know both natural and artificial flies and be able to present flies in a way that will fool the trout into thinking the artificial is not attached to a leader.

Fly Fishing Strategy takes up where *Selective Trout* left off. It explains in detail our techniques for realistic presentation in both moving and still water. It presents proved tactics for times when trout are rising and not rising, plus new pattern developments that are really effective in tough situations.

describes a circular path, more power is applied in directions other than the aimed direction of the cast. These statements stem from the fact that the line tends to flow tangentially or at a right angle from the movement of the rod tip. Therefore, an arcing or circular motion dissipates power in a multitude of tangents and varying directions,

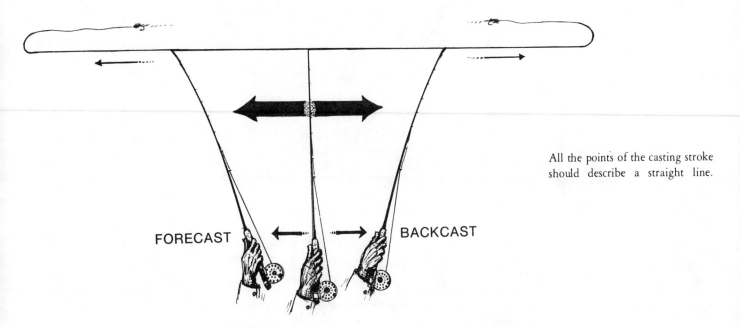

FORECAST   BACKCAST

All the points of the casting stroke should describe a straight line.

while a straight-line motion concentrates all the power in one direction and efficiently deploys the line toward the target.

Casting with the entire arm and shoulder is not only the most efficient method, but also the most practical. Unlike the locked-elbow method, it is a natural motion, somewhat like throwing a baseball or football. It's also less tiring. The various wrist, arm, shoulder, and body muscles are smoothly blended into one fluid motion, causing little strain on any individual muscles. This is important when an angler spends long periods of time on the stream.

In fly casting, the path created by the fly line as it rolls out from the rod tip is called the loop. This configuration looks basically like a candy cane lying on its side, first tilted one way as the backcast forms and then the opposite way as the forecast is formed. The ability to regulate its size, exact shape, and direction is known as "loop control." To become a really good fly caster, this skill must be developed until it becomes instinctive.

Control of the loop size is one of the most important factors in proficient casting. The distance between its upper and lower portions determine whether the loop is "tight" or "wide."

If this distance is in the 1- to 2-foot range, the loop is considered relatively tight. A 5- or 6-foot loop would be quite wide. For most situations, a tight loop is much more desirable, mainly because it has less air resistance. In fact, a very wide loop has so much air resistance that it will often collapse before it can straighten. The inability to cast a tight loop is why so many anglers have trouble with collapsing leaders, even in

Casting with entire arm and shoulder is a natural and efficient motion, very much like throwing a football; every motion contributes to the cast.

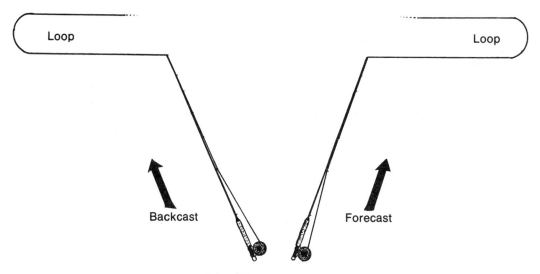

The perfect loop configuration.

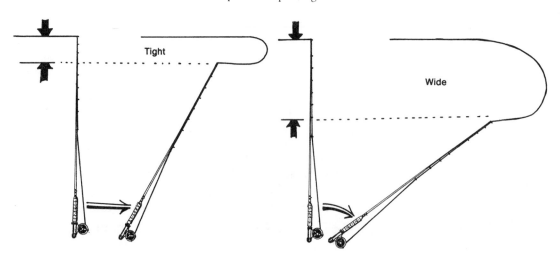

Wide loops are the result of "arcing" the rod tip; the bigger the arc, the wider the loops will be—and the shorter the cast.

light wind. A basic casting principle is that the tighter the loop the farther the line will go with the same amount of effort.

The most practical method of forming a tight loop, at least for the novice and intermediate caster, is to develop a casting stroke that moves the rod tip in as straight a line as possible. This technique, which utilizes an alternating push-pull movement of the entire rod, produces a tight, efficient loop that is one of the trademarks of a good fly caster.

Another advantage of the tight loop is that the power of the cast is aimed in the right direction—*toward the target*. The energy applied to every cast can be broken down into two types, that applied in the horizontal direction and that applied in the vertical direction. Our target is normally located in a horizontal direction so it makes sense that we direct most of our casting power parallel to the water's surface, or horizontally. Power applied in the vertical direction merely widens the loop, which in turn creates more wind resistance; it also dissipates energy that could otherwise be applied in the horizontal plane. Let's direct as much of the energy of the cast as possible toward the target rather than wasting too great a percentage on wide loops.

For most casting situations, loops that are tight, accurate, and dynamic are formed by training the hand to travel in a *straight* line *directly at the target*. If we power the hand straight to the target, the rod tip will follow.

As mentioned, the general shape of the loop is that of a candy cane. Perfect loop shape, the configuration we all strive for but rarely throw, is a candy cane with the top and bottom portions parallel and the front rounded. However, more often than not, most fly casters throw some version of either an *open loop* or a *closed loop*. The open loop is characterized by the top portion of the candy cane angling up and away from the bottom portion. This is typically a wide, nonfouling loop, which has the advantage of reducing tangles and "wind knots" but, unfortunately, has excessive wind resistance that results in poor turnover. Most beginners are plagued by the open loop because they allow their rod tip to scribe too large an arc.

The closed loop is quite a common sight to the average angler. It appears most often when one is trying to reach out a little farther than he can and is most severe when his backcast is excessively high. This loop configuration, sometimes called the "tailing loop," is distinguished by the top portion of the candy cane, angling down toward, and often falling below, the bottom portion. This is the loop that has us "talking to ourselves" at the end of a tough day on the stream. It is responsible for tangled lines, snarled leaders, and broken hooks. These so-called "wind knots" have caused jangled nerves, pierced earlobes, smashed rods, and other forms of streamside violence. The closed loop is one of the most common problems we encounter in our fishing schools and clinics across the country. In fact, we find that at least 80 percent of all fly casters throw some form of a tailing loop. This obviously affects their efficiency and enjoyment of the sport.

Loop shape is directly controlled by the third loop characteristic, *direction*. By loop direction, we mean the relationship, or angulation, between the forecast and backcast. The ideal relationship, and a basic casting principle, is that the backcast and forecast should be in direct line with each other. In other words, they should be separated by 180°. Any casting plane can be used, parallel to the water's surface, tilted up or tilted down, just as long as both loops are thrown in a straight line. A perfect candy cane, top portion parallel to the bottom, is possible only when this straight-line relationship is created.

Perfect Loop

Open Loop

Closed Loop

Tight accurate loops are best formed by powering the hand directly toward the target; the rod tip will follow.

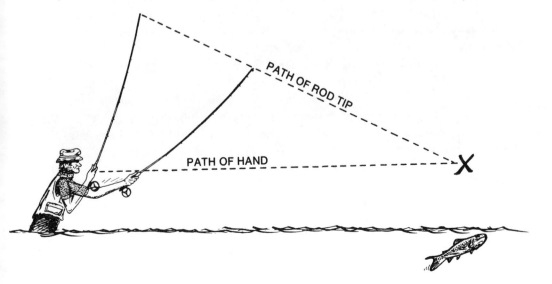

PATH OF ROD TIP

PATH OF HAND   X

A very wide, tailing loop

A medium-wide, well-shaped loop

A tight, tailing loop

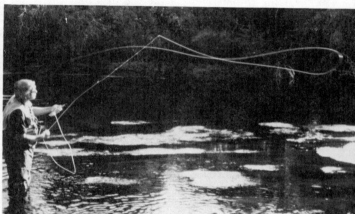

A tight loop, slightly tailing

When front and back loops are separated by *more than 180°*, the resulting candy canes are open. In the stream this situation normally occurs when the angler allows his backcast to fall under the horizontal plane, often slapping the water behind him. This condition is magnified even more when both forecast and backcast are aimed so low that they hit the water's surface, especially on very short casts. Basically, the greater the amount of "angle overthrow" on 180°, the greater the tendency to throw open loops. For example, if our candy canes are separated by 181°, we can barely detect the slight opening effect; however, if they are opposed by 200°, the top portion of the candy cane will be angled up steeply from the bottom.

When front and back loops are separated by *less than 180°*, the resulting candy canes are *closed*. This condition is common to fly casters who have developed the superhigh backcast and to anglers who attempt to throw farther than their ability allows. For some strange reason, certainly unknown to us, most fly-casting instructors and fly-fishing schools across the country advocate and teach this excessively elevated backcast. Possibly they are convinced that some object, such as a bush, or small tree or an ugly grizzly bear, is always positioned directly in the path of the fly fisherman's

8

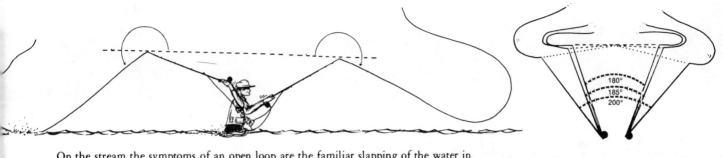

On the stream the symptoms of an open loop are the familiar slapping of the water in front and in back of the caster. The greater the amount of angle "overthrow," the greater the tendency to throw open loops.

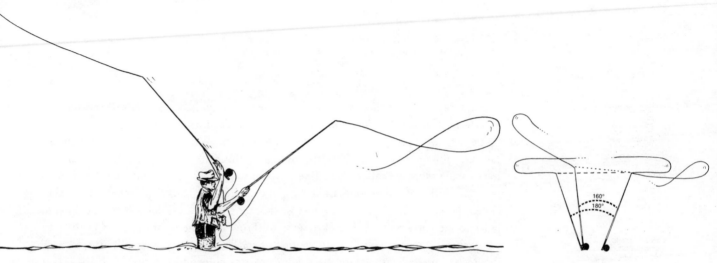

A closed loop on the stream usually results from attempting to throw a high backcast. If the casts are separated by less than 180° an angle "underthrow" results.

back loop. Whatever the reason, they spend many hours of valuable instruction time making sure that each student hurls his line high to the heavens. Instead, emphasis should be put on the fact that loops must be thrown in a straight line.

Obviously, the backcast will be fairly high if a long rod is used to throw at a target only a short distance away, say 15 or 20 feet. But even in this situation where the back loop must be aimed at a high angle, the basic straight-line principle should be stressed rather than high backcast. Actually, the correct angle of backcast can be figured by drawing an imaginary straight line from the target through the rod tip. The target, of course, is normally a point 2 to 4 feet above the water's surface. In order to facilitate the casts required for effective presentation, the knowledgeable angler cants his rod somewhere between 45° and horizontal. This means the rod tip is usually about the same distance from the water as the target, generally 2 to 4 feet, sometimes slightly higher. As you can see, under these conditions, a straight line drawn from the target through the rod tip falls in a plane that seldom varies more than 10° from horizontal.

Next time you visit your favorite stream, take a few minutes and observe other fly casters. Notice the angles at which they cast and the direction of their backcast in relationship to the direction of their forecast. In most cases, you'll undoubtedly see casting planes tilted too far forward and an abundance of tailing loops.

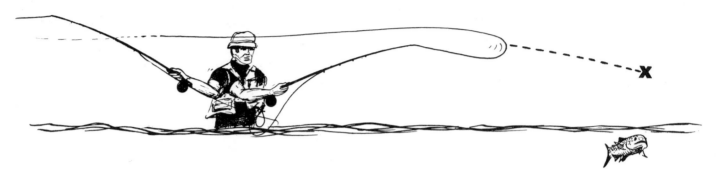

The correct angle of backcast can be figured by drawing an imaginary line from the target through the rod tip.

Some casters argue that they can throw the superhigh backcast and still end up with a perfect, or at least a nontailing loop in front. Indeed, this is true. Anyone can do it by *waiting until the back loop falls* far enough to be in line with the forecast. Unfortunately, this procedure destroys the timing of the cast. Waiting for gravity to take over creates what we call a "dead line," which has lost its power and zing. In order to make an efficient, tight-loop front cast, the angler must take advantage of a well-aimed, properly timed, dynamic backcast. Rather than waiting for a high rear loop to fall into the correct plane, it makes sense to throw it in the right direction in the first place, thereby making ultimate usage of this rod-loading force. Actually, the forecast should be initiated just before the candy cane straightens to the rear. It is important that we use this force to "cock and lever," thus ensuring a powerful forecast.

Another basic casting principle, then, is that the greater the amount of "angle underthrow" on 180°—we call it cheating on 180°—the greater the tendency to throw closed, or tailing loops. If, for example, our loops are separated by 179°, we can hardly see the slight closing effect, but if they are slanted only 150° apart, a definite tail will be seen.

A really good fly caster has the ability to demonstrate loop control. This is the ability to throw tight loops, wide loops, perfect loops, open loops, and closed loops on command, all at any plane of casting, tilted up, tilted down, or level. In fact, this is without a doubt the best exercise for casting improvement. Start with tight and wide loops, throwing several of each and then mixing up the sequence. Shout out the commands, "Wide loop front," "Tight loop rear," "Tight loop front," "Wide loop rear," and immediately follow through with the movements. Practice until you can do them quickly, smoothly, and without mistakes for several minutes. Use varying lengths of line, say 15 to 40 feet, and cast at varying degrees of cant, from horizontal to vertical angulation of the rod. Follow the same routine in practicing loop shape and direction control.

Remember that loop direction controls loop shape. To throw perfectly shaped loops, be sure you carefully *aim* both the front loop and the back loop in directions that are opposed by 180°. *Aiming* is the important part of this exercise. One of the most critical aspects of becoming a good fly caster is learning to *aim each and every loop at a*

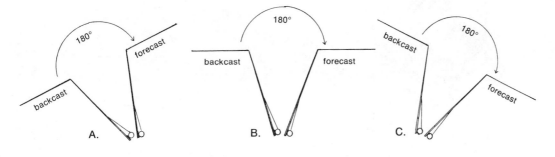

Horizontal Ground Plane

A. High Forecast-Low Backcast   B. Level Fore- and Backcasts   C. Low Forecast-High Backcast

You can learn to throw a perfect loop in any plane. As long as the loops are not separated by more than 180°, the line will travel at maximum efficiency.

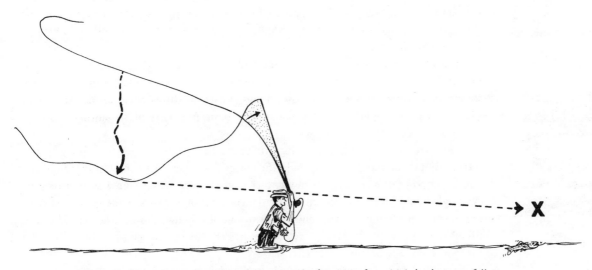

Make full use of the rod's loading force instead of waiting for a high backcast to fall to the horizontal plane.

Good timing will cock the line, assuring a powerful forecast. With the loop on the right plane, you can load the rod at the right moment, just before the "candy cane" straightens out.

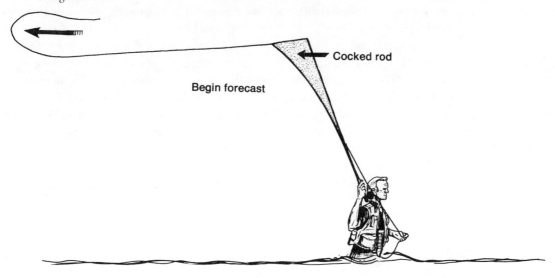

Cocked rod

Begin forecast

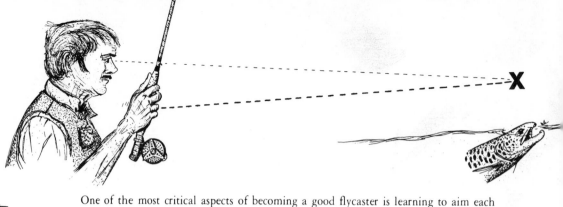

One of the most critical aspects of becoming a good flycaster is learning to aim each and every loop at a target, consciously coordinating eye and hand movements.

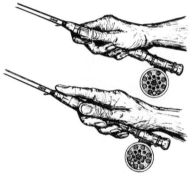

The thumb on top, 180° from the reel.

The "free wrist" grip (*above*) allows the angler to angle overthrow; the index finger on top is not as powerful a grip as the thumb-on-top.

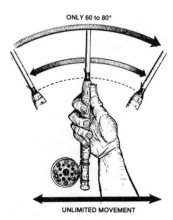

The major advantage of the thumb-on-top grip for the intermediate and novice caster is that it restricts wrist movement and facilitates the movement of the rest of the arm.

target. The targets can be real or imaginary, but you should always have a fixed, visual reference point and direct every forecast and every backcast at the target. Accuracy is developed by consciously coordinating hand movements and eye focus. Learn to drive your hand straight to the target. It is similar to shooting a handgun and, because it keeps the hand high, can be especially helpful in keeping the beginner's backcast off the water. (Though we have always taught students to aim their loops, Pete Merrill of Birmingham, Michigan, gave us the helpful handgun analogy.)

Most of the time spent on loop shape and direction exercises should be utilized to master loops that are perfect, or nearly perfect, in shape. Some portion, however, should be devoted to open and closed loops. Learn to throw them all on command. Only then do you completely understand the basic principles of fly casting and only then can you correct your mistakes.

Before attempting the basic casting stroke, the fly caster must learn proper grip and stance. By far the most practical and efficient grip is where the thumb is on top of the handle, opposite the reel. It is similar to that used when picking up a satchel or suitcase and should be very firm. Squeezing the cork not only develops the important casting muscles in the hand, wrist, and forearm, but also helps dampen the rod. With the thumb on top, 180° from the reel, more power and control can be applied on the forecast, especially on the final delivery.

Two other grips, thumb on the side and index finger on top, have gained some popularity but are not nearly as effective as thumb on top. The thumb on the side, sometimes known as the "free wrist" grip, is not well suited to the beginning or intermediate fly caster, mainly because it allows the wrist more freedom in bending. One of the major faults of most new anglers is the inability to stop their rods soon enough on the backcast. With the thumb on top of the cork there is more resistance to the wrist movement than there is with the thumb on the side. The free wrist grip should be used only by anglers who really understand fly casting and know how to put it to good use. For certain long-distance situations it is useful in maintaining proper rod tip travel and loop control.

Some anglers say that they display much better accuracy with their index finger on top of the cork. Pointing the finger at the target supposedly improves their marksmanship. Frankly, you can be just as accurate, and probably more so, with the thumb on top of the rod and you can certainly throw a lot farther. The index finger simply does not have as much power as the thumb, so it is useless for long-distance casting situations. Also, it is a rather awkward, inefficient grip for some of the sidearm and backhanded casts that are so necessary for good presentation.

Though the stance we use may not seem critical, it is important to the development of proper casting technique. Actually, it is possible to deliver a fly to the target with a variety of stances. We can look squarely ahead with shoulders at right angles to the direction of cast or we can turn to the right or left and operate with at least a fair amount of efficiency. The best stance, and the one we should always use for practice, enables us to look easily back over our casting shoulder. For a right-handed caster, this means turning to the right so that the hips and shoulders are angled about 30° to the left of the casting direction. This is only an approximation and varies with each individual. Some people stand with hips and shoulder almost parallel to the direction of cast while others are almost at right angles. We find the 30° mark about right, allowing good visibility to the rear but not restricting the casting stroke.

The reason, of course, for looking over your shoulder is to obtain a good view of the backcast. How can we expect to improve something we can't see? If we want to develop a good casting technique we must be able to see both forecast and backcast. The loops we throw are highly visual and must be observed closely so that they can be corrected.

We find that few fly casters take the effort to look back over their shoulders. This habit obviously stems from the fact that, while on the stream, most of the action is taking place in front of the fisherman. But fully half of our casting is done behind us. Each forecast is almost always preceded by a backcast. For this reason alone, it is important that we learn to observe and evaluate our back loops. Added to this is the fact that it is difficult to make a good forward cast without first having made a good backcast. If the rear loop is tight, well shaped, and thrown with gusto, about all you have to do is point the rod to get a good forward cast. In other words, if you can't straighten it to the rear you'll have trouble straightening it out front. On the other hand, a wide, misdirected backcast usually results in a wobbly, impotent forecast.

The casting field is where we must learn to observe our loops, both front and back. Casting improvement on the stream is difficult and slow. There are simply too many other problems to contend with during the heat of battle. Discovering the hatch, identifying the species, deciding which stage is important, selecting the right fly, changing tippets, swatting mosquitoes, and fighting off canoes are only a few of the problems that divide the angler's attention. If you can solve your casting problems ahead of time, on the casting field, you are far better off than trying to learn everything at streamside.

Develop the habit, on the casting field, of always twisting your neck back and forth

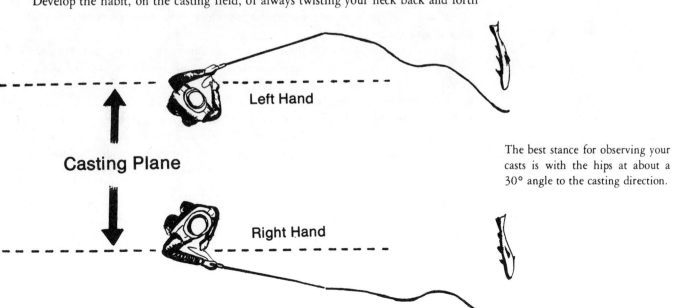

Casting Plane

Left Hand

Right Hand

The best stance for observing your casts is with the hips at about a 30° angle to the casting direction.

on *every* casting stroke, much like watching a tennis or Ping-Pong match. This may seem like a lot of effort at first but, like everything else, you'll quickly adjust and it will become an automatic part of your training. Even on the stream, try to stand so you can look back, at least every few casts, to see what's going on behind you. Acquire this habit and you'll be amazed at the dividends it will pay.

Now we are ready for the real nitty gritty of fly casting. Along with the proper grip and correct stance, let's add the hand and arm movements. The blend of these movements is what we call the "Basic Casting Stroke." Whether you're false casting, picking up from the water, throwing for distance, casting side-arm or backhanded, this fundamental maneuver will be employed. Though the basic stroke is uncomplicated, it is imperative that you learn it well. This requires understanding and practice; there are no magical shortcuts.

When illustrated either on paper or by actual demonstration, the basic casting stroke seems so simple that anyone could do it immediately. But this is where many get into trouble. Even though the individual movements are easy to learn, it takes practice to blend them together so that the entire stroke is smooth and fluid. The whole problem is timing and speed. With slow motion, it takes only a few minutes to learn the fundamental hand and arm maneuvers. Impulses from the brain can trigger crisp, clear-cut muscle response when working at this snail's pace. Unfortunately, timing must be speeded up immensely when the transition is made from classroom to casting field. At the speed required to keep a real fly line in the air, it is much more difficult for the hand and arm to coordinate with the mind. To bridge this gap, one must "dry run" the basic casting stroke, starting with slow motion and gradually building the tempo up to normal casting speed. This dry-run period varies with the individual. Many, especially those with good reflexes and open minds, are ready for the casting field in a matter of minutes, while others, usually those with habits that must be broken or those with closed minds, may require several days or even weeks.

We recommend that initial practice of the basic casting stroke be done using only the butt section of the fly rod. This eliminates the willowy movements of the tip section, which might prove distracting to the beginner. If a rod is not available, use an object such as a ruler, hammer, or pencil—even your bare hand will do. Grasp the rod with the proper suitcase-type grip, thumb on top of the cork, and squeeze firmly. Make a tight fist with thumb on top if you're using your bare hand. Stand a little sideways so you can look over your casting shoulder. Now we're ready to perform the basic casting stroke.

Extend the casting hand a full arm's length in the direction of the cast, keeping the hand at shoulder level, thumb on top of the cork and the rod butt aimed at eleven o'clock. This is the starting position. From it, we'll initiate the backcast, which is the first half of the total casting stroke.

Pull the rod toward your shoulder in a perfectly straight line, parallel to the ground, keeping the rod at eleven o'clock. This is a very slow, deliberate movement. When your hand is approximately six inches in front of your shoulder, suddenly, and with all the power in your wrist, angulate the rod back to one o'clock. This completes the backcast.

After a two- or three-second pause, the time it takes for the back loop to straighten, reverse the procedure by pushing the rod forward, maintaining the one o'clock position. This also is a slow, deliberate movement. When the arm is almost fully extend-

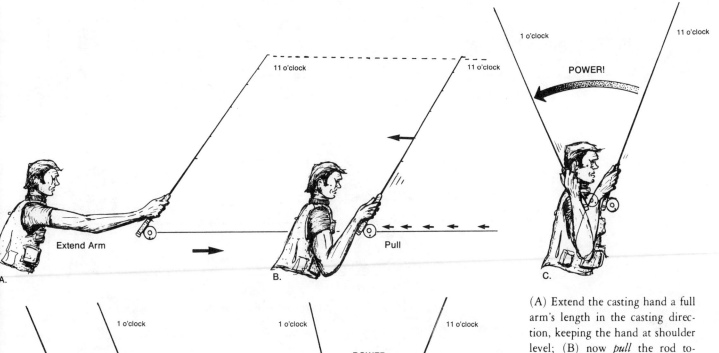

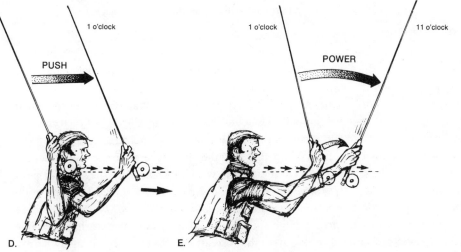

(A) Extend the casting hand a full arm's length in the casting direction, keeping the hand at shoulder level; (B) now *pull* the rod toward your shoulder, keeping the rod at 11 o'clock and parallel to the ground.

(C) When your hand is about six inches in front of your shoulder, bring the rod back to 1 o'clock with all the power in your wrist.

(D) After a two- or three-second pause, reverse the procedure by pushing the rod forward, maintaining the 1 o'clock position; (E) when the arm is almost fully extended, snap the rod forward to 11 o'clock with a powerful wrist action.

ed, suddenly snap the rod forward to eleven o'clock, again with powerful wrist action. This completes the forecast.

As you can see, the basic casting stroke is quite simple. The only real problem is trying to blend the relatively slow "push-and-pull" movements with the very fast, dynamic-tension wrist action. Initially, these dissimilar motions should be emphasized individually but the final goal is a smooth, fluid delivery. For most beginners, it is advantageous to first get the feel of both the forecast and backcast separately. When practicing, it is critical to keep the thumb directly on top at all times. This ensures straighter, truer rod-tip travel, which is very important to loop control. Actually, thumb, wrist, and arm must all stay in the same flat plane. Remember to keep your casting hand at or near shoulder level. If you reach higher or lower you automatically reduce the amount of travel for each stroke. We find that fly casters master the movements more quickly if they are exaggerated, so we advocate the full arm-length reach when practicing. Admittedly, only a 5- or 6-inch stroke is needed to handle 25 feet of line but the mechanics are the same, straight push-pulls mixed with strong wrist movements.

Some beginners have trouble with the position of their arms at the end of the back-cast motion. In this maximum-bent position, the wrist should be on a path aimed so it

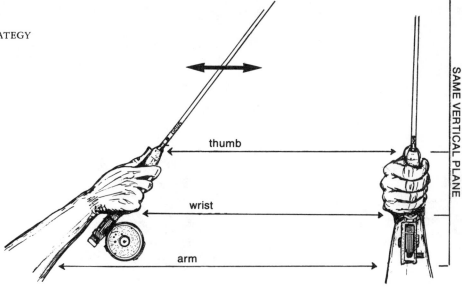

The wrist, thumb, and arm must all stay in the same flat plane.

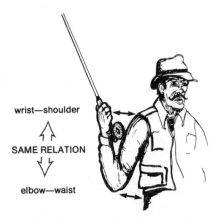

At the end of the backcast, the wrist and shoulder, and the elbow and waist, should be separated by about three or four inches.

will miss the shoulder by about 3 or 4 inches. The elbow should also be aimed to miss the waist by the same amount. Keeping the arm tracked in this plane gives the stroke a more natural, comfortable feel and reduces fatigue.

We find that more confidence and greater progress are attained by the student if we explain the rationale behind our techniques. Far too many casting instructors try to ram a casting stroke down the pupil's throat without ever demonstrating the mechanical principles or logic involved. With this in mind, let's take a look at the reasoning behind our basic casting stroke. Most students want to know why they should push and pull the rod. Actually, there are at least three good reasons. The first has to do with one of the basic concepts in fly casting, *the line should always be straight before the power of the cast is applied.* High-speed photography has shown us that a fly line is almost never straight as it rolls out on the forecast and backcast. It has many wrinkles and sine waves, except for one tiny fraction of a second as the loop finally unfolds. If our timing was computer perfect, we could catch it at this critical moment and apply the power of the cast. This, of course, is impossible, so we push and pull the rod in order to straighten the line. This is accomplished *without* the use of wrist power, which is saved for the cast itself. The real power of the cast comes from the wrist so we should not waste this all-important force in merely straightening the line. Leave the wrist fully cocked during the push-and-pull phases so you can apply as much power as possible when it will really do some good.

Another important reason for pushing and pulling the rod has to do with the fact that as a fly line, which has considerable weight, is dragged through the air it causes the fly rod, a flexible lever, to bend. The more we bend or cock the rod the more power we put into the cast. Once you get on to the basic stroke, you should actually feel the rod bending and "loading up" during the push-and-pull periods. Try to cock the lever as far as possible before bringing the wrist into play.

Pushing and pulling the rod provides even another advantage. It aids in promoting and maintaining proper loop alignment, which, in turn, allows us to throw tighter, better-shaped candy canes. Here is how it works. Let's assume you have selected your target, thereby establishing the direction of your forecast. You draw your mental straight line from the target through your rod tip, thus establishing the direction of

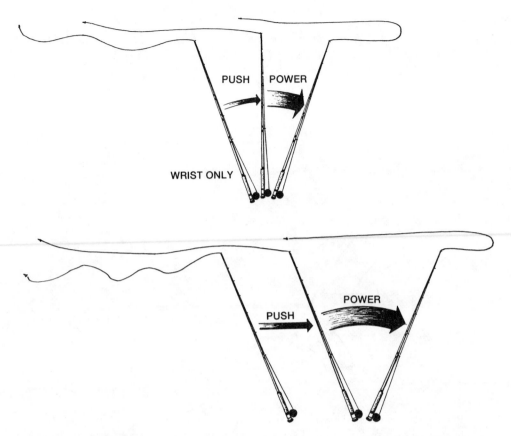

Using the "wrist only" casting stroke means that some of the power stored in the cocked wrist must be used to straighten the line, so that a smaller amount is left to apply directly to the line. By pushing the line straight, all the wrist power may be applied to line direction and distance.

your backcast. When you actually throw your back loop, however, let's assume your estimate was off and you end up throwing 20° high. If you did not push the rod, but merely applied wrist power as soon as the line straightened, your loops would be separated by only 160°, resulting in a badly tailed loop. On the other hand, with a long push preceding the wrist action, the back loop would be pulled down, bringing both candy canes closer to the desired straight line, or 180°, relationship.

It is obvious that you should work hard on the push-pull phases of the basic casting stroke. Without them, you will be doing what we call "waving the rod." To cast well without them requires fantastic timing that takes years to develop. With good push-pull technique, you will do a better job of straightening the line, loading the rod, and lining your loops up properly.

Pushing and pulling the rod—and the fly line—through the air "loads" the rod, much like a lever.

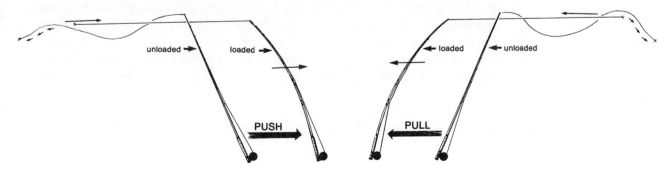

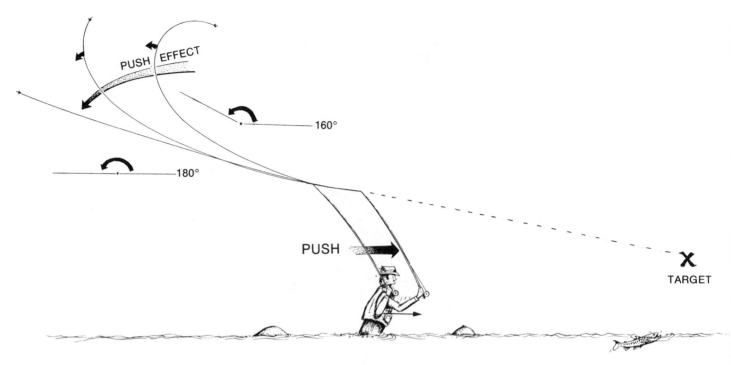

Pushing the rod allows the angler in this situation to correct the angle of his forecast; he threw a high backcast, but a long push will bring it into the proper plane, so that he will be on target. A "wrist only" casting stroke would have resulted in a tailing loop in this situation.

Once the basic casting stroke is mastered in the horizontal plane, it should then be practiced at various angles. Tilted forward, it simulates the pickup from the water; tilted backward, it simulates long-distance casting. We always start with the horizontal plane because it is easier to understand and it is the plane we false cast in. Let's face it, most of our casting time is spent false casting so we might as well practice this position first. We must, however, learn to work at every degree of tilt and how to change angles smoothly.

With ten or fifteen minutes of dry-run practice, most students have developed a pretty good feel for the basic stroke and are ready for the casting field. After assembling the rod and stringing the line through the guides, strip enough line off the reel so that 15 to 20 feet extend past the rod tip. With the line lying out straight in front of you, assume the correct grip and stance. In the beginning, we are only concerned with educating our casting hand; therefore, to eliminate line-handling problems, squeeze the fly line firmly between your hand and cork when you form the suitcaselike grip. This will keep the line from slipping and you will have fewer control problems. Sometimes it helps to put the other hand in your pocket merely to keep it out of the way.

Start the basic casting stroke the same way you did in the dry-run exercise, with an arm fully extended. On the pickup from the grass, of course, your casting plane will

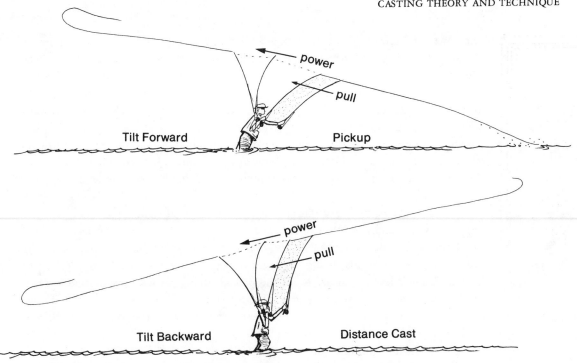

After practicing in the horizontal false cast plane, you should master the pickup and distance-casting planes.

be tilted forward, probably 30°. Just remember the motion is the same, no matter what the angle. With this forward tilt, your extended hand will be a little lower than shoulder height and your rod will be aimed at nine thirty to ten o'clock position, rather than eleven o'clock. With thumb on top, pull the rod up and back in a straight line. At the end of the pull, apply the wrist power, snapping the rod up briskly to approximately the twelve o'clock position. Let the line straighten to the rear—it will not take long with so little out—and then start the forward part of the stroke. If all goes well, and it should if you practiced your dry run properly, make the transition from the tilted plane to the level plane and continue to throw loops parallel to the ground. If you have difficulty, practice only one complete cycle at a time—one backcast combined with one forecast—and then stop. Some students must break their practice down even more, attempting only one backcast or one forecast at a time. This is rare, however, and usually indicates a lack of desire or too little time spent with the rod butt exercise.

Many schools spend hour after hour on the casting field practicing the pickup from the grass, throwing a high loop to the rear, and then driving the frontcast back into the ground. We feel this routine is overemphasized. Probably 80 to 90 percent of all casts, including both false and delivery casts, *should* be made in the horizontal plane. As a result, more progress will be made by *continuous* false casting. After all, you can't learn anything with your line lying on the ground. Keep it moving and observe the loops closely.

For those who experience difficulty in getting the feel of the basic casting stroke, there are some analogies that might be helpful. The motion of throwing a baseball, for example, is very similar to that of fly casting. Even though the hand scribes an arc,

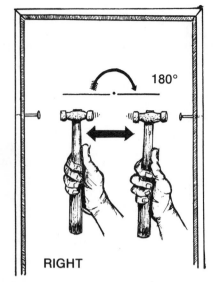

RIGHT

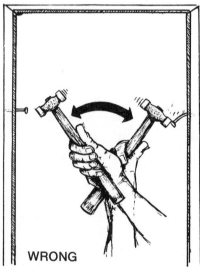

WRONG

The mechanics of the casting stroke are similar to those of attempting to hammer two nails into opposite sides of a doorway. You will see that the hammer and wrist must stay in the cocked position until the very end of the hammer stroke, just as in the casting.

the power and release of the ball are aimed *straight* ahead. If power were applied all the way through the arc, the ball would be hurled into the ground at the player's feet. The balance of the motion after release is "follow-through." A similar situation exists in fly casting. After the power is applied and the line is released toward the target, the rod follows through to a position past the release point. This is also follow-through and it plays a very important role in advanced casting.

The casting motion is also similar to passing a football. Again, the power is straight ahead and the release is high with plenty of follow-through to complete the motion. In our schools, we find that the baseball throw and football passing analogies work quite well, especially with the younger set. Others find the familiar hammer-stroke comparison to be helpful. For this analogy, picture yourself standing in a doorway facing one of the jambs. With a double-headed hammer, drive a nail horizontally into the front jamb with the forestroke and the other horizontally into the rear jamb with the backstroke. The nails should be aimed in opposite directions, exactly 180° apart, and at shoulder level. In order to hit the nail squarely, you will quickly find out that the hammer and wrist must stay in a cocked position until the very end of the stroke. If you apply the wrist too quickly, before the hammer gets close enough, you'll miss the nail completely. Notice how similar this motion is to the basic casting stroke. Long, straight-line, pushing-and-pulling movements are combined with sudden powerful wrist action. Even the angles are the same, the forestroke push cocked at one o'clock and the backstroke pull angulated at eleven o'clock position.

In simulating this exercise, try to drive both nails home with as few strokes as possible and with equal power—to develop maximum straight-line thrust in both your forecast and backcast.

As already stated, the most important exercise to improve your casting ability is practicing what we call loop control. Now that you have the feel of false casting with the real line and rod, it is time to start studying the basics of how to control the various loop characteristics. The first step is to learn how to regulate loop size. To become an effective fly fisherman, you must be able to throw a tight loop when you need it and wide loop when you need it. Most anglers have little difficulty throwing the wide loop, in fact, some never learn to throw anything but the wide variety. The reason for so many "fat candy canes" is that most fly casters equate the casting motion with "circular" movements, perhaps because numerous books and instructors advocate locking the elbow into a fixed position as the stroke is made. During practice sessions, the student is forced to squeeze some object between his elbow and waist. This situation forms a fixed pivotal point, leaving the wrist and forearm no choice but to travel in a circular path. The poor beginner, in order to cast with any degree of skill, must spend endless hours on technique. Even with the proper timing, the locked-elbow style is inefficient for long distance and quickly causes fatigue. Unfortunately, few fly fishermen are able to achieve any great degree of proficiency with this method. Most don't have that much time for practice sessions.

The modern way to cast is to free the elbow and upper arm. In fact, everything should be free and natural. With the old-fashioned, stationary elbow method, progress is slow and fatigue sets in quickly. More important, it is inefficient and impractical for applying the streamside techniques necessary for success. The commonsense way to cast is to utilize all the muscles at your disposal. Rather than relying on wrist and forearm only, let the fingers, hand, wrist, forearm, upper arm, shoulder, and even the entire body all contribute a small percentage to the total casting effort. This blend of power results in a more natural motion and allows you to cast for long periods of time without tiring. It also is a great aid in learning how to throw the all-important tight loop. Combined with push-pull techniques, this free-wheeling approach facilitates straight-line travel of the rod tip. This is the secret of the tight loop. In fact, the most important casting principle of all is that *the straighter the path of the rod tip, the tighter the loop*. On the other hand, *the more the rod tip follows an arcing path, the wider the loop*. The line goes where the rod tip goes.

With these principles in mind, practice tight and wide loop control so you can throw either type any time you wish. Start with a small amount of line, only 15 feet or so, and work up to 35 or 40 feet. Remember to use the basic casting stroke but vary the path of the rod depending on the kind of loop desired. You will undoubtedly find the wide loop easy to throw and the tight loop much more difficult.

Here are a few suggestions that might help you tighten your loop. First, be sure you *control* the amount of arc you put into your wrist as you snap it during the power portion of the basic stroke. Powerful wrist action does not automatically mean the rod must sweep through a large arc. It is possible, with a little practice, to apply great wrist power in a very narrow arc. For the tight loop, practice snapping your wrist with maximum power in as straight a line as possible.

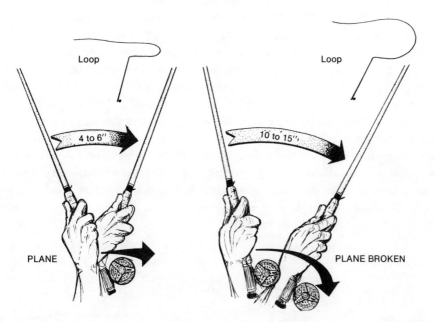

To ensure a tight loop, practice snapping your wrist in as straight a line as possible; you can apply a great amount of wrist power in a relatively small arc.

A routine we've found to be helpful is to find a straight reference line that can be "traced" during the casting stroke. For example, stand near a building in such a position that you can line up your rod tip with a straight roof line. As you practice the casting motion, force your rod tip to follow the straight line of the building. We use a similar routine in our fishing schools, only we begin by casting sideways, or in the horizontal plane. Standing close to a chalk line, the students sight through their rod tips and "paint" the proper path. Usually, only a few minutes are needed to get the

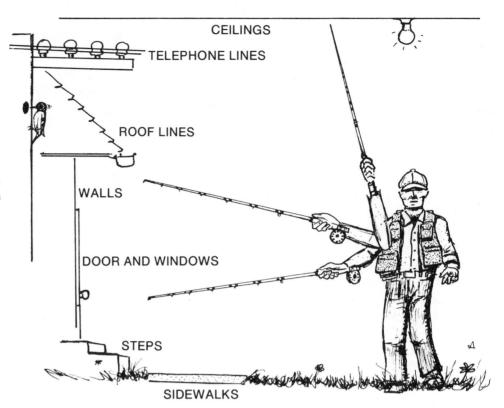

CEILINGS

TELEPHONE LINES

ROOF LINES

WALLS

DOOR AND WINDOWS

STEPS

SIDEWALKS

You can use a variety of horizontal lines as guides for practicing in all planes.

feel of throwing tight, horizontal candy canes. In order to keep the rod tip on the chalk line, or at least in a very small arc, the push-pull motions must be emphasized. As soon as the loops are tight, the plane of casting is slowly shifted from the horizontal to the upright position. If you don't have access to the chalk lines of an athletic field, use the straight lines created by driveways, curbs, walls, or your imagination.

A valuable indoor exercise for learning tight loops involves the use of the mini-rod. This is a miniature rod 3 to 4 feet long, an old rod tip will do, and a piece of wind-resistant yarn. In the typical house with 8- to 10-foot ceilings, there is just enough room to cast with this short rod in the upright, or near-upright position. To improve your tight loop, practice the basic stroke with the rod tip as close as possible to the ceiling at all times, almost as if it were riding in a track. Again, accent the wrist power and use long push-pull movements.

ROD PLANE=ROOF LINE

You can practice the straight rod tip stroke by "tracing" the line of a roof.

Beginning fly casters characteristically throw wide loops but this does not mean they automatically throw *good* wide loops. Actually, there is quite a difference between the wide candy cane of a neophyte and that of an expert. The difference is in the pushing and pulling movements. Without these, the beginner is left with only a waving motion of the rod, which results in casts that are sadly lacking in both power and accuracy. Such loops fail to straighten on the water and often tangle the line and leader. The expert, on the other hand, with his ingrained pull and push motions sandwiched between wrist snaps, can form a smooth, wide candy cane that will lie out straight on the water and deliver the fly accurately to the target. When practicing wide loops, then, be careful not to get sloppy and forget to use the basic casting stroke. Just as you would with your tight-loop practice, use plenty of push-pull but instead of making the rod tip follow a straight path, make it scribe an arcing or curved path. This, again, is controlled by the wrist. The more the wrist is arced during the snap part of the stroke, the wider the loop will be. This is what we call the "depth of arc" principle. The distance the rod tip falls, from the beginning of the power stroke until line speed overcomes tip speed, determines loop size. In simpler terms, the more the rod tip deviates from a straight line, the wider the loop. Again: *the line goes where the rod tip goes.*

To get the feel of good wide loops, practice the same exercises used for tight loops, but make the rod tip travel in an arc instead of a straight line. Use arcing wrist power, not straight wrist power. After you become proficient with both wide and tight loops, throw some of each, varying the sequence on both front and back casts.

Loop direction controls loop shape. The loop shape you want on the forecast will automatically determine the direction of your backcast. Naturally, you will want to throw "perfect" loops as often as possible. To develop the ultimate candy cane shape, practice throwing front and back loops that are lined up 180° apart. Expert fly fishermen almost always direct their front loop in, or very near, the horizontal plane, so to throw a perfect candy cane up front, the backcast must also be aimed in the horizontal plane, in exact alignment with the forecast. This routine should constitute the bulk of your loop shape and loop direction practice. It is helpful, however, if you can throw the "bad" loop when you want to: this will help you to understand the basic mechanics of loop shape and direction. More important, you will be able to correct yourself quickly on the stream, especially when so-called "wind knots" start forming. To throw an open front loop, aim the back loop low so both are separated by *more* than 180°. With a few hours of practice, you should actually be able to feel the difference between 179° and 181°.

Your casting is really starting to gel when you can completely control all three loop characteristics—size, shape, and direction. Thirty minutes a day for two weeks should easily bring you to this point. Sandwich in a little practice with the mini-rod, if at all possible. This will speed your progress even more.

We first suggested that loop control practice be carried out with the line squeezed between your casting hand and the grip. This was to allow full concentration on the major problem of educating the rod hand. When fishing, however, the other hand must be used to perform a variety of functions, so it should be brought into use as soon as the basic casting stroke becomes second nature. Most students are ready for this added refinement after the first hour on the practice field. When this time comes, start practicing with the fly line held *firmly* in the line hand. For a right-handed caster, this would be the left hand. The grip is exactly the same as the rod grip, thumb on top with most of the pressure between the thumb and forefinger. Hold your hand in a comfortable position at waist level. Remember to grip the line as tightly as possible. If not held securely, it will slip in the guides and kill the cast.

In most fishing situations, the angler shoots the line through the guides to deliver the fly to the target. To develop this important ability, the beginner should practice shooting small amounts of line as soon as loop control is mastered. This is accomplished by releasing the line on the forecast. Timing of this maneuver is critical. Release should coincide precisely with the power snap of the casting stroke.With a little practice, a tight loop, and good timing, 25 feet can easily be extended to 40 or more.

Another important phase of each casting session is "plane and tilt" practice. A truly expert fly caster is capable of controlling the size, shape, and direction of his loop, not only in the vertical plane but in every other plane as well. This ability facilitates various streamside casts that are critical to successful fly fishing. Curve casts are best performed, for example, with the rod canted horizontally to the casting-hand side, while a certain wind cast must be thrown back-handed. Various angles of frontcast and backcast tilt are also important to the performance of numerous specialty casts.

An important point to remember is that no matter what the plane of casting— whether sidearm, upright, or backhanded—*the thumb is always the leading edge of every backcast and the trailing edge of every forecast.* This means that when casting forehanded, the fly caster is always looking *directly into his palm* and when casting backhanded, he is always looking *directly at the back of his hand.*

The timing of the release is critical; it should coincide with the power snap of the casting stroke.

POWER SNAP

RELEASE

CHAPTER 2

PRACTICAL APPLICATION AND ADVANCED CASTING TECHNIQUES

FLOATING INSECTS normally move along at the same speed as the current they are drifting in. Sometimes, especially on windy days, they will flip and flutter, changing velocity and slicing across current lanes, but by and large they tend to remain congruent to their line of flow. As their drift dips and sways and changes speed, so do they. The fly fisherman, then, in order to fish effectively, must be concerned with this phenomenon. He must be able to present his artificial in such a manner that it behaves exactly like the natural he is attempting to imitate. In effect, his delivery must allow the fly to drift naturally in the trout's feeding lane, just as if he had gently dropped the fly, without line and leader attached, into the proper current flow.

Difficulty arises because the artificial is connected to a leader-line combination and the cast usually has to be delivered across currents of varying velocities. In the typical stream situation, faster currents between angler and trout cause line and leader to be pulled tight in a downstream direction. The resulting tension increases the speed of the fly and drags it out of the proper line of drift. No matter how realistic the imitation, the trout will usually reject a fly if it acts in this unnatural manner.

Drag is the single greatest presentation problem facing the stream fisherman. To solve this problem, a variety of techniques can be applied to achieve drag-free floats.

The first is merely a combination of simple line and rod handling procedures that will give the angler both control and at least a fair amount of drag-free float. As soon as the delivery cast is made, the line should be transferred to the index finger of the casting hand, the rod tip lowered to the water, and then the rod tip should follow the drift of the fly line. This sequence should be practiced until it becomes instinctive; it is basic to effective stream procedures. In our schools, we call it the "over the finger, lower the rod, follow the line" routine.

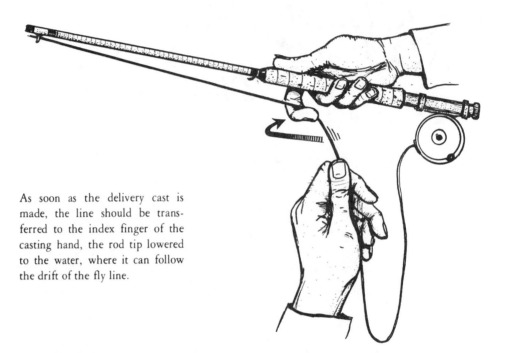

As soon as the delivery cast is made, the line should be transferred to the index finger of the casting hand, the rod tip lowered to the water, where it can follow the drift of the fly line.

Putting the line over the index finger gives the angler *control*. He can better handle accumulating slack line, feed out and strip in, set hooks and manipulate flies with this system. Control is a must, especially in moving-water situations. Lowering the rod tip and following the fly line both help keep tension off the line and leader, which, in turn, delays drag buildup. This three-step procedure should be mastered before the specialty casts are attempted.

The next approach is slack-line casts. These casts have a variety of names—serpentine, sine wave, shaky S, or just plain slack-line cast. It doesn't matter what you call them but it is important that you understand how they work. All operate on the principle of using more line than is required to get to the target. This extra line is distributed in a series of "wrinkles" between angler and fish and its purpose is to buy yourself more time. As the excess line is straightened and played out by the currents, the fly has time to float drag-free. Sometimes, just another second or two of natural drift is all that's needed to draw a strike.

For the beginner, the best method is to use the casting hand as the control for slack-line casts. Observe the front loop closely as it shoots toward the target. Just before it straightens completely, pull your casting hand back abruptly. This causes the line to jump back toward you and fall into the water in a "wrinkled" configuration.

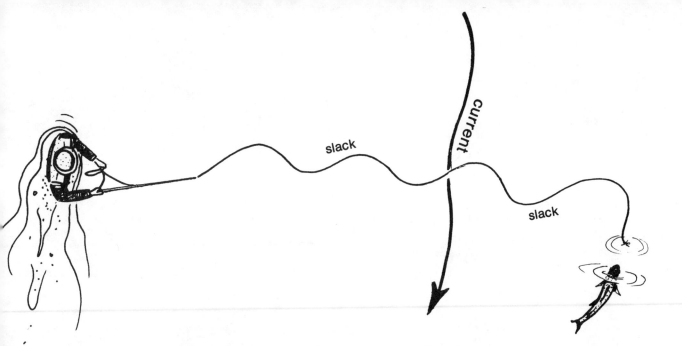

The basic principle of the slack-line cast involves casting more line than necessary to reach the target, so that it will absorb some of the force of the current and allow a few extra moments of drag-free float.

Varying the sudden pull of the casting hand will vary the amount of slack line formed. Before proceeding any further with slack line training, an angler should be sure of his ability to throw a line that has no wrinkles at all. To throw a perfectly straight line, the caster must learn to control the energy put into each cast and to use his casting hand as a shock absorber. First, enough power must be applied so the candy cane will straighten. Then, just before the line straightens in the air, the casting hand must be pushed forward and down, in sort of a soft, arcing motion. This absorbs the shock of uncoiling, allowing the line to land straight rather than rebound into a series of sine waves.

Practice, either on land or water, casting to a target, not only trying for accuracy, but to control varying amounts of slack line. All sorts of exercises can be devised that will increase your ability to throw everything from a perfectly straight to a crooked line. An excellent one is to set a target, such as a hula hoop, out on the lawn at varying distances. Start at about 25 feet. Practice throwing exactly 25 feet of fly line into the target, which means the line must be perfectly straight in order to make it. Then take one long strip off the fly reel, about two feet. This means you'll have about twenty-seven feet of line out. Put the end of the fly line into the target several times; a slight amount of slack line will be required to accomplish this. Then add another 2 feet and notice that a little more slack is required. Keep adding until 40 or more feet are being used for a 25-foot cast. Then work your way back down to 25 feet of line. This will quickly teach you how to control varying amounts of slack. Practice until you can satisfy both conditions and everything in between. An aid in obtaining the greatest amount of slack line possible is to tilt the casting plane up in front. The higher the forecast is aimed, the more time the excess line has to jump back and the more slack is formed.

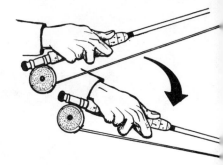

Pulling back on the rod produces lots of slack but this method has a serious drawback. In fly casting, accuracy is controlled by the rod tip being aimed directly at the target. As soon as we start jerking the rod around, this all-important feature is de-

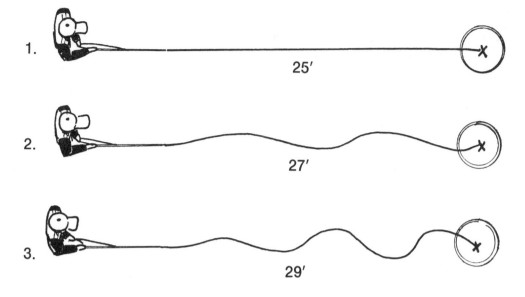

A good exercise for learning to estimate and control varying amounts of slack line: cast to a target 25 feet away, then strip off two more feet of line, and cast for the target again.

stroyed. The next step, then, is to develop a technique where the rod tip is kept in line with the target to maintain accuracy. In this cast, the front loop is allowed to straighten and snap back of its own accord. No pull-back motion is necessary. Just stop the rod tip dead, keeping it aimed at the target, and the wrinkles will form. To master this cast, the angler must have progressed far enough in his casting to be able to throw a powerful, tight-loop cast whenever he needs it.

Bringing the line hand into play adds the final touch of finesse to the slack-line cast. This refinement provides optimum control over distance, accuracy, and the amount of slack that can be produced. As the front loop straightens, rather than pulling back the rod tip or overpowering the cast, apply a subtle flick with your line hand. If timed properly, the line will jump back and drop to the water in a serpentine pattern. Any degree of slack can easily be obtained by varying the timing or power of the flick, the angle of tilt, and the power of the cast. Further control is possible by the action of the casting hand. The abrupt stop or even slight pullback of the rod tip will accent the amount of slack, while a "giving"—or forward-and-down—motion will reduce slack.

Still another method of producing slack line is what we call the "stutter cast." To perform this cast, make the rod quiver or vibrate back and forth in the horizontal plane as the line shoots out. Great amounts of slack can be thrown over great distances with this cast. It works well for covering the far sides of large pools and runs, especially when you're fishing an area rather than an individual riser.

Delivery of the slack-line cast. The rod hand has been lowered and pulled back.

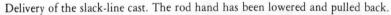

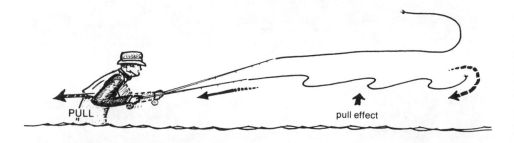

Use the casting hand as the control for a slack-line cast: observe the front loop closely, and just before it straightens out, pull your casting hand back abruptly. This causes the line to jump back toward you and land on the water in a "wrinkled" conformation.

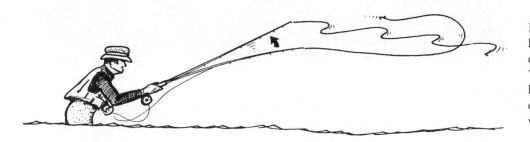

If you can cast a powerful, tight loop, you can make a slack-line cast by simply stopping the rod tip "dead"—on the target. The front loop will straighten and snap back on its own, forming slack line wrinkles.

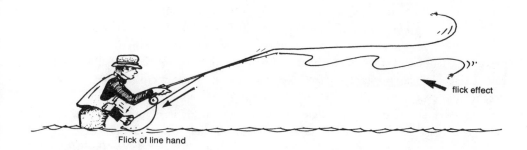

You can also apply a subtle flick of the line to create slack.

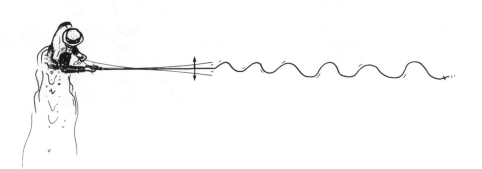

Using a "stutter cast" you can throw a slack line over a great distance.

Serpentine cast

The basic weakness of the slack line cast is that the caster can never be sure that the waves will land on the water in the proper relationship to the current.

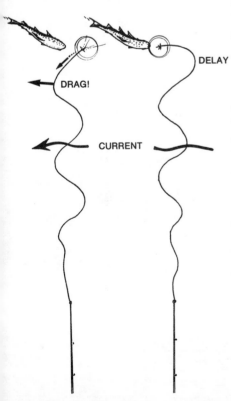

Few anglers progress further than learning some form of slack-line casting. This is unfortunate since there are other methods of obtaining natural drifts that, in many situations, are much more effective. One of these is what we call the *reach cast*. The object of this cast is to put as much of the fly line as possible *upstream* from the fish so that the whole line must drift downstream before drag sets in. This varies radically from the slack-type casts that rely on a series of sine waves. Similar to a chain with a weak link, the typical slack-line cast is only as good as *one* of the sine waves in the cast. Normally there is a critical area between angler and target where currents of varying speeds come together. If the sine wave covering that juncture is curled in the right direction, a fairly good, drag-free float will result, but if this "wrinkle" is not properly oriented, the cast will not achieve its desired purpose. In other words, slack-line casts are often a rather chancy approach to a situation where you need all the help you can get. In many instances, especially when fishing directly cross-steam or cross-stream-and-down, the reach cast is a much more positive and effective solution.

We have found that even neophyte fly casters can quickly learn to throw a reasonably good reach cast *if* they understand the basic principle behind it. As previously mentioned, the rod tip controls everything in fly casting. Remember: *the line always goes where the rod tip goes.* If the rod tip, for example, arcs to the left during the casting stroke, the line will roll out in a left curve and if the rod tip goes through an S curve configuration, the line will follow and lay out in an S curve shape on the water. This is an extremely important concept that can help you solve many casting problems on the stream. It is also the basis for the reach cast.

The first step in performing any reach-type cast is to draw a mental image of where you want the line to land on the water. Assuming you're right-handed, let's go through a typical "crosscurrent left bank" situation, where the flow is moving from left to right. Picture a trout 20 feet away feeding in relatively slow-moving water. The current between you and the fish is moving at a moderate speed. Rather than throwing straight in with a serpentine cast, let's use a "left reach cast." Draw an imaginary line from the target to the tip of your rod when it is extended horizontally to the left

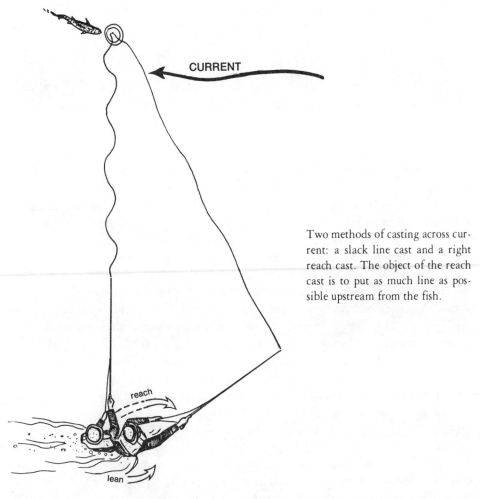

Two methods of casting across current: a slack line cast and a right reach cast. The object of the reach cast is to put as much line as possible upstream from the fish.

across your body. In this case, the target should be a spot 2 or 3 feet upstream, or to the left of the trout. With a 7-foot rod and a long-stretching reach, your rod tip should be almost 10 feet to your left. Under these conditions, your imaginary line will be angled 25 to 30 degrees farther upstream from the trout than the direction of the conventional slack-line cast. If you can lay your fly line on the imaginary line, you'll have a great drifting angle on the trout.

To accomplish this left reach cast, throw a moderately powered backcast in the horizontal plane and then come forward with a wide but firm loop. Keeping in mind that the line will go where the rod tip goes, slowly, but with accented, full-arcing wrist action, "paint" your rod tip along the full length of the imaginary line. Your casting hand should sweep across in front of your body at a 45° angle with your thumb on top during the entire stroke. At the conclusion of the cast, you should be leaning and reaching *as far as possible* to the left with the rod tip almost touching the water.

Reaching across your body with a seven-foot rod, your cast should lie on the water along a line ten feet above the line of a slack-line cast.

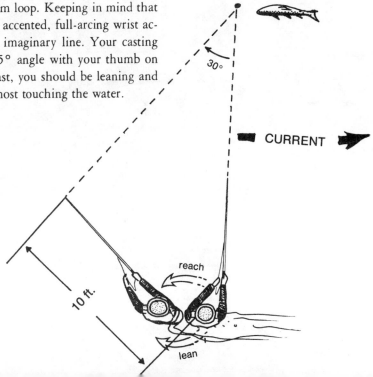

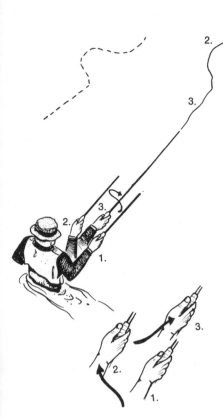

Not only is the reach important during the cast phase, but it is just as critical during the drift phase. As soon as fly, line, and leader begin floating downstream, follow the drift of the line with the rod tip. This reduces line tension to a minimum. Another advantage of the reach cast is realized during the first half of the drift cycle. As the rod tip follows the fly line from the far left position to the center position, it is swinging *toward* the target. This, of course, reduces the distance between rod tip and target which, in turn, further reduces tension on the line. Once the line has drifted past the center (target) position, you must begin reaching to the right. Keep the rod tip at water level all the while. At the conclusion of the drift, you should be leaning and reaching just as hard to the right as you did to the left when the cast was delivered.

If "painting" the line on the water with the rod tip is not helpful in learning the reach cast, maybe a slightly different approach will work. We've said that the line goes where the rod tip goes. It also follows that the rod tip goes where the wrist goes, so another casting concept that should be remembered is that *the line goes where the wrist goes.* In each case, of course, the motions are greatly magnified. A small wrist movement produces a larger rod tip movement, which produces a highly magnified line movement. What this boils down to is that if you can develop the ability to translate a desired cast into a wrist motion, you can easily throw and control the cast. Let's apply this to the reach cast. Again, make a mental image of how the cast should land on the water. Knowing that the line will follow your wrist, stroke the wrist through the same configuration. It's merely a matter of matching the power movement of your wrist to the desired shape of the line on the water.

Another way of looking at this situation is to visualize the casting stroke of the wrist being broken down, or divided into many small increments. Form a mental image of the wrist flexing through its power stroke in superslow motion. Then, firmly imprint upon your mind that the very *first* tiny increment of power application controls where the *fly* will land on the water and the *final* increment controls where the

The line will follow the movements of the wrist in an exaggerated pattern; each wrist movement is transmitted along the line and leader to the fly, so that the first movement will reach the fly and the last movement will determine where the line closest to the rod tip will lie. If you are conscious of this relationship through the entire cast, and practice, you can establish a very high degree of control over your line movement.

The reach cast: (1) throw a moderately powered backcast and come forward with a wide but firm loop; (2) sweep your casting hand across your body at a 45° angle; (3) at the conclusion of the cast you should be leaning as far as possible to the left with the rod tip almost touching the water.
Learning to "paint" the line onto your imaginary line above the target is easier if you remember that the line will follow the path of your wrist.

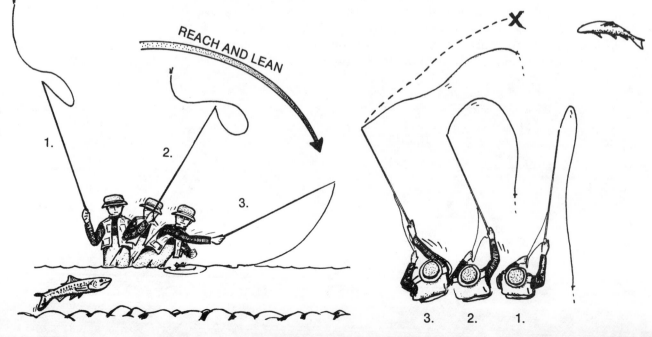

Left reach cast

fly line near your *rod tip* lands. Each increment in between controls corresponding portions of leader and line.

Let's apply this approach to the left reach cast using a long, arcing power application, from twelve o'clock position all the way down to nine o'clock. Again, draw the imaginary line from target to the spot where the rod tip will end up. After the backcast, push the rod forward, keeping it at twelve o'clock. Look at the target and apply the first increment of wrist power in that direction. In the eleven thirty position, the wrist should be aimed a little farther up the imaginary line, at eleven o'clock, farther yet and at ten thirty, it should be aimed exactly at the midpoint. Continue aiming each increment of wrist power along the line until, at nine o'clock, the rod tip stops in the final leaning and stretching position to the left. We have found this type of association very helpful when throwing specialized casts. First, decide where you want your fly to land, where your rod tip should stop, and what the configuration should be in between. Then run your wrist through this pattern a number of times in slow motion. After it feels natural, try it with the rod and you'll be surprised at the various shapes you can throw on the water.

The reach cast to the right is basically the same as the left reach, except, of course, that the directions are reversed. This cast is normally used when the current is moving from right to left. Start with the horizontally directed backcast and come forward with a wide but firmly controlled loop. Aim the first part of the stroke at the target and direct the balance along the imaginary line, ending with the rod tip pointed almost straight out to the right. As the line drifts downstream to the left, follow it closely with the rod tip to eliminate all possible tension. The final, end-of-drift position is an extreme leaning, stretching reach to the left.

For the right-handed caster, the right reach cast is slightly more difficult than the left reach. With the rod in the right hand, it is easy to obtain a long, smooth, reaching motion to the left. A stroke of 3 feet or more can be accomplished when the

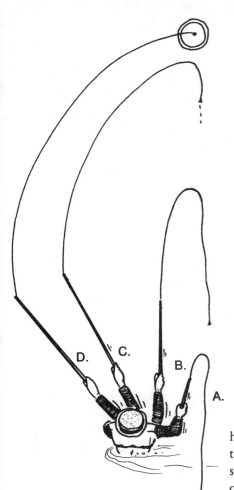

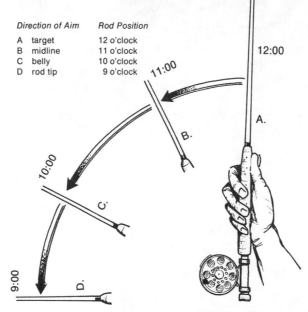

Direction of Aim		Rod Position
A	target	12 o'clock
B	midline	11 o'clock
C	belly	10 o'clock
D	rod tip	9 o'clock

Each increment of wrist power should be aimed along the imaginary line of the cast. (A) The first increment of power from your wrist should be aimed directly at the target, the rod at 12 o'clock. (B) When the rod is powered to 11 o'clock the cast should be aimed at about the midpoint of the imaginary line; (C) at 10 o'clock, the wrist should be aiming its power farther along the imaginary line, continuing until (D) it reaches 9 o'clock and the rod tip stops in the final leaning and stretching position to the left.

hand is swept down 45° from the right shoulder position to a point well to the left of the waist. For the right reach, however, it is difficult to make more than a 2-foot stroke. The longer the stroke the more control you have over the cast. This fact points out the need of being able to cast effectively in every plane. With this skill, the right-handed angler can deliver the right reach cast from the *left* side, or back-handed position, thus allowing a longer stroke and better control. On their first attempts at throwing reach casts, most fly fishermen make the mistake of using too tight a loop on their delivery. With a "quick" wrist, they suddenly apply *all* of the power of the cast at the target. Then, as an afterthought, they belatedly swing the rod tip to the side. The resulting line configuration is a "wrong-way" curve that bellies downstream. You know that you've arrived when you can make all your reach casts land on the water in a straight line.

The real pro can throw *accurate* curve casts, both left and right. It is one thing to throw random curves on the casting field but quite another to curl a fly into a 2-inch feeding lane on the stream. Curves are mainly used to produce better natural drifts but are also valuable for fishing "around corners" and preventing what is called "lining" the fish. The longest drag-free floats can be accomplished with curves that are combined with reaching motions. One of our favorite techniques when the hatch is sparse or nonexistent is to fish dries and floating nymphs downstream with curves. From a position slightly above and across from a good run, throw a curve that places the line well upstream of the fly. Immediately lower the rod and begin feeding and mending line. You can often run the whole fly line out through the guides without creating drag on the fly. This is a deadly technique, especially when used at the end of a hatch or spinner fall.

To throw effective curves, you must be able to cast in a canted plane and control the size of your loops. Both curves, right and left, are thrown with the rod tilted to the side. If you are right-handed, the cast that curves to the left is known as a positive

34

Reach cast right #1

Reach cast right #2

Reach cast right #3

Reach cast right #4

Reach cast right #5

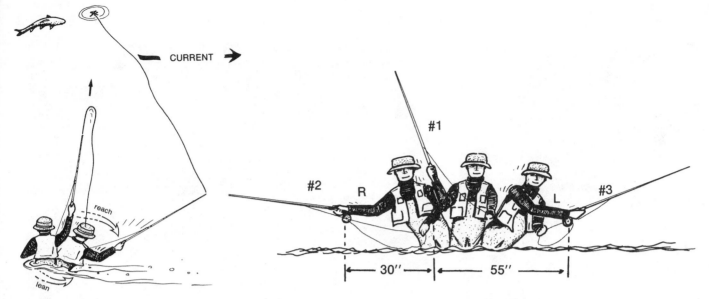

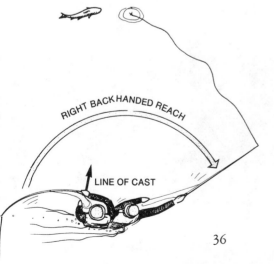

The right reach cast is basically the same as the left reach, except, of course, that the directions are reversed.

The right reach is somewhat more difficult, however, since from the right-hander's starting position, (1) you must power the cast in a shorter stroke going to the right with your right hand, (2) than in the left reach cast (3).

This difficulty may be overcome by learning to throw the right reach cast backhanded, which allows a longer stroke and better control.

curve, because it is thrown with a tight, dynamic loop. With the rod angled about 45° to the right, flick a thin candy cane to the rear in the horizontal plane and then come straight forward with an overpowered forecast. The added thrust applied to the front loop will not only make the candy cane straighten but will kick the end of the line around to form a candy cane in the other direction. This is the secret of the positive curve—applying enough zing to the cast to make the candy cane reverse itself. To give this type of cast more snap, pull back slightly with the casting hand just as the loop starts to straighten, or better yet, apply a quick, but subtle pull on the line with your left hand. Either method, or a combination of both, will add impetus to the curving effect. The positive curve should be mastered completely as it will be used much more frequently than the negative curve. Because of its dynamic character, it is easier to control, especially in windy situations.

The cast that curls to the right, for a right-handed caster, is called the negative curve. This cast is also thrown with the rod canted, but is based on a wide rather than a tight loop. For the right curve, angulate the rod even farther away from the body—almost horizontal is best. The object is to throw a wide, lazy loop and let it fall to the

Another common problem in learning to throw the reach cast results from throwing a tight loop and applying all the wrist power quickly. The angler must reach the rod tip quickly as well, and often the line is traveling faster than the reach; the result is that the line actually bellies downstream.

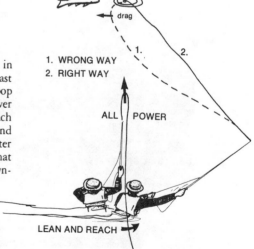

Curve cast   A positive curve with slack line

water before it can straighten. It helps to keep the backcast high and the front cast aimed low. The more quickly you get this cast into the water the less chance there is for the tip of the line to straighten or kick around to the left. Where the positive curve is a live, dynamic cast, the negative type is very slow-moving and underpowered. In fact, you do everything you can to kill or soften it, so that the candy cane maintains its shape. To help deaden this cast you can "give" with your casting hand as the loop starts forward. This is a forward-and-down arcing motion—which, by the way, is a

The positive curve cast: with the rod canted to 45°, bring a thin backcast forward with an overpowered forecast, which will not only straighten out the forecast "cane" but reverse it.

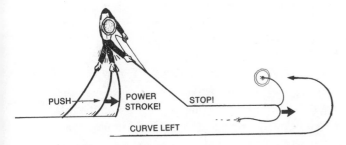

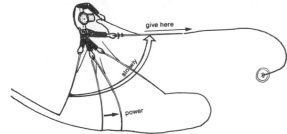

The negative curve cast starts from a wide loop; the object is to throw a wide, lazy loop and get it onto the water before it straightens out.

37

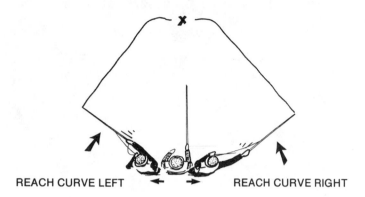

REACH CURVE LEFT   REACH CURVE RIGHT

The combination of a curve cast and a reaching motion, right and left, means that you not only increase the angle on the fish, but your fly curls down to an area *below* the line, creating the ultimate drag-free float.

Right reach curve

basic move to soften the delivery of any cast. At the same time, you can release the fly line from your left hand. This will also help kill the cast.

One of the real secrets of throwing negative curves is to keep the front and back loops separated by *more* than 180°. In fact, if you want to throw a real "roundhouse" job, maintain at least 220°, or even up to 270°, between forecast and backcast. This is one of the many situations where a complete understanding of the basic mechanics of fly casting pays big dividends. Since the cast is performed sidearm fashion in the horizontal plane, you can get away with a large angle between loops. This would be impossible in the vertical casting plane.

Negative curves, which rely on extrawide, underpowered loops, are extremely difficult to control, especially in windy situations. Even with no breeze at all, it is a real challenge to lay the fly into the trout's feeding lane with any degree of consistency. This curve is probably best put to use when you're "fishing the water" rather than individual risers.

The ultimate drag-free cast is the "reach-curve" combination. If you want to achieve maximum natural float, sweeping curves combined with long reaches are the answer. With this technique, you not only increase that all-important angle on the fish but your fly curls down to an area well below the fly line. We find that in most typical cross-stream situations, the reach curve produces at least *three times* the natural drift of the standard slack-line cast. If you can become proficient at reach and curve casting, blend the two together and you will be astounded at the improvement in your dragless floats. And let's face it, the reason you work on improving your technique is to increase your efficiency while on the stream.

Here's an example of just how much your efficiency can be improved upon learning to throw the reach curve properly. The average angler fishing dry flies will make about one hundred and eighty casts per hour. These are delivery, not false casts. During a day when eight hours are actually spent fishing, which is not uncommon for many of us, this means that more than 1,400 casts will be executed. Let's assume one angler, who has the ability to throw only standard slack-line casts, averaged 2 feet of dragless drift per cast. This totals about 2,800 feet of natural drift. Another angler,

38

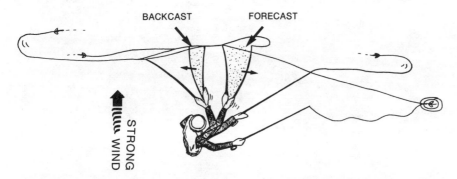

BACKCAST   FORECAST

STRONG WIND

In a very strong wind you can apply the same principles you use in normal casts to a backhanded stroke.

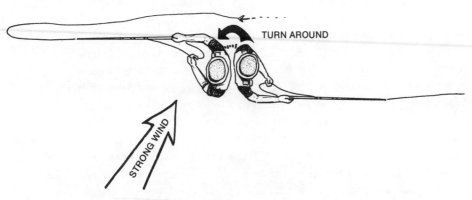

TURN AROUND

STRONG WIND

If you need to cast a distance into a strong wind, try fishing backwards: turn around so that the backcast becomes the delivery cast.

Heavy and uncontrollable winds must be handled differently. Winds of this intensity make it almost impossible to make any casts at all on the casting-hand side. In this case, resort to backhand casting. It feels a bit awkward at first, but a few half-hour sessions in the casting field will permit you to make 30-foot casts with accuracy and ease. The same rules apply—thumb on top, push-pull and straight-line rod tip travel. Backhanded casting is one of the most valuable skills to have in your bag of tricks. It will bail you out of trouble time after time.

When a cast of 30 feet or more is needed in a heavy wind, simply turn around and fish *backwards*. In this position, the back loop becomes the delivery cast. Some accuracy will be lost, but at such long distance, this factor is normally not important. Still another method to use when the wind is strong and relentless on the casting side is to change hands. A few hours practice with your left hand, if you're a natural right-hander, should make you proficient enough to handle many of the less critical situations. It's also a welcome relief to give your regular casting hand an occasional rest.

Mending, feeding, and stripping are three techniques that must be mastered in order to achieve maximum efficiency in the stream. Unfortunately, few anglers ever develop these skills to their proper degree of proficiency. If you observe a truly expert fly fisherman when he's working over a stretch of river, you'll be amazed at how busy he is between each delivery and pickup cast. Whether fishing dry flies, nymphs, or

The mending motion: flip your wrist in a quick arcing motion and the rod tip and line will follow.

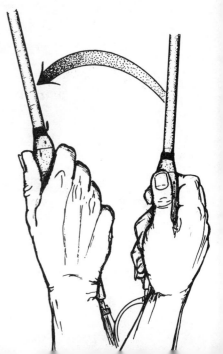

An upstream mend to remove tension from your fly

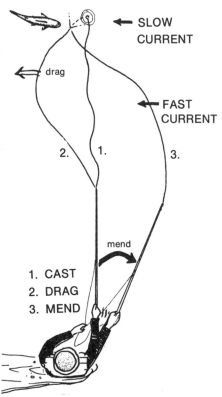

← SLOW
CURRENT

drag

← FAST
CURRENT

2. 1. 3.

mend

1. CAST
2. DRAG
3. MEND

Mending upstream—fast water between the caster and the target.

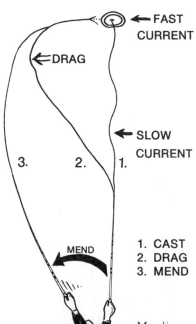

← FAST
CURRENT

←DRAG

← SLOW
CURRENT

3. 2. 1.

MEND

1. CAST
2. DRAG
3. MEND

Mending downstream—slower water between the caster and the target water.

streamers, his hands are almost constantly on the move. Once the fly hits the water, he doesn't simply stand back and wait for something to happen, *he makes it happen* by using one or more of the line handling or line manipulation techniques.

We know many anglers who excel in taking large numbers of trout, yet are mediocre fly casters. Even without the ability to throw reach and curve casts, their effectiveness is quite high, because they have become skillful at mending, feeding, and stripping. Mending is the simple solution for the fly rodder who is unable to make his casts land on the water in the proper drag-fighting configurations. It is a technique where the line is repositioned on the water *after* the cast has been made. It is used both for *reducing* and *increasing* tension on the line-leader-fly system. Mending is used most often, at least by the dry-fly fisherman, to eliminate or reduce drag and is accomplished by flipping loops of line either upstream or down, depending on the situation. Typically, the angler finds himself casting across fast water to a fish that is rising in slow or dead water. In this case, the mend must be made *upstream* with the loop big enough to reach over all of the faster moving water. A *downstream* mend is required when casting over dead water into higher-velocity currents. Occasionally, mends in more than one direction are needed to conquer a series of varying currents.

Reading currents and then figuring out which configuration to mend is possibly one of the more difficult problems of presentation. An aid in solving this problem is to cast straight across the currents in question and observe the line closely. After a few seconds of drift, the line will flow into a certain shape, usually a portion bowing well downstream and a portion staying relatively stationary. The proper mend needed to fight drag is the reverse or mirror image of the observed shape. Taking the typical situation where the angler casts across fast water into dead water, a straight cast would quickly belly downstream. An upstream mend is called for under these conditions. This method works well even for a series of complex currents.

A flip of the wrist is about all that's required to mend line. Remember, the line goes where the rod tip goes and the rod tip, in turn, is controlled by the wrist. So just flip your wrist with a quick arcing motion in the desired direction of mend, and the line will follow. The larger the arc the larger the loop that is mended. Extralarge mends are facilitated by raising your casting arm slightly before the flip of your wrist. To move longer lengths of line it is best to break the surface tension before applying power.

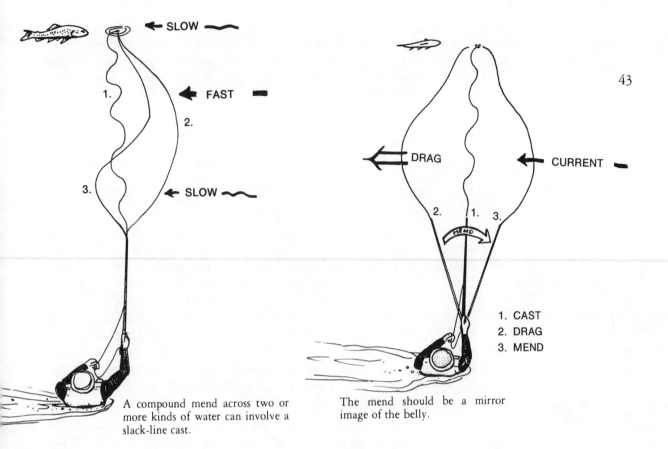

A compound mend across two or more kinds of water can involve a slack-line cast.

The mend should be a mirror image of the belly.

1. CAST
2. DRAG
3. MEND

Mending is not only used to reduce drag but also to increase it. When fishing wet, especially with streamers, it is often desirable to create as much tension as possible on the line. This pressure causes the fly to dive under the surface and swim with great speed across the current. Sometimes both types of mending are used on the same drift, the drag-reducing and the drag-creating types. It all depends on how the angler wants his artificial to behave.

Working extra line out of the guides is called feeding and sounds like a pretty simple process. It is, if you do it right, but most anglers don't. Feeding is the method normally used to lengthen the drift of an artificial fly. When used with dry flies, it is imperative that the feeding process does not create drag or, worse yet, sink the fly. As the artificial nears the completion of its float, drag has usually built up to a dangerous level and it is usually at this point that the feeding process is initiated. So great care

A. LOW ROD—SHORT MEND LOOP
B. HIGH ROD—LONG MEND LOOP

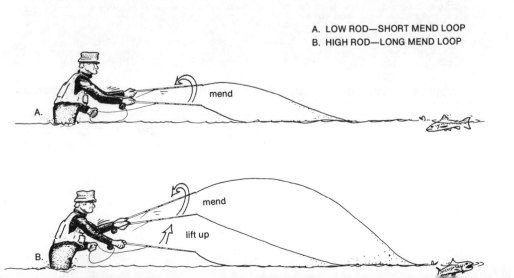

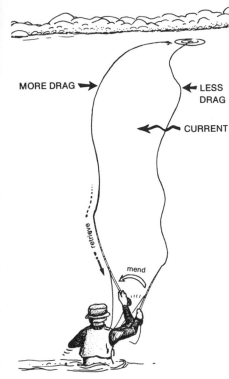

MORE DRAG

LESS DRAG

CURRENT

retrieve

mend

Mending can also be used to *increase* drag when that is desirable, as in streamer fishing.

must be taken not to disturb the freely drifting imitation. If even a small amount of frictional buildup occurs, all is lost. It is at this point that most anglers have trouble. They not only use improper feeding techniques but are far too slow in manipulating their hands. Drag can build up from a variety of sources:

1) Friction in the guides
2) Friction of stripped line being pulled up off the water
3) Friction of the line running through the hands and the resistance caused by clumsy, slow-moving hands

For right-handed casters, the proper procedure is first to strip from the reel the amount of line needed, just letting it lie on the water's surface. Make the cast and then, before the drift is too far along, start feeding. From the starting position, line over right index, grasp the fly line with the left hand 15 to 20 inches behind the right index finger. Release the line being held by the right index finger and replace it with the line held in your left hand. This forms a loose loop of line between the stripper guide and your right index finger. A very quick but subtle flick of the wrist will feed the slack line out through the guides. The wrist movement can be horizontal or vertical depending on whether you want to feed the line out straight or mend it slightly right or left. Quite often small mends are thrown in conjunction with the feed. The governing rule here is to mend in such a direction as to keep the general shape of the drifting line *as straight as possible*. Once a belly or bow forms, drag will set in.

After the first loop of slack line has been flipped or mended out through the guides, grab more line with your left hand, transfer it to your right index finger, and flip again. Repeat until the desired amount of line is fed out. It pays to practice this technique in slow motion at first, possibly to a three-count of "grab, pinch, flip." In actual use, however, at the speed used on the stream, it's more like a two-count. As the loose loop is being flipped out the left hand is grabbing more line. Whatever the cadence, you should practice enough so that this all-important maneuver becomes instinctive. Combined with the reach-curve casts, this technique is one of the deadliest to have in your bag of tricks.

Stripping has a double meaning in fly fishing: pulling line off the reel and pulling line in through the guides. Both may seem simple, unimportant tasks, but at least one type of stripping, retrieving through the guides, is extremely important. Most anglers simply have not developed the speed and agility in their hands to do the job properly.

In our fishing experiences, we often encounter conditions where the extrafast retrieve is not only effective but deadly. This is especially true when fishing in the salt and when using streamers in larger rivers. Both barracudas and browns can really get "turned on" when a minnowlike imitation goes zipping by. The high-speed movement of a streamer probably excites the fish into a frenzy because it looks like an escaping minnow. Rapid retrieves also force a quicker decision by the fish and minimize discrepancies in the pattern.

For proper stripping, the line should go directly from the stripper guide to your "point of control," which is usually the index finger of the rod hand. The middle finger or even two fingers can be used, whichever is most efficient and comfortable for you. Grab the line, just behind your control point, with the thumb and index finger of

44

A close-up of how to feed line out through the guides. First, take line with your left hand . . .

Then transfer line from your left hand to right index finger, forming a loop between your index finger and the stripping guide.

As you shake the rod tip, the hanging loop will feed out through the guides.

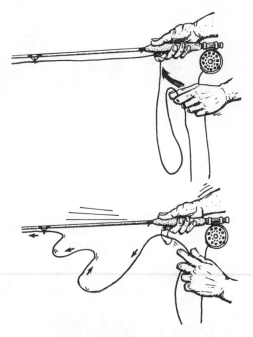

Feeding line through the guides: grasp the line fifteen to twenty inches behind the right index finger hold (*above*); then release the line from the right finger and replace it with the left-hand line. A quick flick of the wrist will feed the line out through the guides.

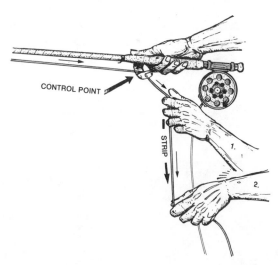

Stripping line: the line should go directly from the stripper guide to your point of control (the right index finger).

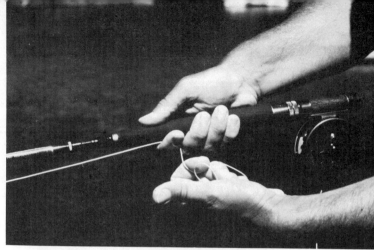

Palm retrieve #1

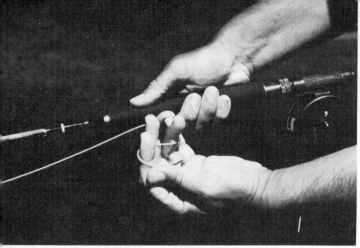

Palm retrieve #2

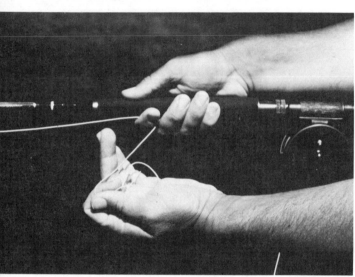

Palm retrieve #3

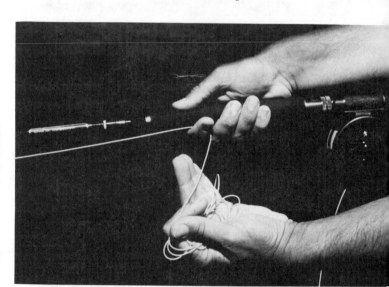

Palm retrieve #4

the left hand and pull or strip the line the desired distance. Practice both long and short strips, from 1 inch to 3 feet, and fast and slow strips. The extrafast retrieve will be the most difficult. You'll know you're getting on to it when you can strip an entire 90-foot fly line in less than 10 seconds. In nymph fishing, a very slow, steady strip is sometimes desired. The figure-eight, or palm, retrieve is very effective in this situation.

The roll cast and the roll cast pickup, which are practically one and the same, are valuable tools of the trade, designed to increase efficiency. When obstructions or special conditions—such as strong wind—severely inhibit a reasonable backcast, the roll cast can be used effectively. But we must violate some of the basic rules of good casting. Without the use of a backcast to build the power and line up the forecast, we must form a large loop of line and then apply enough energy with the rod tip so that it will roll to the target.

There are three important phases of the roll cast—initial rod position, loop formation, and final rod position. To start, bring the rod from nine o'clock up to the one o'clock position with a relatively slow movement. Hesitate until the line arcs down into the water, just off your casting shoulder. Then push the rod forward and snap

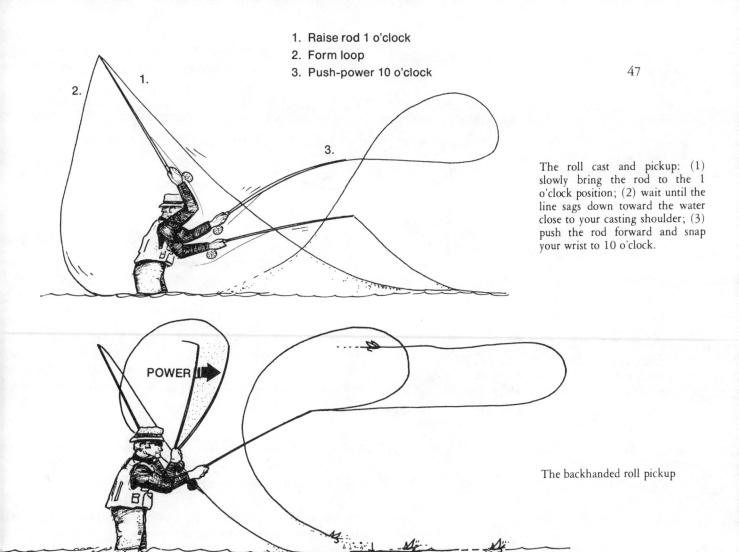

1. Raise rod 1 o'clock
2. Form loop
3. Push-power 10 o'clock

1.

2.

3.

The roll cast and pickup: (1) slowly bring the rod to the 1 o'clock position; (2) wait until the line sags down toward the water close to your casting shoulder; (3) push the rod forward and snap your wrist to 10 o'clock.

POWER

The backhanded roll pickup

your wrist to the ten o'clock position. By stopping the rod high, a tighter, more powerful roll will result. If you come all the way down to the water, the cast will die before the target is reached. The roll pickup is performed the same way except that you aim a little higher on the delivery. The object is to get the fly line airborne with as little effort and disturbance as possible and then begin normal false casting.

You will constantly use the roll pickup in both dry-fly and wet-fly techniques. It is invaluable for removing your fly from the water quietly at any time during a drift, especially when you have to make a change-of-direction cast. Practice this maneuver at every fishing angle, both forehanded and backhanded. The roll or versions of the roll can also be used effectively for such tasks as removing flies from logs, changing the pressure angle on a fighting fish, snapping weeds off a fouled hook, and throwing out slack line. To remove a fly imbedded in a log, flick a hard-driving loop down the line and it will reverse the pull on the fly and often yank it free. Normally a fighting trout pulls in a direction opposite the pull of the line. So, if, for example, you want to make a fish come back toward you, quite often you can move him by roll casting a loop of line that pressures him from the other direction. A roll cast followed by a well-timed pickup motion is also the simple way of snapping weeds from your fly and it can be used to supply large amounts of slack line quickly during or at the end of a drift.

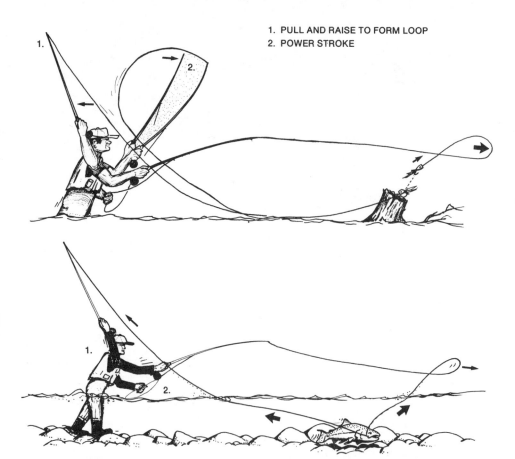

A roll pickup can be used to free your fly from snags.

Rolling a line against a hooked fish can often make him move toward you.

One of the most frustrating sights the angler often encounters, especially in large rivers, is a pod of 2- to 3-pound trout rising just out of casting range. Often these fish can be reached by keeping two or three large coils of line off the water while shooting. This eliminates the friction caused by ripping excess line from the surface while casting. You can hold the large loops in your left hand, or form two loops and hold them with your lips. This will free your left hand for double hauling and is an especially good technique if you are hip-deep in water as is the usual case in these situations.

Long-distance casting is based on the standard engineering equation F=MA, force equals mass times acceleration. It is obvious that if a line is to be cast farther, more force is needed. This leaves us two variables to play with, mass and acceleration. In fly casting, the fly line is our mass. By increasing the weight of the line, we create more force and can cast farther. And this is certainly the case, at least up to the point where the rod becomes too overloaded and the action breaks down. Increasing line weight, however, once the optimum weight for a given rod is reached, is very impractical. First, the loops will start to sag, making control over loop shape difficult; second, heavier lines slap the water harder, creating severe presentation problems; and finally, it's more fun and more satisfying to use lighter lines.

This leaves us with *acceleration* as the variable that can give us more force, hence more distance. Let's go back to the rod tip again. We keep saying that it is the important controlling element in fly casting. It controls the size of our loops, their shape, and their direction, both vertically and horizontally. *It also controls the speed of our loops.* So, if we can increase the speed, or accelerate the rod tip, we can throw farther. This, of course, is predicated on maintaining a constant loop size—in other words, keeping the air resistance factor the same.

Many weapons in our casting arsenal can add speed to the rod tip. We can add more force with our fingers, push harder with the thumb; we can use a more strenuous push-pull motion, flex the elbow more quickly, or simply try to make the whole arm move faster. The very best weapon at our disposal, however, is none of these but, instead, the *wrist.* It is by far the most potent element that can provide acceleration to the rod tip. If you have doubts, take a rod and snap it through a full 180° arc with maximum wrist power. No other set of muscles can begin to induce this amount of speed. Used properly, the wrist can provide the acceleration needed to cast light lines, #3s and #4s, 80 feet or more.

The stroke used for long distance resembles the basic casting stroke in that it consists of relatively slow push-pull movements sandwiched between explosive snaps of the

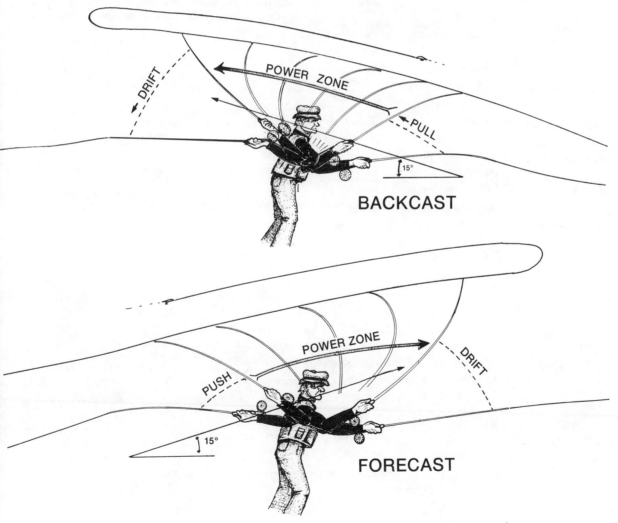

In order to compensate for the power stroke's longer wrist arc, you must raise the rod on about a 15° angle. That keeps the loops in at the proper 180° angle of separation.

wrist, but it differs in the amount of arc scribed by the wrist and the angle of the push-pull motion. In the basic stroke, the wrist works the rod back and forth between eleven o'clock and one o'clock, which is only a 60° arc. For long distance, the wrist flexes through a much greater arc, at least 120° and sometimes up to 180°. These fuller arcing motions are necessary so the wrist can build up higher speeds and unleash more power. Extra angulation of the rod also lengthens the stroke. This increase permits more line to be handled in the air and does a better job of loading the rod and taking the wrinkles out of the line.

With the added wrist movement, you've probably been thinking about air resistance and wondering how a tight loop can possibly be thrown when the rod dips all the way down to nine o'clock on the forecast and three o'clock on the backcast. Obviously, if a horizontal push-pull plane is used with this exaggerated wrist motion, the rod tip will go through a large depth of arc and a wide loop will result. And no matter how much wrist power is applied, the cast will fade or die because of excessive air resistance. Even with extreme wrist power, the loop must be tight in order to achieve distance.

Tight loops mean straight-line rod-tip travel. To make the rod tip follow a straight line, with a full-arcing wrist, the *rod hand must be raised during the casting stroke.* This lifting motion compensates for the "drop" of the rod tip during both the loading and unloading phase of rod movement. Every rod has a different stiffness profile and therefore requires a slightly different compensating motion by the rod hand. Generally, however, the push-and-pull portions of the long-distance stroke are tilted up somewhere between 10 and 30 degrees. After each forestroke and backstroke is delivered, a dropping, follow-through motion must take place in order to get the casting hand back to the proper level for the next stroke.

The long-distance casting stroke begins with the arm extended, hand slightly lower than shoulder level, thumb on top, and rod pointed at nine o'clock. Pull the rod back and up on a 15° angle, keeping your wrist cocked forward. When your hand nears the shoulder position, snap your wrist to the three o'clock position. Keep your thumb on top all the while. Then drop the rod slightly lower than shoulder level as the backcast straightens.

To make the forecast, push the rod forward and up on a 15° angle, keeping your wrist cocked backward. When your arm is almost fully extended and your hand is near shoulder level, snap your wrist to the nine o'clock position. Drop the rod slightly lower than shoulder level as the forecast straightens.

Be sure your thumb stays on top of the rod during the entire sequence. The timing is exactly the same as the basic casting stroke, but the angle of push and pull is different. The 15° is only an approximation; this will vary as the casting characteristics of each rod vary.

Hauling is a method of adding even more speed to the fly line but should not be attempted until the casting strokes are completely mastered. Most apprentice casters begin hauling much too early. Soon after they learn to throw 35 or 40 feet of fly line reasonably well, they get anxious for more distance. Rather than spending their time perfecting the casting stroke and tightening their loops, they take up hauling. With only a small amount of practice, they are overjoyed to find out they can add 10 to 15

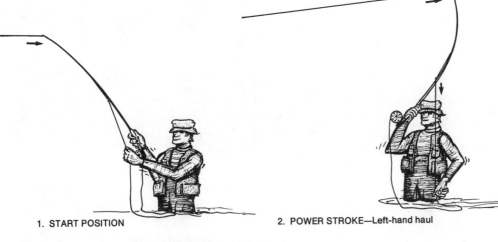

1. START POSITION

2. POWER STROKE—Left-hand haul

feet to their distance. Unfortunately, the development of their casting skills usually stops at this point. In reality, they are doubling the speed of their mistakes, or over-powering their poor technique to get a little more distance.

At any rate, hauling *is* a valuable tool for the fly caster, but *only* when it is added to properly executed casting strokes. The idea is to apply a *quick* pull to the fly line just as the power thrust is being delivered. This greatly increases the speed of the line, causing it to shoot farther.

Dry-run practice is by far the best way to learn the hauling motion. It further simplifies the process if the various parts of the motion are broken down individually. There are four parts or counts to the basic casting stroke, pull-snap-push-snap. Add the hauling movements to each part, one at a time, until both hands can be blended together smoothly.

During the first part of the basic stroke, holding the fly line firmly, *pull* the line hand along with the rod hand, keeping them side by side. During the backcast *snap*, pull the line hand quickly down to the waist area and immediately return it to the casting hand. This completes the backcast and single haul.

On the forecast *push*, again keep both hands together. During the forecast *snap*, pull down quickly and return with the line hand, just as you did on the back snap. This completes the basic stroke and double haul.

In actual practice, the hauling need not come down all the way to the waist area. A very short pull, only 6 to 12 inches, is sufficient. The main point to remember is that the timing of the pull and the snap must be exactly the same. If the pull starts before or lasts longer than the power stroke of the wrist, it will hinder rather than help the cast.

The following are exercises we use in our schools to improve casting ability:

1) *Painting a straight line with the rod tip.* Learning to make the rod tip travel in as straight a line as possible is undoubtly the most important aspect of good fly casting technique. There are several exercises that help promote straight-line movement. Beginners sometimes pick up this concept more quickly by casting sidearm, or in the horizontal plane. Stand facing a chalk line, or other straight line on the ground, and make the rod tip follow the line during the casting stroke. Once the stroke is mastered in the horizontal plane, slowly elevate to a more vertical plane, where such things as telephone wires and roof lines can be used as guides for painting straight strokes. Also, indoors, using a short rod that barely reaches the ceiling, paint the ceiling with your rod tip as you make the stroke. Or pretend the rod tip is caught in a track that runs along the ceiling.

3. DRIFT—Hands together

4. PUSH-POWER STROKE—Left-hand haul

5. DRIFT—Hands together

2) *Lining Up the Planes of Casting.* Not only should the front and back loops be lined up in a straight line when observing from the side, or ground level, but they should also be in a straight line when viewed from above, as from an airplane. The feel of proper plane alignment can be learned quickly by standing next to a chalk line, curb, edge of a driveway, or any straight line and making sure both the front loop and back loop stay directly over the line. Many casters are surprised to find out how misaligned their loops are.

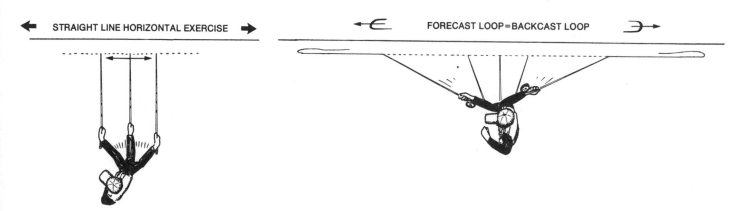

3) *Rod-flexing Exercise.* With proper grip, hold your rod straight out in front of you parallel to the ground. Flex rod in a horizontal plane from right to left. Make rod tip travel a 180° arc with *minimal* wrist movement. The object is to apply maximum wrist power with as short a stroke as possible. Actually try to break the rod with massive power that is applied as fast as possible with minimum arcing of the wrist. This is also a great exercise for strengthening the proper hand, wrist, and arm muscles.

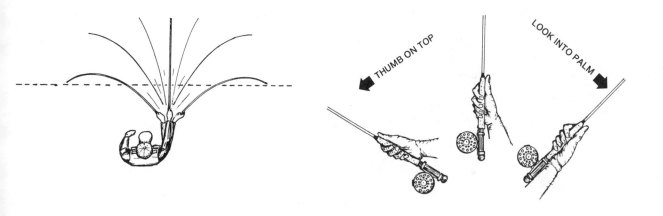

4) *Watch That Thumb*. This exercise might better be called "watch that palm." The thumb should always be on top, the leading side of the backcast and trailing side of the forecast. If you can look directly into your palm during the casting stroke, you know your thumb is right. Another aid that teaches the feel of proper thumb position is to cast with a large, flat sheet of material such as the side of a cardboard box or a piece of sheet plastic. Either cut out a grip at the bottom or attach a wooden dowel. Such a large, flat, lightweight sheet *has* to travel straight as it slices through the air, ensuring that your thumb will stay in the proper position. If turned even a few degrees sideways, it will immediately straighten itself because of the tremendous buildup of air resistance. This exercise not only corrects the thumb but teaches the feel of perfect loop alignment.

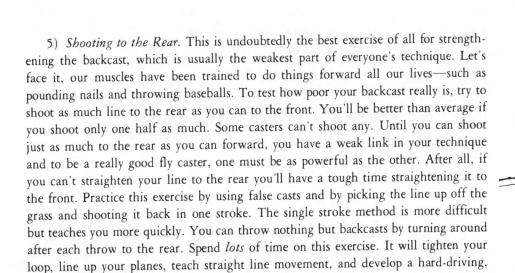

5) *Shooting to the Rear*. This is undoubtedly the best exercise of all for strengthening the backcast, which is usually the weakest part of everyone's technique. Let's face it, our muscles have been trained to do things forward all our lives—such as pounding nails and throwing baseballs. To test how poor your backcast really is, try to shoot as much line to the rear as you can to the front. You'll be better than average if you shoot only one half as much. Some casters can't shoot any. Until you can shoot just as much to the rear as you can forward, you have a weak link in your technique and to be a really good fly caster, one must be as powerful as the other. After all, if you can't straighten your line to the rear you'll have a tough time straightening it to the front. Practice this exercise by using false casts and by picking the line up off the grass and shooting it back in one stroke. The single stroke method is more difficult but teaches you more quickly. You can throw nothing but backcasts by turning around after each throw to the rear. Spend *lots* of time on this exercise. It will tighten your loop, line up your planes, teach straight line movement, and develop a hard-driving, dynamic backcast that will add distance and finesse to your forecast.

6) *The Heavy Rod—Light Line Routine*. Put a light line, preferably a DT- #3, #4, or #5, on a heavy rod, such as a #9 or #10, and practice loop control and shooting. Since the underloaded rod will hardly bend, *you* will *have* to do all the work— and you'll improve your technique faster.

7) *Casting Without a Rod*. This sounds difficult, and is, until you get the hang of it; but when you do get on to it, you'll soon learn about casting. You'll discover why the rod tip is the controlling factor in fly casting because your hand, in effect, becomes the rod tip. To throw any distance in this type of casting, you must shoot a lot of line and if you try to shoot through your bare hand, you'll burn your fingers. Use a small phenolic, or similar, tube to shoot through. With a little practice, casts of over 60 feet are possible.

8) *Lengthening the Stroke.* For long-distance casting, the stroke should be as long as possible—to load the rod more, to smooth out the large wrinkles in the line, and to maintain proper loop alignment. To find out exactly how your longest stroke can be made, stand next to a wall and go through the casting motion with your knuckles rubbing the wall. Do this at various heights—at, above, and below shoulder level—and mark the total reach for each one. You'll find the longest stroke can be made *at* or *very near* shoulder level. Combine body and leg movements into the stroke and you'll see it lengthen by as much as 2½ to 3 feet or more. Rubbing your knuckles along the wall will also help you get the feel of a straight stroke; practice in the shower on a smooth tile wall.

9) *Breaking the Rod.* To help develop a more dynamic casting stroke and strengthen important casting muscles, especially those used on the backcast, devote some of your practice time trying to "break the rod" on both forecast and backcast. In other words apply a sudden but great amount of energy during the final power portion of the stroke. You really won't break the rod (at least we haven't heard of one being broken this way yet), but you'll learn how to make the rod work at maximum efficiency for you. *Use a glass rod!*

10) *The Mini-Rod Trainer.* We advocate the mini-rod used with a piece of air resistant yarn as a valuable indoor training aid. The tip section of an old fly rod or ultralight spinning rod works fine. Certain aspects of fly fishing, such as line handling techniques, cannot be simulated with the mini-rod. Loop control, slack line, reach and curve casts, however, can all be refined right in your own living room or on a smoothly tiled or linoleum floor. Sit down on the floor and slide wide loops, tight loops, open loops, and closed loops across the floor. You can lay out, in stop action, such things as a high backcast and then slide the forecast straight ahead across the floor. Then you can see for yourself, in living color, with the candy canes separated by *less* than 180°, why the front loop closes and fouls itself.

11) *Shooting to the Hoop.* The amount of line a fly caster can shoot is normally a pretty good indication of his casting ability. To increase your shooting capacity, try the following exercise. Lay a hula hoop out on the grass approximately forty feet away, or at some distance that you can easily shoot to. Put that amount of line in the air and drop a perfectly straight cast into the hoop. Then pull in *one* fairly long strip of line, about two feet. False cast the 38 feet of line and shoot 2 feet into the target. Then, strip in twice, about four feet of line, and shoot the 36 feet of line back into the target. Keep repeating this process, adding 2 feet to each shoot, until you can no longer shoot back into the target. Work with this amount of line until you can make it, then take another strip in. This exercise will quickly improve your shooting ability. You're starting to get the idea when you can false cast 20 feet, 10 strips in, and shoot into the 40-foot target.

12) *Shooting Through the Hoop.* This exercise is designed to tighten your loop and improve accuracy. Merely hang a hula hoop from a tree limb, or some support, at about head level and try to throw your front loop through it without fouling. When you can consistently make your forecast go in and out without touching the edge of the hoop, then work on your backcast. This practice will quickly reduce the size of your candy canes so you can easily cast into tight, difficult areas on the stream.

13) *All-Wrist and All-Arm Casting.* This is just an exercise to make you understand casting better. Cast loops using only your wrist and then some using only your

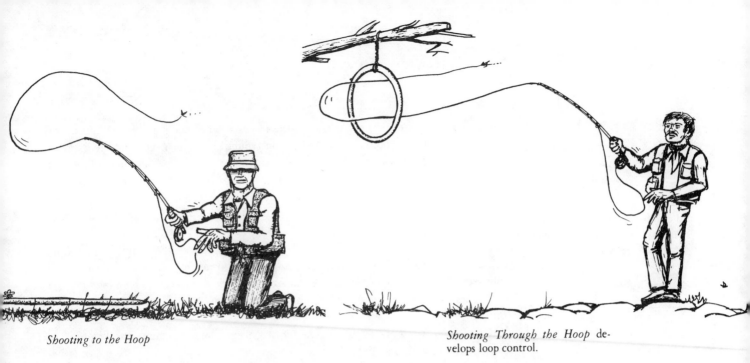

Shooting to the Hoop

Shooting Through the Hoop develops loop control.

arm. To produce straight-line rod-tip travel with your wrist, a strong, but quick, power application must be used. Notice how the rod must be snapped through a very small arc in order to throw a tight loop and how difficult it is to form well-shaped candy canes. Your timing must be absolutely perfect to do well at this.

Now throw some loops with only your arm, using a push-pull, sawing motion to make the rod tip travel a straight line. Notice the lack of power and authority in this type of motion. But also notice that timing is not so critical and that the loops are smoother. What these exercises point out is that a happy blend of arm and wrist is the modern, efficient way to cast. The wrist provides acceleration and power while the arm smooths out the loops and keeps the line from fouling.

14) *Isometrics.* Many claim that fly casting is all technique and that muscle does not play an important role. It is true that technique must be learned first. But once a caster has become proficient at loop control, strength becomes a big factor. Lots and lots of practice will strengthen the proper muscles but the addition of a few isometrics will speed up the process immensely. You can use some of the new isometric gadgets on the market or improvise. The simplest device is a wooden dowel, or better yet, part of the butt section of an old rod, just so long as you have something that's fairly rigid and is comfortable to hang on to. To exercise, merely simulate casting positions, both fore and back, and apply pressure for about ten seconds. You can catch the end of the dowel or butt section in a doorway, in the corner or a room or on a tree limb. Use your imagination. Just two or three minutes a day will work wonders.

15) *Backcast Low and Fast.* For longer and more dynamic casts, especially when working on distance, keep your final backcast extra low and the timing slightly quicker than usual. The lower backcast provides two advantages—higher angle of trajectory on the forecast and the best possible line-to-rod relationship. To gain more distance, the front loop needs more *time* to fight gravity. Considering the perfect loop relationship of 180°, the lower the backcast the higher the front trajectory, hence more time to add distance. Low back loops also create maximum loading of the rod on the forecast.

When the angle between the butt of the rod and the line is approximately 45°, ultimate loading conditions occur. This situation, maximum cocking of the lever, peaks

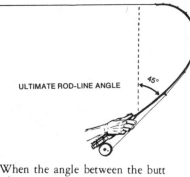

ULTIMATE ROD-LINE ANGLE

45°

When the angle between the butt of the rod and the line is approximately 45°, ultimate loading conditions occur.

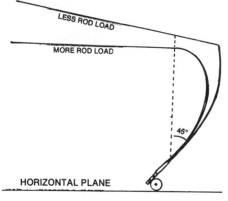

LESS ROD LOAD

MORE ROD LOAD

45°

HORIZONTAL PLANE

A greater angle means the rod is not being loaded to full capacity.

just as the power stroke is concluded on the forecast, when the hand or the butt of the rod is at an angle of about 45° to 55° to the ground. In simpler terms, if the backcast is aimed straight back, or slightly lower than horizontal, maximum loading will result, but if an identical backcast (same size, same power, and same timing) is aimed 30° above horizontal, less loading will occur. This may seem like nit-picking to many, but in long-distance casting it's important to take advantage of every inch of stroke and every ounce of power.

Another aid to more dynamic, longer casts, is to speed up the timing on the final delivery cast slightly. This is a very fine adjustment to make. Start your forecast just a split second sooner so you can utilize some of the backcast energy to help load the rod on the forecast. If you reduce the timing too much, you'll crack the whip and pop off flies.

16) *Laying the Line on the Table.* This concept sometimes helps the beginner to stop his rod at a high angle and align his loops better. Just pretend you're standing between two big tables, both five or six feet high. Try to skim the top of the table behind with your backcast and lay your forecast out straight on the table in front. After the line has settled on the imaginary table, then lower the rod to fishing position. This promotes the proper soft delivery and breaks that habit of "drilling" the line into the water.

17) *Straighten a Short Line.* It's relatively easy to straighten 30 feet of line and leader on the water because of the large amount of mass involved, but much more difficult to straighten only 5 feet of fly line and a 10-foot leader. Practice throwing straight to the target two ways, with only a few feet of fly line out and with just the leader out of the rod tip. The secret is keeping the loop both *tight* and *low* to the water.

18) *Practice in All Planes.* This is very important. Practice loop control exercises in every plane—sidearm, straight up, backhanded, and everything in between. Use the basic stroke, keep the loop tight, and keep your thumb in the same position for every angle. You can acquire this ability with very little practice yet it will pay big streamside dividends.

19) *Watch Those Loops.* From the beginning, form the habit of watching every single loop, both front and back, when you're on the casting field. After all, you can't expect to improve something if you can't see it. Every loop should form a stop-action image on your brain and should then be reviewed. In this manner, timing can also be refined. For example, you don't wait for a tug on your rod to make the forecast—by then it's too late; instead, you *watch* the candy cane and catch it just before it straightens.

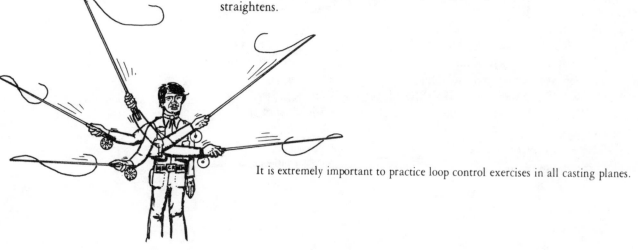

It is extremely important to practice loop control exercises in all casting planes.

CHAPTER 3

FISHING THE WATER—NO SURFACE FEEDING APPARENT

THERE ARE SO MANY METHODS of fishing a river when no hatch or spinner fall is in progress (almost as many methods as there are fishermen), that it would require a computer to list all the techniques. Often, different anglers using diverse methods will all catch some fish and sometimes no technique will work very well when fish are not actively feeding. Many rivers do not have much hatching activity, and even on big rich rivers, the surface activity lasts a relatively short time during a twenty-four-hour period. Thus, a thorough knowledge of attractor fishing is important, otherwise the majority of the time spent on the river will be wasted.

Even in this type of fly fishing, a good understanding of the insect population and hatching periods is useful; some hours before a hatch actually begins, trout will often feed deep on the nymphs that are becoming active prior to the actual emergence. Then a knowledgeable nymph or wet-fly angler should do well. At these same times very large browns may come out of their hiding places to gobble an unwary smaller fish that is gorging on the excited nymphs. The streamer expert with a good baitfish or small-trout imitation will occasionally hook a real trophy trout at such times.

Less known is the fact that the same streamer technique is also effective for very large fish during a hatch.

The very worst time to fish the water is directly after a hatch has ended. There is a

57

good scientific reason for this. Ichthyologists have proved that fish feeding actively during a hatch will gorge themselves to the point where insects are actually coming out of their throats and still keep on feeding. But when the hatch ends and they finally quit, they will not feed again for quite a while, even after some digestion has taken place, and they have plenty of room in their stomachs for more food.

This doesn't mean that it is impossible to catch fish after a rise, for not every fish in a river will feed during a particular hatch, but it is much slower and more difficult fishing.

The various methods of fly fishing when trout are not obviously feeding are:

1) Nymph and wet-fly fishing
2) Streamer and bucktails
3) Dry-fly attractors
4) Dry-fly realistic imitations
5) Dry-fly terrestrials

Each method is a whole field in itself and entire volumes have been written on each. Each method has its adherents who swear that their particular specialty is "the best answer." There really is no single answer, so at least a cursory knowledge of all the styles of fishing the water is necessary to meet specific situations.

An example of the need for versatility would be an angler fishing a spring creek for a period just before a hatch when nymphs are active, and the next day the same angler fishing a large, fast freestoner where no hatch is expected. If the time of day and water temperature were ideal for the season, the expert nymph man would do well on the spring creek and, very likely, a good streamer fisherman would be much more successful on the boulder-strewn, fast-water freestoner. This would not always be true, especially if a big stonefly nymph population was present on the fast-water stream; then the right nymph in the right hands could be even more deadly. The point is, one must know the river, its ecosystem, and have the various methods of attack at hand. Unless you are satisfied to be effective with only one specific type of fly fishing, you must have a working knowledge of all successful methods. A well-rounded fisherman will, over the seasons, catch many more fish and enjoy the sport more than the limited expert.

Trout holding behind a rock.

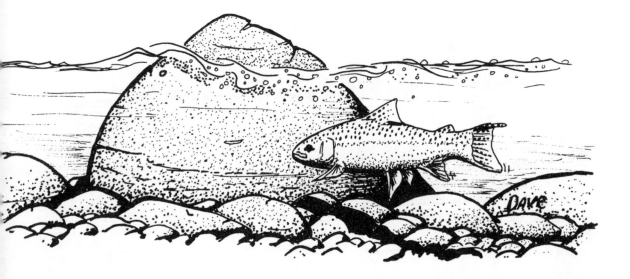

Trout holding under a raft.

WHERE TO FISH WHEN FISH AREN"T SHOWING

Normally, the only time trout will move into open, shallow water is during a good hatch, spinner fall, or at night when they are on the prowl under the cover of darkness. At these times, they seem to lose their native caution and sometimes go almost crazy. Most of the time, however, trout are wary and only to be found around some sort of cover. When they are not in a feeding frenzy, which is most of the time, trout are very skittish. They must protect themselves from predators, and the best way to do this is to hide. Browns prefer overhead cover. Rainbows prefer deep flows with boulders or other obstructions. Cover can mean a large boulder in a riffle that has slow currents in the backwash and broken water above to obscure the vision of flying predators; it can mean an undercut bank, a log lodged in a bend, an undulating weed bed beside a riffle, a deep run, a deep pool, even felled trees and man-made sunken rafts. The possibilities are uncountable. Along with restricted killing regulations, the best way to improve a stream is to improve the cover.

Trout holding under a submerged log parallel to the flow.

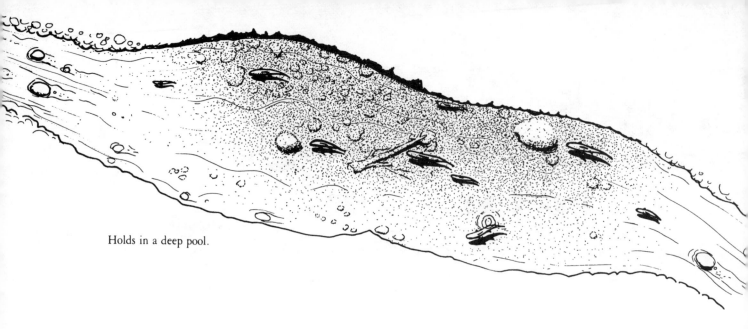

Holds in a deep pool.

When fishing the water in an attempt to catch nonfeeding fish, you must learn to recognize the places where trout rest and the cover they prefer. Whether you pound them up with variants, or drift a weighted nymph, bumping it along a deep run, you'll do best to fish in the places where the fish are. The illustrations here will give you an idea of what to look for initially. Keep in mind that cover need not be a huge boulder or a large sunken tree. A small rock or a medium-size branch can harbor surprisingly large fish.

A very important point to remember when searching the water is: *trout much prefer to hide under or beside cover that is parallel to the flow.* Large sunken logs are a perfect example—and log rafts or fallen trees where at least some of the elements are parallel to the current. A digger log placed at right angles to the flow is one of the very worst places to find trout waiting for a drifting insect; only if nothing else is available will trout linger in such a location. This has been proved time and time again during electroshocking.

Let's take up each method of blind fishing separately and examine the most productive times, places, and techniques for each type.

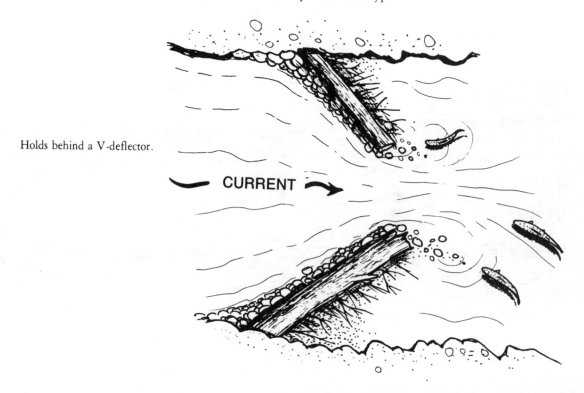

Holds behind a V-deflector.

Holds under a felled tree.

NYMPH AND WET FLY FISHING

Nymph fishing can be the most productive of all methods of blind fishing, particularly on rivers that have a large population of natural nymphs. The presence of a natural population of aquatic insects can be quickly and easily discovered by the use of a simple seine. The seining process will not only tell you if a good population is present, but also what type of natural (flat, oval, long, short); this will dictate the size and colors your artificial should be at a certain time.

Whether on freestone, spring, or tail-water fishering areas, if we are aware of what kind of insects are in or on the water in a particular season, we will be more successful. Alternately, if no aquatic insects are present, or are very slight in numbers, we would be better off using terrestrials or baitfish imitations. Only one piece of equipment is needed to discover what we must know. It is a simple seine—a piece of wire screen tacked to a couple of wooden handles. This is held on the downstream side of the angler, usually in gravel riffles. The angler kicks at the bottom, which dislodges the nymphs and pupas, which are then carried into the screen by the current. The screen is then lifted from the stream and its contents examined.

We first fished the streams in the West Yellowstone area some years ago in the month of August. We had no idea what aquatic insects the many streams in the area held. In fact, we were there to find out, since we were researching for *Selective Trout* and wished to include the important western species. We booked a motel room in town, and arrived at the Madison at dawn. It is a picture-perfect chalk stream in the park and has the appearance of a river loaded with mayfly nymphs. There was no surface activity so we got out the seine and explored the river bottom. We could find nothing at all in the gravel, nothing in the green moss beds, and only a few caddis cases near the bank on the logs and twigs. We fished all day long but there was no hatch at any time. A few caddises did appear at dusk, just as our seining had predicted. At this time of year we found that we were wasting our time on this particular stretch of the Madison.

Holds in a deep run.

A trout holding under an undercut bank.

We tried sections of the Fire Hole and the Gibbon next, with the same results. The third day we decided to try the North Fork of the Snake, about thirty miles west of the park. The results were incredible. On the first lift of the seine, clinging to the wire screening were literally hundreds of mature olive and brown mayfly nymphs, sizes #18 to #22. The river bottom was crawling with life. That day, exactly as the seine predicted, the hatches were spectacular. They started at nine thirty A.M., just as the sun took the mountain chill from the air, and continued until dark. Not one, but four species of flies were on the water that day, in immense numbers, and we had good nymph and later dry-fly fishing to rising trout.

By getting samples of the nymphs on the stream where you are about to fish, you can choose an artificial of the same size, shape, and color, and be confident that you are using a representation of what the fish are surely feeding on. It will give you confidence in your fly, and is a lot better than the hit-or-miss method. It could keep you from nymph-fishing a river that has no nymphs, or from wasting your time on a hatch that will never occur. When matching your artificial to the streambred naturals, size and shape are by far the most important characteristics. Color need only be fairly close for success. If the naturals you find in the seine are #16, slim and rounded, do not select a #14, robust, flattened artificial. Such a mismatch will not be nearly as effective as the correct size and shape.

Our favorite *nymph style*, which we use to imitate mayfly types, is very simple. It can be tied slim, flat, fat, rounded, large, or small. The abdomen is spun fur (sometimes ribbed with gold wire for a little flash). A thorax is made of spun fur with a darker feather wing case and legs. Tails are made of some speckled soft feathers, such as grouse or wood duck. This style dressed in the appropriate colors, size, and shape is good for most mayfly species.

When nymph fishing at times when hatches are not in progress, the flies should be presented deep, either drifting or swimming just over the bed of the stream. This is probably the most difficult technique to accomplish as even a moderate current lifts a dragging fly very rapidly. It can be accomplished by either one or a combination of the following:

1) Weighted nymphs
2) Qwik-sinking lines with short leaders
3) Short lead lines incorporated into the leader
4) Casting upstream and permitting the fly to sink as it comes down without drag
5) Weighted dropper fly on the leader
6) Split shot on dropper

Our basic nymph pattern

The nymph pattern tied in two basic shapes: short and fat, and a longer, slimmer shape.

The main thing is to get the nymphs down deep where the fish are resting, because most of the time they will not move very far to take. You must drift the fly close to make it easy for them, and, of course, the fly should be similar to the natural nymphs they are accustomed to feeding on. Steelhead and Pacific salmon require that a fly be drifted just by their nose before they will take. Drift your nymph close to cover and obstructions except when fish are flashing in the runs just previous to a hatch. At these times, the fish will leave the cover and move to the area where natural nymphs are to be found in the greatest numbers.

The most productive time to fish an artificial nymph is when fish are feeding on natural nymphs. These periods are just before and during an emergence, but the occasional trout will sometimes come from cover to grab a drifting and swimming nymph when not actively feeding, although the success rate will not be anywhere near the catch at the ideal time.

Other than the techniques of deep drifting, swimming, or twitching, a large, fat, furry nymph, fished with a very short leader and a sink-tip fly line, can be allowed to sink to the bottom and stripped back at various speeds. We vastly prefer the soft, fur-bodied nymphs, which show natural translucency, over the more realistic hard artificials, which sometimes even have the small detailed marking of the naturals painted on. These flies look good to the fisherman but for us they are not appreciated by the final critic of our fly-tying skill, the trout.

Probably the most natural way to present a nymph to nonfeeding trout is the use of a lightly weighted or an unweighted artificial, cast up and across stream. As the nymph floats down with no drag, it sinks to the bottom; the drag-free float is maintained by mending line in the proper direction, so a very long, natural float can be achieved. As the float finally comes to an end, the fly is raised to the surface and twitched slightly with the rod tip to simulate an emerging nymph.

This technique is not only effective, but is the most pleasant way to fish a nymph, as no weight is required. Weighted flies and split-shot are abominations to cast and completely destroy the aesthetics of fly fishing. This is, however, the most difficult method of sinking a fly to the bottom. Here is our basic technique for fishing any unweighted fly (wet, nymph, or streamer):

1) You must first pick your primary target area—that is, the spot in the flow where you want the fly on the bottom. This would be a spot where you believe trout to be resting.

2) It takes time for the fly to sink to the bottom, so you must figure out how far to throw the fly upstream, above the target area so it will have enough time to drop to the desired level. This will vary depending on the speed of the current and the depth of the run. A little experimentation may be necessary. When you have picked this spot upstream (the secondary target area) cast a straight-line cast one foot past this spot and break the surface tension with a pull of the left hand. This submerges the fly and leader, and puts the fly into the proper line of drift.

3) As the fly and line float downstream, you will find that the line will eventually acquire a downstream "belly." If left unchecked, this belly will drag the sunken fly up toward the surface. So, as this belly begins to form, we mend the line with upstream loops to eliminate tension on the sinking fly.

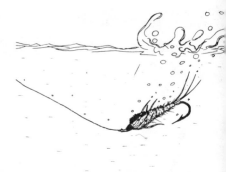

A weighted nymph heads right for the bottom, taking the leader with it.

Casting up and across stream allows the nymph to sink and float in the current in the most natural manner.

A nymph on a quick-sinking line and a short leader is pulled to the bottom by the fly line.

64

The straight-line cast, a valuable
technique for nymphing

You can establish a constant tension
factor and maintain it by raising your
rod during the first phase of the drift.

Continue to maintain tension by raising your rod. When your fly is directly
across stream from you, the rod will be at its highest level.

You can maintain tension as the fly drifts below you by lowering your rod and reaching downstream. Feed line out for longer drifts.

This is the proper position for the double-hand strip, used for extrafast retrieves.

4) Also, as the fly begins coming downstream toward you, begin to raise the rod to establish tension and to keep the line as straight as possible, but without any pull on the fly. The rod tip is at its highest level when the fly is directly across-stream from the angler's position.

5) As the fly drifts downstream from the angler's position, the rod tip is slowly lowered, while maintaining the same tension on the line. The rod tip can be lowered to the water, and "reached" downstream for a longer drift.

6) At the end of the complete drift, or at any other point where you believe a concentration of trout exists, various actions can be given to the fly, including complete dead drift; dead drift with twitches; twitching rising fly in front of bulging fish; dead swing, in which fly is permitted to swim up to the surface and across current, at the speed of the current; fast, escaping rise (by stripping line); a broadside swim (as the fly passes downstream from the angler, line can be fed out and *mended downstream*. The fly can be made to swim almost all the way across the stream by this technique).

When drifting the fly downstream, remember that the fly goes where the line goes. To work a fly around an obstruction, such as a protruding log, or next to a grassy undercut bank, mend the line next to the problem spot and the fly will follow.

When the current is too rapid or the water too deep to allow the fly to sink to the bottom, an unweighted tail fly and a heavily weighted large dropper fly, possibly a stone fly nymph, will often accomplish the desired effect. The light tail fly will swing and drift in the natural manner while the heavy dropper will occasionally be taken. This technique is sometimes preferable to using a large hunk of split shot, since the shot has no chance of enticing a strike while the heavy dropper fly does. The dropper should be attached by short stiff piece of mono, which will prevent twisting and fouling around the main leader.

Another way of getting a fly deep—whether a nymph, wet fly, streamer, or bucktail—is to use ultrafast sinking line and leader materials, such as lead-core trolling lines and stainless steel leader wire. Segments of these materials, varying from 4 to 36 inches, can be incorporated into a regular nylon leader, normally about a foot back from the fly. We fabricate these "mini-heads" at home and carry an ample supply in our vests. Form loops at each end of the segments to facilitate tying onto the leader.

At the end of the drift, you can let the nymph hang in the current at a dead drift.

Twitching the rod will add a little movement to the dead drift technique.

A lead core section of line incorporated into the leader

Lead Core Section

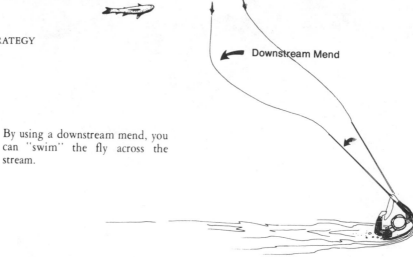

By using a downstream mend, you can "swim" the fly across the stream.

By pulling the line back with your left hand, you will break the surface tension.

By far the easiest, and currently the most positive method of getting the fly on the bottom is the split shot on a dropper technique. A long tippet (2 feet) is tied on the end of the leader with a blood knot. One of the ends of the blood knot is left untrimmed and an overhand knot is tied at the tip. Split shot is then pinched on the dropper. This rig is cast slightly up and across stream, and the shot is permitted to "tink" along the bottom. If the correct amount of lead is attached, you can easily feel the shot bouncing on the gravel stream bed. It is a deadly technique and can be used whenever a completely bottom drifting fly is needed for trout, steelhead, or salmon. Of course you will lose some "rigs," and it may be the understatement of the year to mention that it is not much fun to cast this kind of setup.

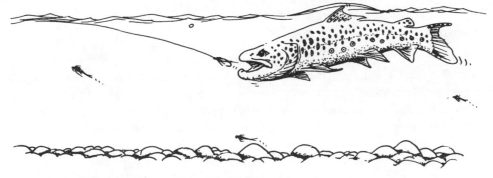

Twitching your rising nymph in front of bulging trout can be a deadly technique.

We have a number of favorite nymph patterns that we use at different times, on various types of water. One of the best is the Hexagenia Wiggle Nymph, #2-#6. Natural *Hexagenia* species are burrowing nymphs found in muck beds. We fish them on cloudy days along the banks of such rivers as the big Manistee, which has large numbers of naturals. It is especially effective in late June and July, when the naturals are emerging, but it is good all year (even in the winter) as the nymphs must emerge from their burrows every time they shed their skins. This occurs about thirty times from egg to maturity. These *Hexagenia* nymphs are allowed to sink to the bottom, and then retrieved with a twitch or fast swimming motion.

On large, fast, boulder-strewn streams, such as the Yellowstone or the Madison, a stone fly wiggle nymph is often devastating. It is the best fly we've ever used on the big cutthroats in Yellowstone Park. It should be fished very deep in completely dead drift. Wiggle nymphs fished dead drift have action of their own and are often twice as effective as rigid nymphs.

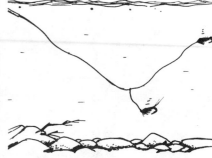

A weighted dropper fly will help sink your fly in deeper water.

A small olive nymph of the standard mayfly type, in sizes #18 to #24, imitates many species of *Baetis, Pseudocloeon, Cloeon,* and *Ephemerella,* and is good on all rivers that have mayflies. A size #18 is best for searching the water. Mayflies can be fished dry, just under deep, dead drift, or twitched.

Certain rivers have more caddis than mayfly hatches, especially below dams. A size #18, green or brownish-tan caddis pupa is the best pattern for searching this type of water, especially when fish are bulging. We fish them dead drift, 6 to 8 inches below the surface. As they come into the bulging area, we twitch them to the surface *actively.*

The most universally effective nymph during late April, May, and June, in the East and Midwest, is the Slate Brown Emerger #14, #16, or #18. We have had good fishing with it on the Beaverkill when Hendricksons, *Paraleptophlebias,* and *Baetis vagans* are all emerging at the same time. This pattern is a good prototypal fly for most emerging spring mayfly species. It is best fished slightly subsurface and twitched occasionally.

A piece of split shot on a dropper is no fun to cast, but it is by far the easiest method of getting the fly to the bottom.

Dave Whitlock has evolved a whole series of fuzzy, impressionistic nymphs for the tail water fishing areas of the South. While most of these patterns do not attempt to imitate a specific species, they are good general flies for many species, and we have found them effective on all trout waters, not just the streams for which they were originally designed.

Wet-fly fishing is the old traditional method of starting a boy fly fishing. The standard wet-fly patterns represent emerging mayflies, caddises, stone flies, nymphs, and small minnows. All the techniques used in nymph fishing can be applied to wet-fly fishing. Many volumes have been written on the patterns and use of the old traditional wet fly, and we need not repeat what is voluminously recorded elsewhere. This is still a very effective method of fishing the water, and usually this type of artificial is given some action as opposed to the well-known dead drift of the nymph fisherman, although dead drift works well with wet flies, also. Some of our favorite wet fly patterns are:

1) Gold Ribbed Hare's Ear
2) English March Brown
3) Black Gnat
4) Leadwing Coachman
5) Grey Hackle
6) Light Cahill
7) Royal Coachman

Wet-fly and nymph fishing are more productive on certain waters than others, and some of the best types are the new tail water areas found in the southern states. They were created when great hydroelectric dams were built, which turned smallmouth bass streams into great trout rivers. The water is taken from under the surface of the lakes to run the generators. The result is that the river below the dam maintains a constantly cold temperature, summer and winter. Trout grow to huge sizes in these tail water areas, due to the twelve-month growing season plus an overabundance of food. The White and Norfolk rivers in Arkansas are prime examples. Fish grow from 1 to 1½ inches a month in these waters and browns close to 30 pounds are not unheard of.

The water level varies greatly depending on generating requirements, but the streams themselves remain clear and at a constant temperature. The best fishing is at low-water periods, which usually occur once or twice a day for at least a few hours. A few of these rivers, such as the Norfolk, have good mayfly hatches; *Baetis* can be observed emerging in the middle of winter. Other rivers, such as the White, are better known for their huge shrimp and crustacean population.

Due to the change in water type from warm to cold, our traditional trout-stream hatches were never present on these tail water areas and most of the warm water species were wiped out. Only insects capable of adapting to the change were able to survive; and even these adapted species are periodically decimated during extremely high water. Wet flies and nymphs imitating shrimp, scuds, sow bugs, and fairly large impressionistic mayfly nymphs and small minnow imitations are the most productive artificials.

SHRIMP AND SOW BUGS

Since this southern tail water fishing is good in both summer and winter, it makes a great break for northern anglers in December and January, as the weather is almost never too cold and fly fishing is possible all winter long. Here the nymph and wet fly are kings.

No esoteric equipment is needed for wet fly and nymph fishing. Some fly fishermen say that a special soft rod is mandatory for feeling the strike. Not true; we often fish nymphs before the hatch, and dries during the emergence. It would be ridiculous if we started with one rod and had to trot back to the car for another when we wished to change methods. We use the rod with the *action* we like and can mend line with. A rod that mends line well will not be too floppy in the tip. It will generally be easier for the beginner to cast, mend, and handle line with a longer rod, say an 8-footer. A more experienced angler can go shorter, say 5½ to 7 feet, depending on personal preference and ability.

We like a bright yellow line for good visibility, weight forward for shooting and because a minimal amount of false casting is needed so the wet flies and nymphs don't dry out. It should be kept clean and greased so it shoots and mends easily.

The ideal leader would be a 10 to 12-footer with tippets as fine as possible (depending on size of fly) for natural action in the water. A Qwik-sink, flat butt would be best. A sinking solution should be applied to the fly and the leader.

Polaroid glasses are often a great aid in anticipating a strike. When you perceive a soft strike you should set the hook quickly, but not hard. Often the take is vicious and the fish will actually hook itself, but the tip of the line should be watched closely, since most takes are gentle. Any unnatural hesitation should be met with a soft, quick strike.

STREAMERS AND BUCKTAILS

Knowledge of effective streamer and bucktail patterns and how to use them provides the angler with one of the most deadly attractor techniques, especially for large trout. In most streams, trout under 10 inches feed mainly on aquatic insects, but as they grow bigger, they become more dependent on minnows and small trout to satisfy their diet. Extremely large trout, especially browns over 20 inches, devour many pounds of smaller fish each season, even though they may feed heavily at hatch time. For this reason, the fisherman equipped with the proper patterns and casting techniques can consistently score well when the fish are not feeding freely on insects.

By and large, streamers and bucktails are tied to imitate small fish or minnows but they can also be fabricated into excellent nymphal and crustacean patterns. The typical minnowlike imitation ranges between 1 and 4 inches in length with the tiny variety, down to ½ inch, and the monstrosities, up to 8 inches, being the exception rather than the rule. Most stream minnows run in the 1- to 3-inch range, a fact that should be kept in mind when tying or buying artificials. Concentrate on total length of the fly rather than hook size. A size #6, for example, can vary from 1½ to over 4 inches, depending on shank length, the amount of overhang past the bend of the hook, and even the tying style of the flytier. It makes sense to use a fly that is consistent with the size of the natural minnows found in the stream being fished.

The basic difference between streamers and bucktails lies in the material used for the wings. Feathers are the principal ingredient for streamer wings while hair is the predominant material used for the wings of a bucktail. Both fly types have advantages and disadvantages. Bucktails are a pleasure to use since they rarely foul the hook; but their action underwater is not the best. Streamers have great action—but the wings continuously tangle around the bend in the hook. It's frustrating having to check your fly every few casts to see if the wings are fouled or not.

Our favorite streamer, and one that solves the tangling problem, is the Matuka. This fly is not new, but we've run into only a handful of anglers around the country who use it. We started fishing the Matuka about seven years ago and it quickly became one of our favorite attractor flies, even topping the effectiveness of the Muddler Minnow. Originally, we tied our Matukas in shades of brown and olive, but now we carry every color in the rainbow and tie them from tiny #16s all the way up to large saltwater sizes. Our most popular sizes for trout are #6, #8, and #10. Olive, brown, black, grizzly, and dark grey are the most effective colors.

The Matuka-style tie has a number of advantages over the standard streamer, which accounts for its effectiveness. First, the wings on a typical streamer join the body just behind the eye; this creates a "scissor effect" between the wing and the body as the fly is stripped through the water, which of course is not a natural movement of a small fish or minnow. The Matuka wing is lashed down at the bend of the hook; this keeps body and wing in a straight line and prevents the unrealistic scissor movement. The wing is also tied down over the top of the body in such a way as to form a series of slanting spines. These groups of fibers fan up when the fly is underwater to form a much more natural-looking, minnowlike silhouette. By lashing the wing all along the top of the body and at the bend, the feathers are much less likely to tangle around the hook. In fact, if tied properly, they never tangle.

The Matuka, then, provides an excellent combination of realistic imitation, great action, and trouble-free operation. It has all the advantages of both streamers and bucktails but none of the disadvantages.

For the very best-looking Matukas, ones with full outlines and many spines, use at least *three* pairs of wide hackles. In fact, try some with hen hackle that has lots of web. Be sure to pick out as many hackle fibers as possible along the top of the body. Quite a few fibers will get lashed down in the tying process, so you must pick them out with a dubbing needle. The more spines, the better the fly looks and the greater its effectiveness.

Another version of the Matuka that we've found to be very effective is the Wiggle Matuka, a takeoff on our Wiggle Nymph, which has a hinged tail section.

The Matuka can be fished in the typical across-and-down manner but we normally use a perpendicular-to-the-bank technique. With this system you try to keep your fly line at right angles to the bank during most of the retrieve, and mend in such a direction as to maintain the 90° relationship. This presents the fly sideways to the trout, which certainly must look more tempting, and gives you a much better hooking angle. Normally, you must mend *downstream* to keep the line at right angles to the current. This also keeps plenty of tension on the line so you don't have to worry about setting the hook.

The fast, escaping-minnow retrieve seems to work best with the Matuka—not always, but most of the time. Be flexible in your technique. Try varying retrieves and varying casting angles. Sometimes a cast straight downstream followed by the fastest retrieve possible is the only thing that will work. At other times, a long, upstream cast with a complete dead drift return will produce best. Try every angle of the clock, at every depth and at every speed. There's almost always a combination that will score, *if* you have versatility in your technique.

Matuka

Another of our favorite streamers, and one that has many of the advantages of the Matuka, is Whitlock's Serpent Fly. Dave developed the Serpent for bass fishing and it is absolutely devastating. It is undoubtedly just as effective as the well-known plastic worm. Dave gave us some of these flies several years ago and, like fools, we never thought of trying them on trout until a year ago. Our first attempt was on the no-kill section of the Beaverkill. It was late one afternoon in mid-May and feeding activity had completely stopped. During those periods of desperation, you're ready to try anything. Traditionalists would have cringed at the thought of tying on such a monstrosity, fully 6 inches long. We did, though, and it worked spectacularly. It was an abortion to cast, especially with #4 weight, 6-foot rods, but it gave us an extra hour and a half of unbelievable streamer fishing. Large browns, which had previously been superselective in taking our delicate, hatch-matching imitations, came flashing up from the depths to attack this weird invader. Since then, we've put the Serpent to great use in many similar situations across the country. Like the Matuka, it is such a tempting morsel and has such great built-in action that fish find it difficult to leave alone. For smaller streams and ease of casting, we now tie the Serpent in much smaller sizes, down to 1½ inch in length. The secret of the Serpent's action lies in the selection of the hackles, which should be as soft and willowy as possible. A fast, pulsating retrieve usually works best.

Dave's Serpent Fly

Marabou streamers are another of our favorites, especially in salt water. They are difficult to tie so that the feathers don't tangle around the hook, but their breathing action in the water is unbeatable. Adding the new extrafine strands of mylar makes the Marabou, or any streamer, even more effective. It works beautifully in the water and has just the right amount of minnowlike flash.

Another type of Marabou, one we call the "Super Streamer," is tied with complete Marabou hackles. With this method, you can fabricate extralarge streamers, 8 inches and longer, that are light in weight and easy to cast. We originally designed these for king and coho salmon in the Great Lakes and their tributaries. They also produce well for large saltwater species, such as giant tarpon, kingfish, and sailfish.

The wings on standard streamer patterns are traditionally constructed of slim and willowy saddle hackles. Saddles have excellent action but sometimes lack enough bulk to provide a good fishlike outline. To correct this poor silhouette, try some wide, webby hen hackles on your favorite streamer patterns. Grizzly hen hackles make realistic, all-purpose imitations.

The muddler is our favorite bucktail, though we also use the Black-Nose Dace, flies. It has taken more large trout than any other bucktail-type fly. Almost every serious fly fisherman carries a selection of Muddlers in his vest. They are easy to cast and very effective, but most of all, they are extremely *versatile*. They can be fished on the bottom, slightly subsurface, or right on top. Or wet and dry on the same cast. Dead drift, dead drag, twitch, dart, or swim. They imitate minnows, sculpins, crustacea, nymphs, stoneflies, grasshoppers, and crickets. Muddlers adapt to more fishing situations than any other fly. They are devastating on the big rivers of the West. Our favorite method is long-casting to the far bank, quickly throwing several large downstream mends, and then actively stripping the fly perpendicular to the current.

Muddler

The Muddler is our favorite bucktail, though we also use the Black-Nose Dace, Squirrel Tail, and Little Brown Trout. It pays to carry a well-stocked streamer box.

Marabou Muddler

SEARCHING THE WATER
WITH THE DRY-FLY ATTRACTOR

There is nothing more pleasant than searching a dancing riffle with one of our favorite attractor patterns on a cool, clear day. Even if rises are scarce, just casting and observing the fly drifting naturally in the currents, drag-free and upright, makes a day on the river worthwhile.

Patterns used for dry-fly attractor fishing are usually heavily hackled affairs—spiders, variants, bivisibles, and hair wings; and the water fished is normally moving fairly fast as these patterns work best in broken water and riffles. Other favorite dry attractors are badger peacock redtag and the groundhog wing, shoulder-hackle patterns that represent both caddisses and stone flies that are often found hugging the riffle at almost any time of the day.

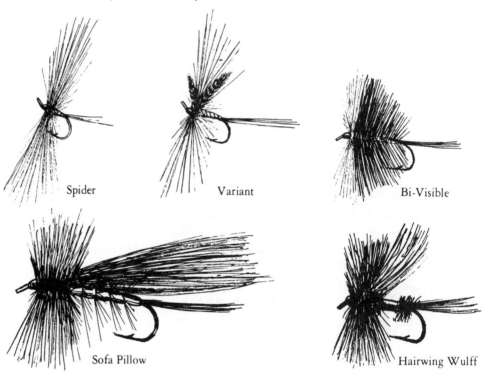

Spider   Variant   Bi-Visible

Sofa Pillow   Hairwing Wulff

Groundhog Caddis

Badger Peacock Red Tag

Our very favorite caddis attractor pattern is the Henryville Special. We tie it in all sizes and colors to represent the various species of caddis. Although it is heavily hackled and a good attractor, it is also an exact imitation of a flying, buzzing caddis. It is the greatest hackle pattern we have ever used and can be fished drag-free, skittered, or even wet and dragging.

The normal method of fishing these attractors is to cast quartering upstream and let the fly float dead drift over likely holding spots. Search out and cast close to any likely-looking bit of cover so the fish need not expose himself more than necessary when taking. Spiders, variants, and caddis imitations can be skittered across the currents, giving them a fluttering action with the rod tip. This often entices a fish to chase the fly quite a distance.

We have fond memories of the huge flat pools of the Muskegon River where this works well. We skitter very large spiders, #14 to #16, that are brown and grizzly or all black, with a long rod, and 18-inch browns hit, busting the quiet stillness of the pools. We've tied some conventionally, but perhaps the most effective were tied horizontally, parachute style.

For some reason, the Humpy (a typical attractor) often works wonders on western rivers when no activity is apparent. It has given us good fishing on such streams as the Gallatin, Madison, Yellowstone, and Gibbon. Perhaps it reminds the trout of a stone fly. Who knows? It works!

In midsummer, a Dry Bee pattern is many times the deadliest attractor of them all. For our midwestern streams, we fish it dead drift with an occasional twitch.

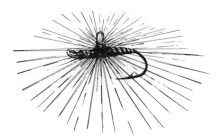

Parachute Spider

Attractor-type dry-fly fishing is usually rather unproductive on the placid spring creeks, but really comes into its own on tumbling freestoners where the fish are lean and hungry. Freestoners, like spring creeks, are not peculiar to one section of the country. They are found in abundance from the Adirondacks and the Poconos in the East, to the Upper Peninsula of Michigan, across the lake into Wisconsin, and in lavish numbers on both slopes of the western mountains. Their riverbeds are mostly stones, ranging in size from fine gravel to boulders the size of houses. Rarely do they have much weed growth, mudbanks or sandbanks, or submerged log jams. The phenomenon that freestone streams share in common is their rather barren bottoms. They undergo great seasonal variation in water level. In summer, and especially dry weather, they are low and clear with interspaced slow pools and fast riffles. At these times, the streams actually have beaches of gravel that provide plenty of room for backcasts. During the spring runoff and other periods of heavy raifall, they suddenly become dark raging torrents, scouring the banks and riverbeds of newly accumulated debris. Often even a small shower will raise and darken the water. This is because the melting snow and the falling rain do not soak into the ground, but run off the land into the river. Because of this, the Yellowstone is unfishable during the salmon-fly hatch seven years out of eight, but if you hit that one year, it's fantastic!

Deer Hair Dry Bee

These great variations in water level somewhat limit the families of insects. For example, burrowing mayfly nymphs would not be found in significant numbers, as there would be little mud for them to burrow in. On some of these streams, stoneflies are perhaps the most common insect and would provide a large portion of the fishes' diet.

These rivers are mostly fast water with occasional pools, and the classic method of fishing them is with a heavily hackled dry-fly attractor.

The fish are generally not selective because the food is scarce; blizzard hatches are not everyday occurrences, trout are lean and hungry, and the artificials whiz by in the rapid current. The fish have little time for a leisurely examination. They grab what they can, when they can, so large buglike dry-fly attractor flies are effective. These fish like a mouthful and must be quick to get it.

There are periods, though, especially during low water in quiet pools, when delicate casting and realistic imitations are needed. On these occasions, the canny angler will revert to the same techniques so successful on the spring creeks.

In the fast water, between pools, trout rest in the least turbulent areas, which are in front, behind, and to the sides of large rocks and other obstructions. From these resting positions they will dart out into the faster currents to pick up large, drifting dry-fly attractors.

The fish in the slower pools will rest deep in the channels, moving into the head or shallow tail to feed during the hatch. In the fast portion of the stream a large meaty imitation is required to entice the fish to surface feed. They must expend too much energy to bother fighting the heavy current for a small reward. The slow pools, of course, are a different matter. Here, even the tiniest of insects may produce a rise. Thus many eastern freestoners have good summer fishing to the *Tricorythodes* spinners. Fish feeding on small flies will usually move back from the holding water to the tail of the pool, where the water is slow and shallow. When larger flies emerge from the rapids above, fish will come to the deeper head of the pool, as the size of the flies makes fighting the current worthwhile.

These freestone streams have greatly changing moods, and a wide variety of fishing. They are lovely, tumbling, intriguing places to fish.

A typical eastern freestone river

DRY-FLY REALISTIC IMITATIONS

In many situations, it's even more effective to search the water with dries by using a realistic imitation. These are a little more difficult to see on bouncing riffles but they more nearly resemble the natural food trout are accustomed to, and short strikes, which attractors are notorious for, are almost nonexistent with realistic duns and spinners. We are referring to the No-Hackle Duns, Paraduns, Hen Spinners, and Partridge Spinners that we developed for fishing the rise—and to the spent caddisses.

Nothing is more deadly on nonfeeding fish than a fairly large (#12 or #14) full-spent Dun/Brown Hen Spinner early in the morning. If a fish is on the lookout for food, even though not freely rising, which would it accept more readily—an attractor, which looks little like anything in nature, or the clear-cut outline of an insect form he is very familiar with? This sounds good in theory and works well in practice. A No-

Hackle Dun, especially a Slate/Tan searching a singing riffle in midafternoon, is unbeatable. These should be tied sidewinder style with wings from duck shoulder feathers, or with a pair of turkey breast feathers as recommended in *Selective Trout*. Wing materials of this type are indestructible and scores of fish can be landed on a single pattern.

The worst fly to use in blind fishing is a fragile pattern. These can be worn out just by repeated casting, and in fishing the water you can expect plenty of casting between strikes. Presentation is important; long drag-free floats over productive water are essential. The curve-reach cast will give you the longest and the best natural floats possible in most situations. And this cast is one of the most deadly techniques we have. Here, we are not throwing at one fish in particular, but rather to a long, attractive run of 40 to 50 or more feet long. The preferred casting angle is about 45° up and across from the beginning of the run.

When fishing to the left bank (looking downstream), use a left reach cast, lower the rod tip, feed line and mend in such a manner as to keep the general orientation of the line as straight as possible. When a large bow forms, drag will set in.

When fishing to the right bank, use a reach curve, reaching to the right and curving to the left.

With the reach-curve-feed-mend technique, the *whole* fly line can be run out with *no* drag setting in. It provides a great presentation angle, because the fly goes over the fish first, with no chance of "lining" the trout. Hooking is easy if you don't hurry. Let the fish turn with the fly and he will hook himself. If you strike too fast, you'll pull it out of his mouth. Don't set hard; take up the slack and pick up the rod tip.

The technique has other advantages. It is great for twitching or skittering a fly, as well as providing enormously long, drag-free floats; and it works well for no-hackles, since the upstream pull of the line on the fly creates a planing effect, keeping it high and looking alive.

When searching the water we prefer to wade downstream and cast slightly up and across. This type of fishing is really hunting. You are hunting for a fish that might be hungry enough to rise from cover to a surface fly. The more water you cover, carefully and quietly, the longer the float and the better the chance you have of finding a greedy fish. Downstream wading is far quieter and much easier walking. We still cast to cover, shelter, and obstructions, which are usually directly across stream from our first casting positions. Actually, this is similar to the more traditional upstream approach, for even then, the cast is across, not directly upstream, which would "line" a rising fish.

Rivers that seem tailor-made for searching the water with realistic imitations are a type we call seepage spring creeks. These are not quite as placid as the streams we usually associate with the term spring creeks nor are they as rapid as the freestoners where unhackled flies are more difficult to follow in the heavy current.

Some spring creeks have their genesis from one or two giant springs and are actually the emergence of underground rivers. The Letort in Pennsylvania, the Castilia water in Ohio, and Armstrong Creek in Montana are examples. They are usually short streams, not exceedingly wide, and very smooth. This type does not have so many different insect species, but the hatches usually occur over a longer period of time. Most spring creeks are from 1 to 10 miles long, then run into another river or lake. If longer, they soon change character, acquiring run-off water, and after a while begin to resemble freestoners.

The seepage spring creek starts from many springs at the headwaters, grows to medium size, and then becomes a great, broad river from the addition of thousands of springs along its entire length. These long seeping spring creeks have the greatest number of insect species of all types of rivers. The Au Sable of Michigan is typical. Long though it is, it receives very little runoff, due to the character of the country it runs through. It is surrounded by mixed pines and hardwood forests, and the ground is very sandy. The forest holds back groundwater and the sandy glacial drift sucks up water like a sponge. When the water finally soaks down to the river, it is pure, and cold, cooling the river and maintaining a steady even level during its entire 200-mile length.

A typical western spring creek

What mainly distinguishes all spring creeks from freestoners is the supreme consistency of the flow found in the former. High water on the spring creeks means a rise of 1 or 2 inches. Discoloration is nonexistent, a mere clouding, barely noticeable. Normal conditions are a slow, even flow, with possibly a few gentle riffles, and water as clear as triple-distilled gin. These streams get little or no runoff, either from rain or melting snow. The regular spring creeks are placid rivers, decorated with pods of watercress on their banks, and swaying clumps of bright olive vegetation in their flows between clean white gravel channels. They are rich alkaline waters with consistent levels, and a veritable cornucopia of aquatic insect hatches. The clear smooth currents enable the trout to take a long leisurely inspection before taking or refusing a floating insect.

Since the water is seldom rapid, the fish can "tip and sip" even the smallest naturals because little energy is required for them to hang suspended in the flow. Because bank cover and bottom channels are not periodically scoured by floodwater, many more nymphs survive. Some of these rivers produce more varied hatches and larger blizzardlike hatches day after day. Muck banks do not get decimated in the spring, so burrowing mayfly species have a place to live. There are plenty of slow waters for the crawlers and clamberers, and the constant temperature, due to the steady flow of springs, doesn't alternately freeze and cook the insects.

The spring creeks are the supreme water for the dry-fly enthusiast. They are "match the hatch," "selective trout" type streams, par excellence. They are the sister streams to the chalk streams of England where the dry fly was born and nurtured for so many years. Their rich sparkling waters demand excellent patterns, the lightest of leaders, and delicate deliveries. Their undulating submerged moss beds create swirling difficult currents, which makes the mastery of curve casting mandatory for any degree of success whatsoever.

As great as they are, the smaller, quieter limestoners are not very good dry-fly streams when no hatch is in progress. It usually takes an emergence of naturals to get the fish interested in surface feeding. One is much better off using nymphs when "searching" this type of water. A few exceptions do come to mind. On the western spring creeks, a #16 to #18, Grey/Yellow, No-Hackle Dun is often very good before the *Ephemerella infrequens* hatch starts. On the spring river at Mammoth Springs, Arkansas, an #18 to #20 Grey/Yellow *Baetis* Dun imitation works great when the water looks dead. On the Kennekenic in Wisconsin, the Grey/Yellow #18 *Baetis* pattern often produces fat browns that jump like rainbows.

Seepage spring creeks are another matter entirely. These by their very character are ideal for searching with realistic imitation. Some fish are always looking to the surface for food; heavily hackled flies are not usually successful for the water is not extremely fast; the lower riding no-hackle patterns are easily followed in the flow. We have had exceptional fishing on the Au Sable's north and south branches with Dun/Brown Hen Spinners early in the morning. Sizes #12, #14, #16 are best. This pattern is successful because it has a good mayflylike outline, and the color is representative of about 90 percent of all mayfly spinners. Hungry fish, still cruising from the night before, seem to relish a stray spinner, flush in the film.

Strangely enough, these seepage spring creeks offer some spectacular night fishing with realistic dry flies. Large browns feed avidly at night and are on the lookout for the occasional *Hexagenia* or Brown Drake Dun. A large Paradrake #6 to #10 can produce some truly spectacular catches.

The North Fork of the Snake is another example of this type of river. Although one of its origins is a large spring, it receives no runoff water in the Island Park area. Realistic imitations are very productive in its great runs, Hen Spinners work well in the morning and Slate/Tan No-Hackles during the afternoon.

TERRESTRIALS

Although good, steady rising to terrestrials does occur—as to a large migration of flying ants, for example—most times an angler is imitating the occasional hopper, juicy cricket, moth, beetle, or other land-bred insect that has accidentally fallen or been blown into the stream. The object is to have an artificial that will imitate insects native to the area and season. Again, we search the cover, rocks, logs, cut bank, and jams with our artificial, but in particular, we cast near the shoreline. Cut banks are ideal; trout can hover close to a protective area and still be in a position to spot the occasional green oak worm or hopper that finds its way into the currents.

There is an ideal stretch of the Upper Madison in Yellowstone Park that is wide, shallow, and riffly with cut banks. In late August and September, the browns hug the hollow stream edge waiting eagerly for the sun to warm the bank grasses and for the big western hoppers to become active. One glorious August morning we hit this stretch at about ten thirty when everything was right and hooked many browns of a size we had never dreamed would be found in this section of stream. We stalked the banks, casting upstream ahead of us, and splatting our #10 Dave's Hoppers just off the grassy banks. After a short drift we would twitch the hopper a little and the fish would come from under the banks with a rush. The strikes were small explosions.

Fishing the tiny jassids is similar (fishing close to the banks), but the rise form is often a mere dimple; sometimes the fly just disappears. We have seen large rainbows sipping #12 red beetles in western streams in the same manner. Thousands of these *Coleoptera* somehow become waterborne on warm spring mornings in late June, and the trout gorge on them.

Each type of terrestrial has its season, and of course the season varies from river to river, and from East to West. The larger ant flights seem to come both in August and September. Most of the others, such as green oak worms, hoppers, jassids, night moths, beetles, and crickets, all feed on bank vegetation and the height of the plant-growing season is a good time for fishing terrestrial imitations. On many streams this usually comes at a time when the large ephemerids become scarce, happily extending the season for large juicy insects that often bring large fish to the surface.

Terrestrial fishing is highly productive on meadow streams. It is here that the na-

Polypropylene Green Oak Worm

Flying Ant

Calcatera Ant

Dave's Hopper

Cricket

Calcatera Beetle

turals live and have a greater opportunity to fall into the flow. Although a typical forest-bordered river will have a few land-bred insects, it will not be as productive as a lush meadow stream, with such few exceptions as oak worms and night moths.

When you are fishing terrestrials with no surface activity apparent, try to fish sections of the stream running north-south through a meadow area. The prevailing westerly winds will blow more insects into these sections. When fishing forest sections during late May and June, look for white birch trees. That's where you'll find the most green worms. Very large fish seem to be on the lookout for these juicy morsels, which hang from the branches by a single silken thread. This type of fishing runs in cycles. On a year when the green worms are heavy, the fishing can be spectacular.

Large hoppers are the most deadly dry-fly attractors in the West, from August through October. Size can be *very critical*, depending on the season (early or late). You should carry large, medium, and small ones. Dave's Hoppers are by far the most effective patterns we have found. They must be thrown very close to the bank, and if you can pull them off the grass bank, that's even better. It's terribly important to grease your line, leader, and fly. The higher the hopper floats, the easier it is to impart effective action. They often draw the most strikes when twitched occasionally. They are sometimes excellent when fished wet, dead-drift, and dead-swing.

Black Ants are very good when used as attractors in sizes #16 to #18, fished in quiet pools. We have had especially good luck fishing the spring creeks with them. When fish are actually feeding on a flight of ants, they become extremely critical, not only of size and color, but even of the body shape. An imitation without the bulge for thorax and abdomen and a thin waist is useless.

Fluttering a white moth across the stream in the evening, and even after dark, is a good way to raise cruising browns. Forest streams provide the best of this often spectacular angling. A 5- or 6-pound cannibal trout smashing the surface in pursuit of a skittered #6 or #8 Night Moth in the dead night is guaranteed to give you the shivers.

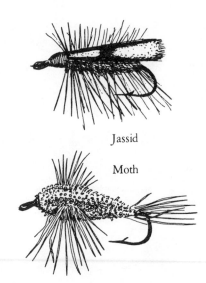

Jassid

Moth

CHAPTER 4

FISHING THE RISE

A FEW CUMULUS CLOUDS drifted in the blue afternoon sky as we parked our rental car below the hill at the fence crossing and walked through the meadow. Stark brown peaks surrounded the lush green valley through which a silver ribbon sparkled in the sun as it wound its way toward a sun-parched desert. In a few moments we came upon the smooth deep runs of Silver Creek.

The banks of the stream were boggy and thickly overgrown with reeds and tall bushes. The flow was strong and difficult to wade. The pungent odor of new-mown hay drifted on the wind, and our hands trembled slightly in anticipation. We had given a slide presentation at the Federation of Fly Fishermen's annual conclave in Sun Valley, and this was the first time we had been able to get away to fish.

The stream's placid surface was carpeted with emerging Blue/Winged Olive Duns, about size #18. We captured one, and sure enough, the species was *Callibaetis coloradensis*, size #18. We tied Slate/Olive Sidewinders to our 12-foot 6X leaders, and again our hands shook as fat rainbows dimpled the water in every direction. We had been anticipating this all summer: fishing the rise on a beautiful western spring creek. Minutes later, we were both fast to leaping trout.

Fishing Silver Creek in Idaho, and other spring creeks like it from Pennsylvania to Montana to California, is the ultimate in dry-fly angling. Their weed-choked channels

80

Silver Creek in Idaho—an exquisite limestone river

harbor great, well-conditioned fish and a veritable cornucopia of insect hatches. This, more than any other experience, is what makes dry-fly fishing so addictive—casting over freely rising trout, fishing the rise.

In some ways it is the easiest brand of fly fishing, but in another way it is the most challenging and difficult. It is often easy because the fish show you where they are. You need not have much experience in reading water, learning lies, or coaxing fish out of resting positions. They are up, in the mood, and gorging on naturals. You can see it all for they are exposed, betraying themselves to the angler. But being in the middle of a great pool that is alive with feeding fish, yet unable to draw a rise, getting nothing but refusal after refusal, can be the most frustrating experience imaginable.

When fish are taking naturals all around yet ignoring your imitation, you are doing something wrong. You may not know what it is, but something is not right and it is obviously your fault.

The hatch can be the toughest time because the fish know what they want (after seeing a few hundred drift by) and usually want it drifting by in a natural manner (drag free). A fly drags when a faster, or slower, current catches the leader or line, and pulls it so the artificial travels faster or slower than the surface of the water it is floating on, often leaving a wake. Thus the angler is faced with two problems:

1) Selecting a suitable pattern (one that will resemble the naturals closely enough to trigger the feeding reflex of the trout);

2) Presenting the artificial properly in a natural manner (usually, but not always, drag free).

The solution to the first problem lies with some basic knowledge of entomology, and either tying or purchasing the proper fly patterns. In *Selective Trout* we detailed the fruits of our studies on this subject.

A dragging fly creates an unnatural pattern on the water that is clearly visible to the trout from beneath.

The solution to the second problem takes time, experience, and thoughtful practice. This is because about 80 percent of all casts to rising fish should be slack line, reach, or curve casts. No matter how realistic your pattern, if it does not act like the naturals you will not hook many fish, especially the larger ones.

The slack-line casts, such as the lazy S, are effective and much easier to learn. But the curves and the curve-reach casts are usually even more effective, though more difficult to master. You *must* study the chapter on curve and reach casting and deliberately practice these casts. This cannot be emphasized enough. Master the slack line, the reach, and the right and left curve casts. Without them you are practically helpless.

The best position from which to cast to a riser is usually directly across and slightly downstream from the taking position. This ideal position must often be varied considerably due to obstructions, difficult crosscurrents, and deep unwadable water. It can vary all the way from a straight upstream cast to a straight downstream cast. These are compromise positions, so when at all possible, get as close to the ideal position as you can. Get as *close to the rise as is reasonable*, but not so close as to disturb the trout; around twenty feet, if you can do it, is best.

The longer the cast the more chance for a sloppy presentation. Also, even a steady riser will allow many naturals to go by, and since your fly is in direct competition with many drifting naturals, *the shorter the cast the more casts you can get over a fish before the hatch is over.* The more drifts you can get over a fish, the greater the chance of averages working in your favor, and the more likely an eventual taking rise.

During a heavy hatch on a stream with a good population of trout, it may not be necessary to move much in order to cast to rising fish. At other times, during sparse hatches, cold weather when fish are lethargic, or areas where trout are rather scarce, it is often necessary to range rather far in order to find "risers." Here again we usually (but by no means always) wade downstream as we search for a surface feeder. When

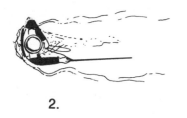

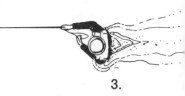

2.

X

3.

The best position from which to cast to a riser, across and slightly downstream (#1), in this illustration would call for a left reach cast. Casting from directly upstream (position #2) would call for a slack line cast; from directly downstream (#3), a curve cast would be best.

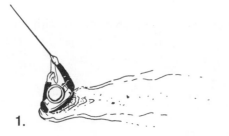

1.

Rising trout on a spring creek

we do find one we carefully get into a casting position, which again is across and slightly downstream from the riser. The reason we wade with the current is simply because it's easier and quieter than fighting your way upstream against a heavy flow; also, much more water can be explored.

A *careful* downstream approach does not disturb fish preoccupied with emerging insects. On small streams, walking the banks is probably the least disturbing. Of course, if a good fish is spotted surface feeding upstream from your position you may approach from the downstream side, but you must wade slowly and carefully so that too much splashing does not alarm the fish.

If you are across from a riser in the ideal approach position, with the current moving from right to left, you would give him a left curve. If the flow is left to right, the best cast would be a left reach. A shaky S or a slack line cast would also be effective. A fish directly upstream would need either a right- or left-hand curve. A fish directly downstream requires a slack line cast.

The fly should land gently a few feet above the rise. (This distance can vary quite a bit according to circumstances.) The closer to the surface a fish is hovering, the closer to the rise a cast can be because the window gets smaller as the fish gets closer to the surface.

On the first cast to a really worthwhile fish—one worth spending time on—you should cast the fly a little short so that it doesn't float directly over him. This is especially true if the fish is feeding close to the bank or some cover. Then, if you get some drag, misjudge the distance or the current, a bad drift will not put him down. Only when you are sure that you have all the factors worked out do you increase the length of the cast, so the fly drifts directly into his feeding lane.

When a fish takes, only a very gentle strike is required, a mere raising of the rod tip. If he wants the fly he will usually hook himself. *Short strikes are invariably due to bad patterns or a bad presentation, not because the strike is too weak.* The fish may come up to look but at the last minute refuse to take, although the disturbance made by his turning in the current may give the appearance of a true take and is often mistaken for a true strike.

At certain times an action float is needed, for example, during caddis and stone fly hatches and egg-laying flights. At these periods, a rather heavily hackled downwing

Henryville

Groundhog Caddis

Palmer Hen Caddis

pattern works well, either a Henryville, a groundhog pattern, or a palmered Hen Caddis type. These insects often bounce up and down on the surface expelling eggs. The fly in this case is cast above the rise and bounced across the stream in short jerks.

During a rise (and often before) a nymph, cast far upstream, allowed to sink to the bottom, then raised to the surface in a short jerky retrieve, will simulate a natural nymph swimming to the surface. This method is quite deadly at the right time. Another effective way to fish the nymph during a rise is dead drift in the surface film. A drag-free float is needed and, here again, the angler needs to master the curve casts. Sometimes a straight cross-stream cast is made and the nymph is allowed to swing down and across the current with no action; or alternately, a short series of twitches can be employed.

One of the most universally devastating methods of fishing the rise is with a *high floating nymph*, exactly like a dry fly. We have found in the last few years (by the use of a stomach pump) that *more nymphs are taken dry than are winged duns during a hatch*. A trout will take three or four floating nymphs, then one or two winged flies, and then go back to the nymphs again. They do not take all nymphs, then switch to all duns as was previously thought. *This is a very important observation, for a nymph tied on a 3X fine wire hook and well greased will quite often outfish the dry subimago two or three to one.*

At times, a nymph fished right on the bottom is the only way to get action, even when there are flies apparent on the surface. Fish flashing deep in the runs are a dead giveaway to bottom feeding. This is especially apparent during *Ephemerella* hatches. Several methods are available to get the fly on the bottom. The use of a short leader (2 or 3 feet) and a fast sinking line is one method. Weighted flies, lead on the leader are some of the best ways, and the use of various lengths of lead-core trolling line (depending on depth and speed of current) between a short leader and the fly line is another. Sometimes only 6 inches are needed. We carry 4-inch, 6-inch, 1-foot and 2-feet lengths. These can be added to, or subtracted from, as necessary. A short, jerky retrieve is good in this situation.

Since some insect species uncase their wings, anywhere from just off the bottom to 4 inches from the surface during the emergence, emerger patterns are often very good.

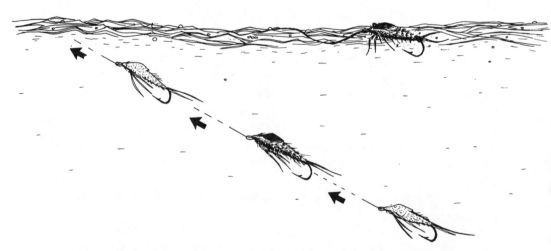

Two productive ways to fish a nymph: short, jerky retrieves from the bottom, imitating the rising nymph; and floating in the surface film.

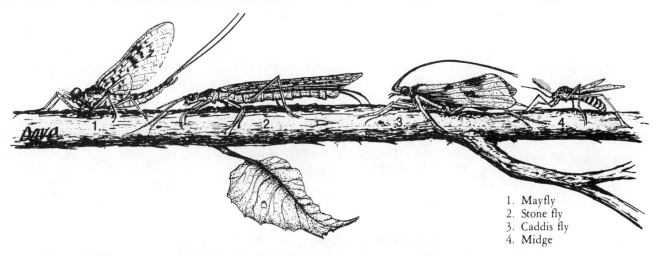

1. Mayfly
2. Stone fly
3. Caddis fly
4. Midge

These can be divided into wet and dry emergers. The wet emergers are tied on wet-fly hooks and the body is the color of a natural nymph body. The wings are usually hen hackle tips tied short, and sloping back over the body. The dry emergers have the color of the natural subimago body, and short duck feather wings tied sidewinder style. They are extremely effective fished dead drift in the film. Their effectiveness is increased anytime the duns have difficulty drying their wings, such as on very cold days or in cool drizzly weather.

Matching a "simple" hatch is often ludicrously easy. Anyone can do it successfully if he takes a little time. Any of the recommended pattern types will work when used in the correct size and at the correct time. If the fish are feeding, find out what they are feeding on: it's that simple—especially if you're getting refusals with what you think will work. Do not keep trying pattern after pattern blindly. *Find out what is actually on the water.* Insects observed flying at a distance look quite different "in the hand." They are usually much smaller and of a slightly different shade.

The most useful hatch-matching aid an angler can carry is a simple goldfish net, or, better yet, a tropical fish net. This can be dipped in the water so that the current carries the drifting naturals into the fine mesh. Now the insects can be examined closely and an artificial of the correct size, shape, and color selected. The scientific names need not be memorized, though you should at least be able to distinguish among the four major trout-stream insects: stone flies, caddis flies, mayflies, and midges. Mayflies are the only ones with upright wings. Stone flies have perfectly flat wings, and caddis flies' wings are folded in an inverted V over their backsides. Midges are tiny creatures with down wings shorter than their bodies.

The types of pattern effective for each stage are as follows:

MAYFLY DUN TYPES

1) Sidewinder No-Hackle Dun
2) Paradun
3) Paradrakes (for very large flies)
4) Standard tied sparse

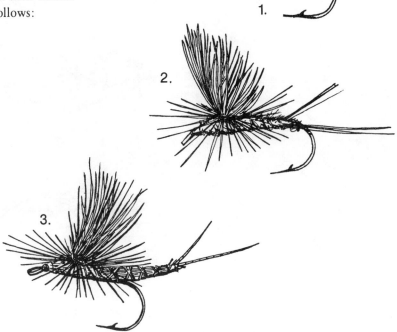

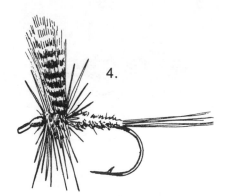

MAYFLY SPINNER TYPES

1) Hen Spinners tied one-half spent
2) Partridge Spinner tied one-half or full spent
3) Full Hackle Flies, no wings

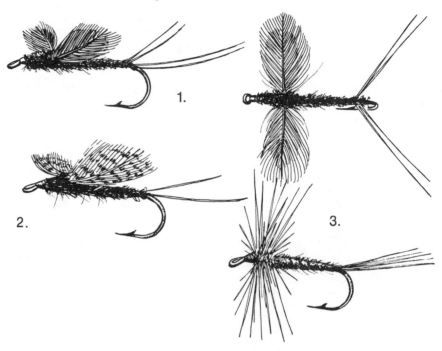

MAYFLY NYMPH TYPES

1) Standard fur-dubbed duck sections thorax nymph and wiggle nymph for slow water

2) Emerger nymph for slow water

3) Floating nymphs with large fur wing cases (elytrons) and split tails

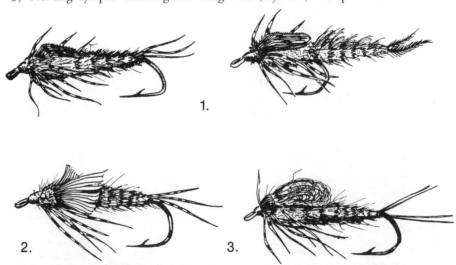

STONE AND CADDIS IMITATIONS
1) Hen Caddis
2) Henryville Special type
3) Caddis at rest
4) Dave's Stone Fly (Whitlock)
5) Caddis Pupas

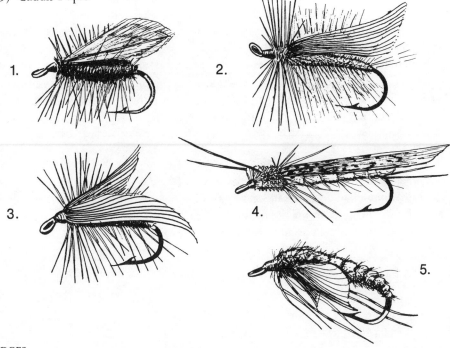

MIDGES
1) #26-#28 Hackle Fly
2) No-Hackle Midges
3) Midge Pupa

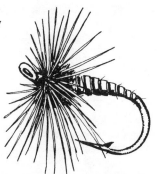

The no-hackle patterns work quite well even on fast, riffly water, although they are sometimes more difficult to follow with the eye. It is true that trout are much less critical in an extremely rapid flow, especially choppy riffles. Here, heavily hackled patterns do work and are much easier to see. Standard hackle patterns also work on quiet water if tied correctly; the rub is, they are hardly ever tied correctly. It is simply much easier to get a fly tied completely without hackle, which does catch fish, than to get a hackle pattern tied sparsely enough to be really effective. Even expert, experienced flytiers invariably use too much hackle of fiber that is too long until finally the wing is obscured, if not totally obliterated.

Sometimes one pattern, in a few sizes, can be a good representation for many species of naturals. This allows a reduction in the number of patterns needed for a well-stocked fly box. The following list would be effective for approximately 95 percent of all hatches you might run into across the country.

___

NYMPHS
1) Standard dark brown fur body, in sizes #6-#22
2) Standard medium brown fur body, in sizes #6-#22
3) Medium olive fur body, in sizes #14-#26

By far the majority of mayfly nymphs are dark to medium brown; a few are olive, especially in spring creeks or any streams with lush weed bottoms.

___

DUNS

Any of the following types may be used:
1) No-Hackles
2) Paraduns
3) Standard patterns and V hackles if tied very sparsely

The first word in the name is the color of the wing, the second word pertains to the color of the body. The tails are usually the same color as the body, and the hackle is usually the same color as the wing.

Remember, if you are using standard patterns, keep the hackle sparse.
1) Slate/Tan, size #12-#26
2) Grey/Yellow, size #14-#22
3) Slate/Brown, size #14-#20
4) Grey/Olive, size #12-#26

___

SPINNERS

Either one-half or full-spent Hen Spinners or Partridge Spinners can be caried for any of the species.
1) Dun/Brown spinner, size #6-#26
2) Dun/Olive spinner, size #14-#22
3) Dun/Yellow spinner, size #10-#18

___

MIDGES

1) Pupas should be tied on size #24s and #28s in grey, black, yellow, and green with fur bodies.

2) Adult midges, hackle flies, palmer and no-hackle midge type in colors grey, black, green, and yellow.

CADDIS FLIES AND STONE FLIES

1) Caddis Pupas—fur bodies in colors; green, tan, and brownish black, size #14-#20.

2) Caddis Adults—either or both the palmer caddis type, or the caddis at rest type in colors; black, tan and olive, size #14-#20.

3) Stone Flies—use groundhog patterns. Body colors should be yellow, black, and olive. Normal sizes are #14-#18 with a very few large #4-#6-#8s. Hackle is brown and grizzly mixed.

In our experience in fishing the rise, size and shape are much more important than trying to match the exact shade or color. The excuse often given that "my fly was the wrong shade of pinkish tan" has little validity. The imitation is probably too large or too bushy, or possibly the fish were nymphing or feeding on emergers.

The color of mayflies varies considerably, even in the same hatch on the same riffle. It varies to even how many seconds have elapsed after the actual splitting of the nymphal case. The longer after the emergence from the case, the darker the fly. So don't worry too much about exact shades, rather get the pattern clean-cut in outline and be sure you are fishing the right stage (nymph, emerger, dun, or spinner). Above all, get the right size! Even one size off will cause many refusals.

When a fish takes an insect on the surface he usually leaves a bubble on the water. Knowledge of rise forms can also be very helpful at times, especially during the multiple hatches, and in determining whether a trout is taking duns from or just under the surface. It can be stated more or less as "the law of rise forms" that: "the larger the insect, or the more likely it is that an insect of any size can escape, the more likely the rise form is to be splashy and noisy." Conversely, "the less likely the insect's escape from the surface of the water and/or the smaller the insect, the quieter the rise." Thus, small spinners caught in the film with no chance of escape will evoke steady quiet feeding, often with just partially observable rings and even no ring at all. The fly often merely disappears. Just because it is a quiet rise form doesn't mean large fish are not involved; in fact, the opposite is often true. Large, meaty duns struggling to escape the film, or caddises that escape quickly, will cause noisy, splashy rise forms. Here, very small fish can make a lot of noise. Much time can be wasted by the neophyte on inferior fish. Only experience can cure this fault.

Certainly the law of rise forms can be helpful during a multiple hatch. For example, if two species of ephemerids, both duns and spinners, emerging caddis flies, egg-laying stone flies, and spent midges are on the water simultaneously, and the rise form is very steady, quiet, and deliberate, the chances are that the fish are feeding on spent spinners or midges. The most difficult time to match the hatch is during the multiple hatch and spinner fall, and there may be no simple answer other than to allow the knowledgeable angler an edge on what to try first. These multiple hatches will be covered fully in following chapters.

Another rise type is the jump rise, when trout jump clean out of the water after fluttering caddises or stone flies. The best way to handle fish like these is to cast a palmer hackle fly to the spot as soon as possible.

All types of trout will feed during a hatch or spinner fall, but it is generally agreed upon that browns are the best surface feeders, with rainbows second, and brooks third.

Browns usually stay close to the banks near cover, while rainbows and brooks feed toward the center of the runs. Browns are the toughest to fool—but no large trout nowadays got that way by being stupid.

Here are some tips on fishing to specific common hatches:

1) Hendrickson (*Ephemerella subvaria*)

A dry slate/tan emerger with duck shoulder or quill segment wings tied short has given us our greatest Hendrickson dun fishing. For the spinner fall, it pays to carry both *full spent* hen spinner and *full hackle* patterns. The latter can be trimmed to half-spent with scissors.

A new point: *many* Hendrickson spinner falls occur on warm mornings from 9:30 to 11:30, not as previously thought in the evenings! These flies need warmth and warm evenings in early May are very rare.

2) Pale Evening Duns (*Ephemerella dorothea*)

When you run into a hatch at dusk or after dark, the duns must float high and the casts must be accurate. Work into the fading sun for visibility. Stand in quiet, shallow water, not in heavy fast water or you won't be able to see or hear fish feed. Be alert for the fish switching from duns to spinners at dusk. Use short casts (10-15 feet) at dusk. Nymphs are especially effective in the deep gravel riffles before a *dorothea* hatch.

3) Tiny blue-winged olives (*Pseudocloeon*)

These naturals usually emerge below clumps of green aquatic vegetation; floating nymphs are very effective. Bodies on nymphs, duns, and spinners must be *very* slim. Cloudy, nasty days are best for hatching.

4) Light Cahills (*Stenonema canadense*)

All the literature says these flies hatch sporadically during the day and are pale creamish in coloration. Our experience has proved otherwise. We have seen many heavy hatches at noon on cloudy days and from 5:00 to 7:00 P.M. on bright days. The duns have yellow wings flecked with grey and orange-yellow bodies. The spinners have speckled hyaline wings and orange bodies (before egg-laying). There is a group of pale cream *Stenonema* mayflies that emerge later in the season, but *Stenonema canadense* is not of this group, at least on our rivers and from positively identified nymphs reared in the aquarium.

5) Slate/Olive Dun (*Ephemerella lata*)

The duns of this size-18 fat-bodied mayfly are always on the move so skitter a No-Hackle or use a Henryville type. The hatch is sparse but trout really relish the duns. At dusk the spinner fall is much more concentrated; this fast fishing does not last long, so get ready just before dark.

6) Little Black Caddis

Fluttering imitation good, use a Henryville type or Adams. The new sparkle-yarn pupas are very effective.

7) *Tricorythodes*

When the fish are gorging on the minute spinners, you need as many drifts as possible. Stand close, keep false casts to a minimum, and keep float distance short. Try hitting fish on the head to gain attention. The Hen Spinner is usually best but try a Bronze Blue Dun Hackle fly on stubborn risers.

8) *Hexagenia* and Brown Drakes (*Ephemera simulans*)

Duns hatch all day on cloudy days. We twitch and swim nymphs and emergers around mud banks. At dusk we twitch spinners to imitate the writhing of naturals. Spinners are usually very dense on the water so we get very close to a riser and practically dapple our imitation, allowing more casts. At the end of the fall we let the artificial swing across current to simulate a drowning spinner.

9) Spinner Fishing—All species

One wing cocked up is often the most effective pattern. Always try Hen Spinners *wet* at the end of the fall. Dead drag best (hold rod still and let fly swing at the speed of the current).

10) Midges and all very small mayflies

Be sure hooks are sharp, offset the bend and bend the shanks up for better bite. An upstream angle is best for hooking but don't set hook quickly. Let the fish turn down on it and he will hook himself.

CHAPTER 5

THE MIMICKING AND MASKING HATCHES— COMPOUND HATCHES

WE PARKED THE CAR in a cut-off and opened the door to a breathtaking sight. We had stopped on the sheer edge of a rocky cliff that dropped sharply, one hundred feet or so. Drifting up was the mixed bittersweet odor of fern and sulfur. Below was an incredibly green meadow through which wound a river shrouded by the smoke from hot springs; the river gleamed like a hidden jewel in the early morning air.

We were in the misty valley of the Firehole. To a flyfisher it is one of the most beautiful places on earth. We had heard the river had come back since the Park Commission had thoughtfully imposed more stringent fishing regulations, and as we approached the bank, we saw that this was true. The river was alive with rising trout. The hatch in progress was the *Ephemerella lacustris*, a fairly large #18 Pale Morning Dun. We tied delicate grey-yellow sidewinders 6X tippets and cast above a nice rise. The brownie took the fly confidently and soon a nice plump 14-incher was landed and released.

It was like that for two full hours during this overcast, cool June morning. The hatch was fairly heavy and persistent, as often is the case in grey drizzly weather. Then, at about 1:00 P.M., we suddenly stopped raising fish to our patterns, although the rise to the naturals continued. They wouldn't even come up to inspect our offer-

The valley of the Fire Hole River in Yellowstone Park

ings. We changed to Paraduns. Still no interest. We tried standard hackle flies. Nothing!

We tried nymphs, we tried emergers. The fish kept right on rising but not to our artificials.

Finally, we did what we should have done in the first place, we waded out to a good flow where the fish were feeding and put the little tropical fish net in the water to capture some floating naturals. Upon close examination we discovered, along with the larger, more showy sulfurs, many tiny dark-brown-bodied duns, #24. They had very dark slate, almost black wings and were practically invisible on the dark water. A #24 Slate/Brown Paradun was all we needed to start hooking and releasing fish again.

We call this particular phenomenon the "invisible" or "masking hatch." *The masking hatch occurs when the presence of a larger, more brightly colored insect effectively masks the presence of a much smaller, darker insect, which is almost imperceptible in the flow.* For some reason, the fish often prefer the smaller fly. This phenomenon is quite common and many anglers never do figure it out, merely because they will not take a few seconds to observe closely.

Most anglers, when they think of fishing to the hatch, think only in terms of the *simple hatch.* This is when only one type of insect is emerging at one time. But we have found that simple hatches are actually less common than compound hatches. Such hatches require the fly fisher to be alert, for, if too much time is spent using the wrong imitation, the hatch may end and a golden opportunity be wasted. Good rises are precious and must be hoarded.

The masking hatches are not restricted to mayflies. A few years ago, one early June evening, we were fishing the North Fork of the Snake on the Harriman Ranch. A hatch of *Emphemerella flavilinea* (#14 Slate/Olive Duns) began about 7:00 and the fish rose well. Then about 8:30, we stopped getting action; realizing that something was wrong, we began observing the stream's surface. A very small dark caddis fly, almost unnoticeable in the gathering dusk of the evening, had appeared and the rainbows switched their feeding pattern, completely ignoring the still present ephemerids. If we had not changed patterns, our fishing would have been over for the day.

The "mimicking hatch" is somewhat similar and is almost a daily occurence on spring creeks, although it happens on all trout streams at one time or another. The best example we know of takes place on Armstrong Creek in Montana, practically all summer long.

One morning in August, a fine hatch of #18 Pale Morning Duns (*Ephemerella infrequens*) was in progress when, suddenly, a smaller, lighter *Baetis* species began emerging and the fish immediately switched their attention. It was apparent the trout had been waiting for it. The new fly was only one size smaller (#20) and the coloration was exactly the same as the larger *Ephemerella*, even to the yellow coloration of the leading edge of the forewing. Yet the fish would not take a size #18, even though the large naturals continued hatching in numbers. Instead, they took exactly the same pattern in a size #20 very well. The difference between the two sizes is about 20 percent, a fairly large variation when you think about it.

We first became aware of the mimicking hatches some fifteen years ago on Michigan's legendary North Branch of the Au Sable. This was before we started using No-Hackle sidewinders, and our favorite pattern was the Marinaro Cutwing Thorax Dun, which is usually quite effective when tied correctly. Hendricksons were on the water, and browns and brookies were responding well to #14 imitations. Working downstream, we suddenly came upon a long smooth run with cedar sweepers on the sides. Good fish were working near the bank but our Hendricksons failed to interest them. We flailed the water for thirty minutes with no results, until, at last, we barged over and captured some naturals. To our surprise they were not Hendricksons at all, but a #16 *Paraleptophlebia* species. Observing the insects in the air we could discern no difference between the two species. We switched to a #16 fly of the same pattern and it worked.

A little later that same day, we came upon a pod of brook trout feeding close to the bank in some quiet water and our #16 imitations did not result in any takes. We switched back to a #14 and these were equally worthless. Again we waded over and captured samples. To our surprise, the natural turned out to be a number 18 *Baetis vagans*. We switched to a #18 Thorax Dun of the same pattern and we were again into fish.

Here we had the emergence of not one but two different species of mayflies being masked by the large Hendrickson. Both smaller flies are very similar in appearance to the Hendricksons and are indistinguishable on the wing.

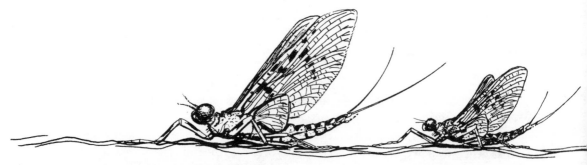

In a "masking hatch" situation the trout may actually prefer to feed on a smaller fly that is less visible to the angler: always check to see what is really in the water during the hatch.

The lesson of all this is: if you have a good pattern and it doesn't work when you think it should, find out what is going on, even if you must wade out and disturb the fish to do so.

To redefine these compound hatches: the masking hatch occurs when a large, fairly conspicuous insect is emerging at the same time as a much smaller, almost invisible fly, and the fish often prefer to feed on the minute fly for somewhat obscure reasons of their own. The combination may be large yellow mayflies and small dark mayflies, but it also may be other insects. For example, large mayflies in combination with small caddises or midges, and large stones and small ants. Any time you run into an obvious hatch of insects that trout will not strike a good imitation of, look closely at the surface film. The fish may be gorging on a masking hatch.

The mimicking hatch is so common on all trout streams that everyone should be alert for it. In a mimicking hatch a large insect emerges simultaneously with a slightly smaller fly (one or two sizes smaller)—the two so close in shade and color as to be almost impossible to distinguish except under very close observation.

Examples of the mimicking hatch are the Pale Morning Dun of the West and the light *Baetis* or *Pseudocloeons*. Hatches of Quill Gordons and *Baetis vagans* on the eastern rivers are often confusing. Also, Hendricksons and *Paraleptophlebia*s present the same problem.

These compound multiple hatches are very important and one of the major reasons knowledgeable anglers do not do as well as they should during a rise.

Just when you have the masking and the mimicking compound hatches figured out, you will run into the "complex multiple hatches"—which will probably drive you completely up the wall, as it has us on many occasions. But that is a whole chapter in itself.

CHAPTER 6

THE COMPLEX HATCHES

THE ALARM CLOCK had been set for 7:00 A.M. This is early for western fly fishing, but we wanted to be on the river earlier than usual to see if anything was emerging that we were not aware of. From the window of our motel room in Last Chance, Idaho, we could see the North Fork of the Snake. There was steam and mist rising from the river, although the sun was just coming up, and the sky was bright blue.

Usually, nothing happens on the Snake until the sun burns the fog off the water. So we decided to run up to Pond's Lodge for a quick breakfast of their delicious honey and homemade scones. We had some streamside lunches packed for us at the Lodge, and hurried back to the river. There was still some fog on the water, but it was lifting. We donned our waders and walked down the path to the first bend. Just as the last touches of mist disappeared from the river, we noticed some large mayfly spinners floating in the film. They were Green Drakes, and they had appeared almost magically. That was the first time we had ever seen Green Drake spinners on the water. They must swarm over the meadows, we decided, because there were none in the air—and all the naturals seemed to be females.

As we got down to the first big bend, more flies appeared on the water. Small fish had been rising, but here the really large fish came out. There were four big hogs

The North Fork of the Snake in Idaho

feeding tight toward the inside bank. They were wallowing in the shallow water, taking flies quite noisily. Each fish was a rainbow of at least 20, and possibly up to 24 inches. We tried a #10 extended bodied Partridge Spinner (tied half-spent) with just a little bit of hackle. This is a very good imitation of the first stage of a large spinner fall. Almost instantly, we were both attached to silver dynamos, and soon landed and released two identical 23½-inch hen rainbows. This was great! This was just the way it's supposed to happen during the rise.

But that's not the way it did happen. What really happened was, we stood in that bend for two and a half hours casting to those four big hogs and never got a single rise! After five or ten minutes of refusals to our imitation spinners, we decided something was wrong. They must not be feeding on those Green Drake spinners after all. So, we got our little nets out, looked closer on the water, dipped some naturals out and examined them. It was soon apparent that there was a lot more going on than just a Green Drake spinner fall.

We showed the trout dries, wets, nymphs deep and in the film—ants, beetles, caddis flies, stone flies and midges . . . *Nothing!*

"Maybe they're taking emergers just under the surface."

No luck.

We counted the different naturals on the water. There were three species of caddis flies, two species of stone flies, and God knows how many midges. There were two smaller *Ephemerella* duns emerging, and two other species of *Ephemerella* spinners falling. There were also some little beetles floating submerged in the film, and a few ants.

Now, when there are this many different types of insects on the water at the same time, and you must decide which stage of which insect the fish are feeding on, it's complicated! Nymphs, duns, or spinners? Of which species? You also have a time problem. There are tremendous numbers of patterns you must try by trial and error if you are going to find out what the fish are hitting. (In this case, fifteen different stages of all the flies.) This is assuming that you know exactly what is going on in the first place, and that you have very good patterns for all stages. This, then, is the

During most hatches, a trout will feed on floating nymphs in a ratio of 2 to 8 over winged flies.

phenomenon of the "complex multiple hatch," possibly the most difficult problem in fly fishing and hatch matching.

Of course, if you fish relatively unfertile rivers, you don't have this problem, or at least not often. But if you fish the rivers that have great hatches, especially the limestoners and spring creeks, which are highly alkaline, then this problem is quite common. In fact, on the North Fork of the Snake it is almost a daily occurrence—which is why the Snake is one of the hardest rivers in the world for fishermen to clean out completely. There is just so much going on that even the experienced angler can't always figure it out.

During that morning at the first bend, we finally discovered that the fish were feeding on the smaller species of the caddis flies. But by the time we found out, those four big lunkers had stopped feeding. Oh, sure, we caught some of the smaller ones, 14, 15, 16 inches—but those big ones remained untouched.

On these occasions, a knowledge of rise forms will help the angler considerably. By knowing the different types of insects that elicit quiet, splashy, noisy, or jump rise forms, you can cut down on the number of choices of flies by at least 50 percent. Of course, in retrospect, if we had known that we were not going to raise those big fish on the first big bend, we would have waded over to their feeding lane and seen for ourselves what flies were the most numerous in that flow. However, you can understand us being very reluctant to disturb four 24-inch surface-feeding rainbows. Such fish don't come along every day. Not even on the Snake. And, of course, you're faced with many other problems: Is it your fly or your presentation? Is the pattern correctly tied—in the right size, and not too bushy? Or is it the wrong pattern entirely? Then, too, on rivers like this, with so many, many hatches, and so many individual insects on the water at the same time, the fish must pass up quite a few naturals while feeding. Therefore, you might even be using the correct fly with the correct presentation, but the fish just happen to take the naturals before and after your pattern passes overhead. It may require a few casts to the fish to find out if your pattern is correct. (Many more casts than in a simple rise or sparse hatch where there aren't so many insects on the water.)

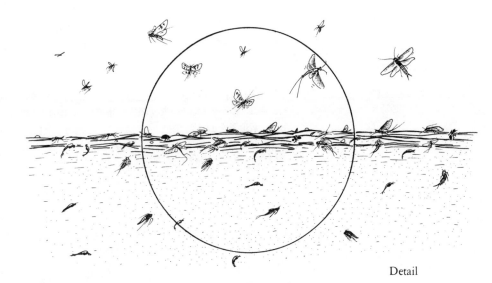

Detail

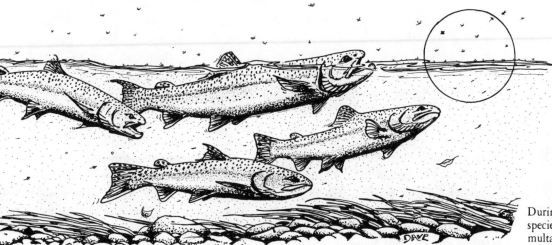

During a complex hatch, when species of insects may be active simultaneously, the angler must determine which ones the trout are really taking.

Often fish, especially large fish, will have a feeding rhythm that will help you when there are thousands of flies on the water at the same time. This often consists of a fish coming up and taking one, two, three, four or more flies in rapid succession, then going down and resting for a period of 30 to 60 seconds. If you keep track of the individual rise pattern, you'll learn when to cast, timing your motions so that your cast will be over the fish at approximately the right time.

Many anglers are reluctant to change patterns quickly enough. This is often because they are really not very proficient at tying on flies to the tippet with a turle knot, or at adding new tippets to the leader with the blood knot. If you change flies often, you must also be able to add tippets, otherwise you are quickly into the heavy end of the leader. Learning to do these things rapidly will give you more incentive to change your patterns when you know you should, without fear of losing valuable time during a rise.

One cardinal rule—don't waste a lot of time on the wrong pattern, especially in simple rises where there aren't too many insects on the water. Often, in this case, the fish will take practically every insect that goes by. So, if after two or three minutes you are not getting any action, switch flies. Again, the real solution is to wade as close to the flow as you can, get your head right down in the water and see what is going on. Even if you do disturb the fish, this is by far the quickest answer. In most cases, you can find another fish equally as large as the fish you are disturbing. However, if there is a big old lunker over there in front of you, and you don't want to disturb him, you'll have to take your chances and keep switching until you hit the right fly.

Matching the hatch is undeniably difficult during the complex multiple hatch. There is no simple solution—only experience, judgment, observation, and lots of luck.

There are, however, some ideas that may help you during these difficult situations. For instance, the new pocket-size binoculars can be of great value if the light is good. These instruments are so small they can be carried easily in your shirt and are quite powerful, 6 or 7 power. With them you can observe a trout's feeding position and quite often actually watch a fly disappear in a swirl.

Observation of a phenomenon we call the "pounds of meat" law will help you during complex hatches. We are sure that fish will feed on the particular stage of the particular insect drifting over his lie that represents the greatest pounds of meat. This is why fish feed on smaller insects so often. They normally come in such great numbers that they represent a much greater weight of food supply than the less-dense, or lower-intensity large species. It's the total volume of meat that turns fish on. Hundreds of size #20 *Baetis* add up to a lot more poundage to feed on than the occasional #14 Hendrickson or #16 Pale Evening Dun. A hungry fish wants to eat. Why wait two or three minutes for a large fly when it can suck in smaller ones, one after the other? As this balance of poundage switches from species to species, stage to stage, so do the feeding habits of the trout.

The stomach pump (which is available from Bud Lilly and Orvis) is the best tool for finding out what the fish are really feeding on. We learned more in one season about the feeding habits of trout than we ever had before. We pumped more than four hundred fish this year and each time we learned something. Often we were astonished at what we found. Probably the greatest single discovery from the stomach pump is the fantastic number of nymphs that are taken by fish that are definitely feeding on the surface. This explains why floating nymphs are so effective. *This can't be stressed too much. During most hatches, two to eight floating nymphs will be taken for every winged mayfly.* This is actually dry fly fishing—the nymph floats like a dry fly and you can see it like a dry fly though it has no wings.

Of course, to use the stomach pump, you must catch at least one fish. When you do, you know *exactly* what the fish are feeding on. There's no guesswork to it.

Here then is a step-by-step method to solve the problem of a compound multiple hatch.

1) Put your nose down to the water and observe as closely as possible. Try to figure out which insect on the water represents the most pounds of meat.

2) If that doesn't work try binoculars. Try to see the fish take a particular fly.

3) If that doesn't work, go into the line of drift and use the net. This will tell you everything that is on the water and will at least narrow down the problem of fly selection.

4) Identify what you captured in the net and determine which stage and species is being taken, either by observation or "pounds-of-meat" law.

5) Use the stomach pump to verify what the trout are really feeding on.

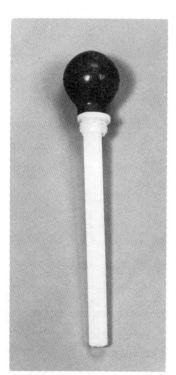

The stomach pump is an excellent device for determining the contents of a trout's stomach without harming the fish.

Here are some further tips. If you can't observe what the fish are taking, get into the line of drift to collect samples, or catch at least one fish to use the stomach pump on.

1) Flies size #16 and larger, especially duns, should be visible to the naked eye. Before trying what you think is the right pattern, *watch* the flies drifting through rises. If fly after fly floats through unmolested, you probably have a masking hatch or floating nymphs.

2) If the fish are feeding on the fly you see on the water, and you simply cannot catch a sample, match the wing color and size to the best of your ability. Remember that most flies *look* larger on the water than they really are, especially the light ones. So if the fly looks like a #14, it would probably be best to use a #16. If the fly is a dark-colored mayfly Dun, a Slate/Olive or Slate/Tan would undoubtedly work while a Grey/Yellow would be a good choice if the fly is light. If the flies are spinners, clear wings, you use the Dun/Brown Hen Spinner.

3) If you have a masking hatch or can see no flies at all on the water, then you must rely on your knowledge of rise forms, time of day, time of year—and experience. Splashy, showy rises invariably mean small caddises. For this situation try a #20 or #22 Dark Henryville or another fluttering caddis imitation. Gentle, unhurried rises at dusk usually mean medium- to small-size spinners or tiny duns. Dun/Brown Hen Spinners, sizes #18 and #24, and a size #20 or #24 Gray/Olive No-Hackle Duns would quickly test out these possibilities. Brown or Dark Olive Floating Nymphs in a couple of sizes could also be used. We usually find the answer from this list of flies when we simply cannot get out into the line of drift to collect samples and cannot observe naturals being taken by risers.

Probably no one will ever figure out these complex multiple hatches completely, and rightly so. If it was always easy, fly fishing would quickly lose its appeal.

CHAPTER 7

THE STILLBORN DUNS

THREE SEPARATE INCIDENTS led us to realize the vast importance of a whole range of new patterns that imitate a stage of many aquatic insects, hitherto relatively unnoticed and unexplored. This is an important discovery because trout seem to prefer this stage of many species of natural flies; as we explore this phenomenon, we will see there is a good, rational reason why fish behave in an often frustrating manner to our offerings.

The first of these incidents occurred on one of the many small spring creeks of the Gallatin Valley in Montana. We arrived very early in the morning, hoping to discover any rise that might occur before the usual Pale Morning Duns at eleven o'clock. It was a warm, blustery day, and the fish started working at seven twenty. There were absolutely nothing but small dark midges, #26, on the water and they were definitely emerging, not laying eggs. We tried all types of usually effective midge patterns: No-Hackle Midges, standard hackle patterns, and the pupal type fished deep, rising, and drifting in the film. None of our artificials worked. Oh, sure, we caught fish occasionally, but not nearly as many as we felt the good rise warranted.

About halfway through the morning, we put our rods up and began to observe the rise forms and the insects more closely. We eventually noticed that many adults were getting stuck in the pupal shucks and that some never did get off the water, either drowning or being taken by the trout. Also, the fish seemed to prefer the "stillborn flies."

The next day we returned to the river at the same time, but armed with plenty of newly tied patterns that had wings partly out, but with the tips stuck in the pupal shuck which trailed past the bend of the hook. These strange-looking new flies not only worked, they were deadly.

We considered this experience merely an interesting interlude and put it to the back of our minds. Then, next spring, we were out early in March collecting nymphs for our basement aquariums. We keep the water an ideal 62° to 65° for fast nymph growth in order to get nymph hatches much sooner than on the rivers. One afternoon in April, the tank erupted with as fine a hatch of Hendricksons as you could ever want in your basement.

The room where the aquariums are located has only one window, and the flies all seem to collect there. We examined the windowsill and collected a few individuals for picture taking. Then we noticed on the surface of the water in the tanks that there were fully as many duns with their wings stuck in their cases, drowning or dead, as had escaped the film and flown to the window. We wondered if this happened on the swift rivers as frequently as it seemed to occur in the relatively calm environment of a tropical fish tank. It probably does, we decided. But nature takes care of the loss by producing many more individuals than needed for the survival of the species, so the hatches continue year after year despite the great loss of the "Stillborn Duns."

A short month later, the little black *Chimarra* caddises were heavy on the Au Sable. The weather was warm and the fishing was great. For a while, that is. After an hour the flies got really thick, and our patterns would entice only an occasional small fish, while being ignored by most good risers. We tried No-Hackle caddis, spent caddis, Palmer-Hackle caddis, Adams and Henryville types, but none really worked well. The pupal imitations were mostly refused. All were taken occasionally, but none seemed to be what the fish really wanted. Then we noticed the same phenomenon we'd seen with the midges in Montana, and the mayfly Duns in our basement aquariums. Many individual caddises were failing to get their wings completely uncased and were drowning in the surface film. The fish were taking these "stillborn" caddis almost exclusively.

The next day we arrived with newly tied stillborn imitations and they worked extremely well. The large fish took them confidently.

These three widely separated incidents couldn't be dismissed casually. What if, we thought, this phenomenon isn't as rare as we assumed, but instead quite common? In many later instances we discovered that it is not only common, but usual.

Why, though, do trout prefer the stillborn flies, often to the complete exclusion of the normally hatching insects? After some discussion we had to say that it is simply easier for the fish to take the trapped flies that can't get away. When you consider the whole matter, it must be frustrating for a wise old brownie to rise up through the flow to engulf a floating insect, only to have it fly away just as he thinks he is closing his jaws on it. This does happen and we've all seen it. When flies escape quickly from the film, trout hurry to capture the fly before it can get away, often causing a splashy rise form. *But trout don't like to hurry!* This requires extra energy, and fish don't waste energy if they can help it. It naturally follows that when they find they can rise leisurely and not worry about the natural getting away, they will feed on that stage—the stillborn duns of the mayfly, caddis, and midge.

We have since found this type of feeding extremely common and patterns tied to imitate the stillborn flies are very effective for selective trout. The wiser and larger a fish, the more apt he is to feed on stillborns.

The manner in which certain species of insects emerge creates this type of phenomenon. The pupas of many caddises and midges swim to the surface and the adult will then pop from the case and immediately take to the wing with no long drift in the current. This does not leave much time for the fish to rise and take the natural—which requires the hurrying that they abhor.

Many species of mayflies get off the water rather quickly, especially on warm sunny days, or during windy weather that dries their wings. Here again the fish will take the fly he knows will not get away. The stillborn patterns will take many a large selective riser for you, and it is the pattern of choice for fully 50 percent of all periods of emerging. Many times when trout seen to be nymphing but will not take artificial nymphs, they are really taking stillborns.

These patterns usually work better than normal emergers, *even when the stillborn effect is not common during a specific hatch*, when the great majority of insects do manage to escape the surface film successfully. The reason, again, is logical. The trout simply realize that a fly halfway out of its nymph case can't escape as fast as one that has completely emerged and is drying its wings. The latter might fly away at any moment. The fly struggling to rid itself of the nymph or pupal case must take longer, thus allowing the fish a more leisurely rise.

We all know emergers, flymphs, or whatever we wish to call them, are a very effective pattern during a rise. But emergers must emerge from something. That something, of course, is a nymph or pupal case. *To imitate the emerger, but not the case from which it is emerging, is to imitate only half the insect.* It is completely illogical to dress these fly types without the cases attached; but the proof of the theory is in the practical application on the only critics we have for our patterns, the trout.

The new fly looks rather weird to the hidebound traditionalists, but it works—often spectacularly!

Over the past several seasons, since our initial discovery, we've encountered many situations where the imitation stillborns proved to be the fly of the hour, bailing us out of tough hatches time after time, from east to west.

Only recently, on the no-kill stretch of the Beaverkill, a multiple spring hatch of Hendricksons, *Baetis* and *Paraleptophlebia* was driving us crazy on a cold, blustery May afternoon. The School House pool was alive with dozens of steadily rising trout. An emergence was obviously in progress as hundreds of slate-winged duns danced and drifted on the slow-moving current.

Baetis and *Paraleptophlebia* were on the water in much greater numbers than Hendricksons so either a #16 or #18 Slate/Tan No-Hackle *had* to be the answer. To save time, one of us tried the larger pattern while the other tried the smaller. To our utter amazement, *neither* fly worked at all. After a dozen or so drifts over steady risers, we concurred that we both had underestimated the intensity of the Hendrickson hatch and quickly reached for our fly boxes. The hurried switch to a size #14 Slate/Tan was greeted with more refusals.

Then we did what we should have done in the first place. We put our rods down, moved into a smooth line of the drift, where visibility was good, and put our noses into the water. By getting the light just right and observing closely, we could see long, dark forms floating on the surface. Whatever they were, they appeared even longer than the Hendrickson, possibly a size #10 in length. Netting a few specimens revealed the reason for the elongated appearance. These long slim creatures were *Paraleptophlebia* stillborns with their wing tips trapped in the trailing cases. The dark coloration of the slate wings and mahogany body with dark brown shucks combined to make this rather large fly almost invisible on the water—invisible to the angler, that is. To the trout, who had the advantage of plenty of backlighting from the sun, they were not only visible but represented a juicy morsel that was not about to flutter away.

As usual, putting our rods down and studying the situation for ten minutes had paid big dividends. We excitedly changed to #16 Slate/Brown Stillborns and found the fish very receptive to our offerings. The School House pool had never been particularly kind to us in the past, but thanks to these new patterns, this uncomfortable spring day turned out to be a day to remember.

So far we have mentioned only mayflies, caddis flies, and midges. On occasion, these patterns work well when stone flies are hatching. Normally, due to either the method or intensity of stone fly emergence, the stillborn imitation is not effective, but there are exceptions. On Michigan's Au Sable River, for example, there's a heavy hatch of small yellow stone flies that occurs simultaneously with the peak of the Pale Evening Duns, around the first week in June. These #18 to #20 downwings are of local importance only when the intensity exceeds that of the sulfurs. Slightly before and after the peak of the hatch, with only moderate numbers of flies on the water, the fish seemed to relish feeding on the skittering adults. At these times, a yellow-bodied Adams or Henryville type works best. During the peak of the hatch, however, those few evenings when the river is blanketed with naturals, most of the trout prefer to feed on the stillborn variety.

The Little Yellow Stone is usually at its best on warm evenings, well before sunset, and has a tendency to become very active as soon as the nymphal shuck has been freed. In order to take the fluttering adult, a trout must expend more energy than he would receive from devouring the minute natural. Thus, the more accessible stillborn becomes the prime target. For this particular hatch, we prefer an imitation with a yellow body, tannish grey wings, sparse ginger hackle, and a medium brown case. The float should be completely drag-free.

A similar stonefly situation provides some of the best fishing of the early season on another of Michigan's blue-ribbon rivers, the Pere Marquette. This hatch comes slightly earlier in the season, the last week in May, but takes place about the same time of day, six to eight in the evening. It is known locally as the Little Olive Stone Fly, and causes great excitement for about a week, bridging the gap between a fading Hendrickson and the initial phases of the sulfur hatch. Without the competition of other major hatches, this #16 to #18 olive-bodied stone achieves great importance in the trout's diet.

Heavy emergences of the Little Olive cause frustration and much consternation among local anglers, many of whom resort to large streamers and bucktails in efforts to ignore the hatch. These flies hatch like most mayflies, in the main currents, and, like the Yellow Stones, become very active as adults. Hackle-flies, especially an olive-bodied Henryville, are effective at times but, during peak emergences, the stillborn is supreme. Our favorite pattern has a medium olive body ribbed with fine yellow thread, grey wings, sparse bronze hackle, and two dark-grey hen-hackle tips for the extended case. The hackle should be clipped flat on top and V'd slightly on the bottom. Duck quill segments or hen-hackle tips, tied in at the bend and lashed down at the eye, make excellent wings.

Toward the end of the Little Brown Caddis hatch, late in May, another caddis, known locally on the North Branch of the Au Sable as the "popcorn hatch," dovetails into the scene. This is a much larger fly than the Chimarra, size #14 to #16, having an olive body and wings that look about the size and color of a freshly popped kernel of corn. Actually, the wings are light grey, but in the sunlight they appear almost creamy white. These flies "pop up" all over the stream in great numbers, causing local anglers much anxiety. Feeding activity is rarely heavy, however, as most of the flies are in the air and not on the water. Many of the adults leave the water quickly and only the smaller fish will try for the elusive targets.

To fish the Popcorn Hatch effectively, one must be armed with both the Henryville and stillborn type of flies, and cover as much water as possible. Numerous large fish can be found feeding if two or three miles of river can be waded in an afternoon and most of these better fish are real "patsies" for the stillborn caddis. An effective pattern for the Popcorn caddis has an olive body, light-grey wings, blackish-grey case, and sparse slate hackle. The wings can best be fashioned from either duck quill segments or strands of light grey Poly II, and should be kept more to the sides of the body than directly over the top. This better imitates the wing position of the naturals. Allow the wings to "bow out" slightly between the front and rear tie-down points. This also adds to the realism of emerging wings, promotes better floatation, and provides excellent visibility.

The trailing pupal shuck is well imitated by double hen-hackle tips, blackish grey in color, mounted flat and parallel to the hook shank. Dark-grey hackle, mounted well back behind the eye, clipped flat on top, and slightly V'd on the bottom, is not only realistic in appearance but cocks the fly on the water at just the right angle. This pattern style is effective for all stillborn caddises. Just match the color of your favorite caddis hatch to these materials and you're in business.

These new fat-tailed flies are now playing such an important role in our western fishing that we wonder how we ever survived without them in the past. Use of the stillborns has added immeasurably to our pleasure and success on such rivers as Henry's Fork, Firehole, and the spring creeks. Though we've been using these patterns only a few years, they've already helped us solve many hatch problems that previously left us frustrated and empty-handed.

Over the years, one of the most perplexing problems has been trying to solve various midge hatches on the gin-clear spring creeks of the West. Rising trout in such situations can be extremely difficult. Sometimes the pupa works, sometimes the hackled adult works, but quite often, *nothing* works—at least not with any degree of consistency.

The problem with the midges, of course, is that the flies are so minute, usually #24 or smaller, that it's difficult to see what's really happening *in* and *on* the surface film.

Large mayflies, especially dark-colored ones, are hard enough to see, but midges are almost impossible. Empty cases can be quite easy to spot on the water; they are light-colored or whitish, after the adult frees himself, but they don't tell us much except that something has just emerged. It is much more meaningful to see what has happened *during* the actual emergence process. We want to know *exactly* what stage the flies are in as they are being taken by the trout. This is more difficult because the flies are darker and more opaque while the adult still occupies, or partially occupies, the pupal case and, of course, darker objects are harder to spot on the water.

This is the problem we faced several years ago when we discovered the spring creek stillborns. On that unforgettable morning, the trout started feeding between seven and seven thirty. They were rising in large but well-defined pods located just downstream from high concentrations of aquatic vegetation. These bright-green weeds, which are so characteristic of the western spring creeks, grow almost to the water's surface where they create a myriad of tiny currents and eddies. Millions of midges are born and bred each season in this vegetation. The trout are aware of this, so at hatch time they congregate slightly downstream where they can tip and sip with ease. On most western spring creeks, such occurrences happen every day, not only once, but usually several times. During this particular day, the first major hatch period took place between seven and ten thirty A.M.

Most spring-creek anglers arrive at streamside just in time for the Pale Morning Dun emergence, which begins around eleven A.M. Arriving early, we had things to ourselves and it was great to see so many rising fish. We were really going to have a terrific day—or so we thought. All the patterns we tried—pupas, hackle and no-hackle adults—were consistent at *not* taking fish consistently.

At first, we were positive that a pupal type imitation *had* to be the answer. But this was the *least* effective of all, producing an occasional false rise. The best patterns, ones that actually caught a few fish, were sparsely hackled adults and partridge no-hackles. The surprising thing was that the most effective size was a #18. This was confusing because the naturals we could see on the water and in the air appeared to be #26 in size.

Landing only a few fish in several hours of fishing was frustrating, especially since there were dozens of large trout feeding right under our noses. After what seemed like an eternity of refusals, we finally laid the rods aside and observed closely.

We waded into an area, not only where numerous fish were rising heavily, but where the current was smooth and slow and provided good visibility. It took a while for our eyes to focus properly on the small flies but we finally saw what was happening. At first, it appeared that #24 to #26 dark midges were on the water. They were pretty standard-looking, except that their wings seemed awfully short and out of position. Closer examination revealed why the wings looked different. The tips were stuck in the pupal case, which was still clinging to each adult's body. In effect, the fly was trapped in its own shuck, and the wings, instead of being free, were being held down tight over the back of the body. The position of the flies on the water was also unique. They were angled up at about 20 to 30 degrees from the water's surface. The weight or drag of the trailing case pulled the rear portion down, causing the front, or thorax portion of the fly to be higher in the water than normal.

Coupled with the different shape and unnatural position on the water was the fact that the total length of the stillborn was *double* that of the adult midge. This explains why the size #18 was at least partially effective during the hatch.

Once we learned to see the exposed wing segments glistening in the sun, we immediately realized that this was the stage the fish were feeding on. Time after time, individual trout would ignore the fluttering, skittering adults in preference to the stillborns. We'd found a whole new world of fly fishing.

That evening, we worked late into the night on strange new patterns. To imitate the trailing pupal case, we used two dark grey, almost black, hen hackle tips tied in flat, one on top of the other. They were mounted in the regular tail position parallel to the shank. We tried a variety of materials for the wings—duck quill segments, shoulder feathers, hen-hackle tips, and strands of Poly II. The hackle was a mixture of grizzly and dark blue dun and, after winding, we trimmed it on top to facilitate mounting the wings. It was left full on the bottom so that the fly would tilt upward in the front. When completed, these little creatures looked somewhat similar to the Goofus Bug or Humpy. In fact, the stillborn phenomenon may explain the effectiveness of these popular western patterns, at least in the smaller sizes.

The next morning we arrived at streamside bright and early, prepared with our funny-looking patterns. Of course, nature can be fickle, so we knew full well that the hatch might have changed, or at least the stage of the hatch that the fish would feed on. We were especially worried that the previous day's experience would end up being a once-in-a-lifetime or at best, once-a-year happening, rather than a common occurrence. After all, with over fifty years of fly fishing experience between us, why had we never recognized the stillborn phenomenon before?

But nature was kind to us that morning. The midges started moving right after seven and by seven thirty several dozen fish were feeding in a large pod, 25 to 30 feet long, just below the green weeds. We purposely left our rods on the bank and waded into the line of drift. Before making a single cast, we wanted to be absolutely sure what the fish were working on. Several minutes of observation in a quiet slick were all we needed. This day we knew what we were looking for: long dark bodies, short wing segments glistening in the sun, and that unique, upswept position on the water. Almost immediately, we spotted the stillborns and watched a half dozen disappear in large, fanning rings.

This was the signal for action. We stumbled back to our rods on the bank, moved into casting position, and waited for the risers to come back to their feeding station. They were rising steadily within a few minutes. It didn't take long to find out whether our new patterns would work. For almost two hours we thought we were in Fly Fishermen's Heaven. Practically every big fish that had passed up our offerings the day before now took in a firm, confident rise. Refusals, false rises, and missed strikes were almost nonexistent. It was "our" day and we enjoyed it to the hilt.

the humpy pattern and a natural stillborn

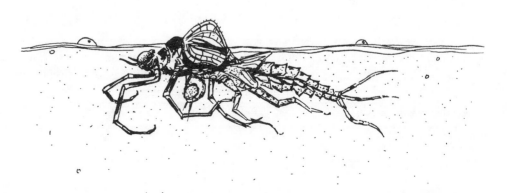

stillborn dun awash in the film

Stillborn Midge

stillborn midge

        Hook: #20-#28   3X   FW
Pupal Shuck: two hen hackle tips
        Body: Fly-Rite Poly dubbing
       Wings: Poly II fibers
      Hackle: cock hackle trimmed flat on top

Stillborn Dun

stillborn mayfly

        Hook: #10-#24   3X   FW
Pupal Shuck: cock hackle tip, tied reversed
        Body: Poly II or spun fur
       Wings: duck quill segments tied down at both ends, or very short and
                slanted back
        Legs: cock hackle, tied DeFeo style, or none

Stillborn Caddis

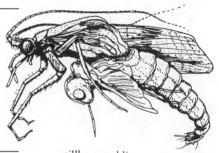

stillborn caddis

        Hook #14-#22   3X   FW
Pupal Shuck: hen hackle tip
        Body: spun fur or Fly-Rite Poly dubbing
       Wings: hackle tips or duck quill segments tied down at both ends
        Legs: cock hackle, tied DeFeo style

Stillborn Stone

        Hook: #10-#20   3X   FW
Pupal Shuck: cock hackle tips tied reversed
        Body: Poly II or spun fur
       Wings: duck quill segments tied down at both ends
        Legs: cock hackle, clipped top and bottom

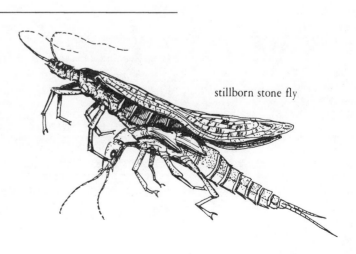

stillborn stone fly

wings: hackle tip
shuck: cock hackle reversed

wings: shoulder feathers
shuck: hen hackle, cut to shape

wings and shuck of Poly II fibers

wings: partridge
shuck: hair

wings: turkey
shuck: turkey fibers

wings: quill segment
shuck: hen hackle, cut to shape

LIST OF PROTOTYPICAL PATTERNS

MIDGES

Green body	light grey wing	dark brown shuck	grizzly and brown hackle
Yellow body	light grey wing	dark brown shuck	grizzly and ginger hackle
Black body	light grey wing	blackish grey shuck	grizzly and dark grey hackle

CADDIS

Green body	tan-mottled wing	dark brown shuck	slate hackle
Tan body	tan-mottled wing	medium brown shuck	partridge hackle
Black body	light grey mottled wing	dark brown shuck	slate hackle
Black body	dark grey wing	dark brown shuck	dark brown hackle

MAYFLY DUNS

Tan body	dark grey wing	medium brown shuck	tan hackle
Yellow body	light grey wing	light brown shuck	honey hackle
Light olive body	light grey wing	dark brown shuck	light olive hackle
Dark olive body	dark grey wing	dark brown shuck	light olive hackle

As with the No-Hackle duns, one color in different sizes can imitate many mayfly species. Following is a list of species the four prototypical colors will match in the correct sizes.

TAN BODY
Henderickson #12-#14, Quill Gordon #14-#16, *Leptophlebia* #12, *Paraleptophlebia* #16-#18, *Baetis* species (such as *vagans*) #16-#20, *Rithrogenia* species #16 Brown Drake (*Ephemera simulans*) #10-#12, *Hexagenia limbata* #6-#8, American March Brown (*Steno. nemafuscum, vacarium,* and *ithaca*) #10-#14, *Siphlonurus* #10-#14 (Grey Drake).

YELLOW BODY
Pale Evening Dun #16-#18 (*Ephemerella dorothea*), Pale Morning Dun #14-#22, (*Emphemerella inermis, infrequens,* and *lacustrius*) light *Baetis* species #20-#22, Light Cahills (*Stenonema canadense*) #14-#16, Pale *Epeorus* species #16-#18.

LIGHT OLIVE BODY
Pseudocloeon, Cloeon, Neocloeon, Centraopolitium #20-#26.

DARK OLIVE BODY
Ephemerella attenuta #18 (Blue-Wing Olive), *Ephemerella lata* #18, *Ephemerella flavilinea, coloradenis* #12-#14, *Ephemerella grandis* #10-12.

A typical stillborn situation: a trout rising smoothly and regularly in a weedy area during a heavy hatch.

TIPS ON FISHING STILLBORNS

1) Look for high concentrations of nymph or pupa-bearing vegetation; risers will congregate below weeds.

2) The heavier the hatch, the higher the chances of fish feeding on stillborns.

3) Quiet, deliberate feeding during heavy hatches indicates a high probability that the fish are taking stillborns.

4) Splashy, erratic, frenzied rises during a heavy hatch indicate a very low probability that the fish are taking stillborns.

5) Pinpoint casting is necessary because the hatch is normally heavy when the fish are taking stillborns (resulting in narrow feeding lanes) and trout will not move very far to take flies that are relatively motionless.

6) Absolutely drag-free floats are essential for most stillborn situations.

7) Stillborn artificials should float as high as possible. Use a good floatant: first spray the fly well with silicone dry-fly spray, then work in a silicone line dressing paste with your thumb and forefinger.

Four pattern types imitate the stillborn stage of midges, mayfly duns, stones, and emerging caddises. They are "type" patterns, and of course the size and the color of wings and bodies must be matched to specific species present at a particular time.

stillborn pattern with both wings tied

stillborn with both wings, one wing free

stillborn pattern with both wings free of case

TYING THE STILLBORN DUN

A typical Slate/Tan Hendrickson with both wings free (can also be tied with both wings caught or with one wing in the nymphal shuck).

1) Fix a #14 3X fine wire hook to vise and attach a medium-brown cock hackle tip reversed (as in two-feather mayfly technique) with three fibers left back for tails. Use brown Nymo thread.

2) Spin tan Poly II on tying thread and wrap on body.

3) Tie in a matched pair of duck primary wing segments, sidewinder style, as in the No-Hackle Sidewinder technique (See *Art Flick's Master Fly-Tying Guide*). Wings should be short and sloping back.

4) Tie in light tan or honey cock hackle DeFeo style, or No-Hackle style, form head and tie off.

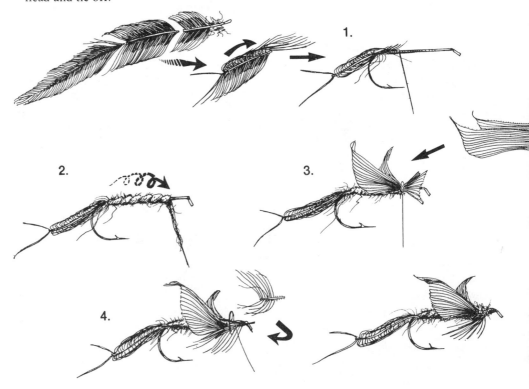

TYING THE STILLBORN CADDIS

A typical olive caddis with both wings stuck in pupal case.

1) Fix a #14-#18 3X fine wire hook in vise and tie in two light brown hen-hackle tips, stacked on top of each other at the bend, with dark brown nymo thread.

2) Tie in a bunch of brown partridge hackle fibers at bend of hook.

3) Spin tan fur or Fly-Rite #3 olive Poly on tying thread and wind on body.

4) Wrap brown cock hackle in front of body and trim on top.

5) Pull partridge wings forward over top of body and tie off at eye.

TYING THE STILLBORN MIDGE

A typical grey midge with both wings stuck in pupal shuck.

1) Fix a #20-#26 light wire hook in vise and tie in two dark grey hen hackle tips stacked on top of each other at bend with very fine olive tying thread.

2) Tie in a clump of light grey Poly II fibers at bend of hook.

3) Spin a very slight amount of Fly-Rite #7 Poly on tying thread and wind on body so it is very thin.

4) Take two turns each of grizzly and dark grey hackle just behind head position and clip flat on top.

5) Take free end of Poly II clump and tie in at the head, form head, and tie off.

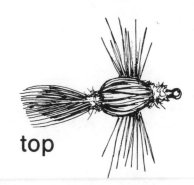

top

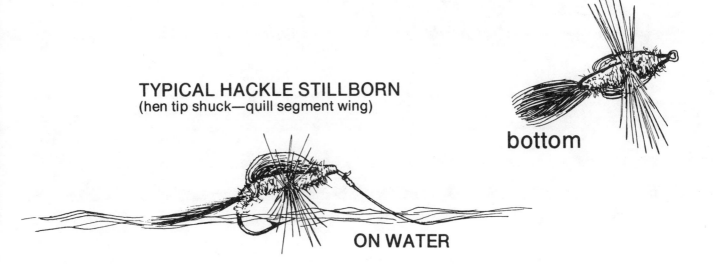

TYPICAL HACKLE STILLBORN
(hen tip shuck—quill segment wing)

bottom

ON WATER

TYING THE STILLBORN STONE FLY

This pattern is for a typical olive stone fly with both wings stuck in the nymphal shuck.

1) Fix a #16 or #18 light-wire hook in the vise, and at the bend, tie in two hen-hackle tips, a dark grey stacked on top of a medium brown. Use dark olive or brown tying thread.

2) Tie in a clump of medium grey Poly II fibers and a short length of fine yellow thread at the bend of the hook.

3) Spin Fly-Rite #15 olive Poly on the tying thread and wind this on the body. Rib body with yellow thread.

4) Take three or four turns of bronze hackle and clip this flat on top.

5) Take the free end of the Poly II clump and tie it in at the head. Form the head and tie off.

CHAPTER 8

NEW FISH OF THE MIDWEST–STEELHEAD, PACIFIC AND ATLANTIC SALMON

"YOU CAN'T CATCH NO STEELHEAD on flies in Michigan," said Wiggler Joe. "You got to use spawn sacks or live wigglers." Wigglers are the nymphs of the largest mayflies in the Midwest (*Hexagenia limbata*) and Joe got his name by catching them and selling them to bait stores. That was ten years ago, and at that time, at least, Joe was right. Up to that point, using flies only, we had landed only two small steelies and experienced one hell of a strike. At that time we were fishing the Manistee River, two miles below Tippy Dam, in the area known as the Sawdust Pile. This is a river well known for its incredible white gravel and huge spawning migrations, and Wiggler Joe, who lived on its banks in an old shack, had killed over ninety big fish the previous September and October. He was the acknowledged expert on midwestern steelhead. He fished every day of the run and knew the river like a book.

It took us ten years, lots of study, and a new "flies only" section on a major spawning river, the Pere Marquette, but we found it can be done. These fish can be regularly enticed to hit a fly.

By now, most people are familiar with the resurgence of the Great Lakes as a trout and salmon fishery. The lamprey eels, which had just about decimated the lake and rainbow trout population, were finally controlled and the waters were restocked, not only with the original species, but with Pacific, king, and silver salmon. The Lakes, which had become overrun with such baitfish as smelt and alewives, were loaded with food, so the newly introduced game fish actually grew faster than in their native Pacific Ocean. Fish released as smolts returned two years later as 15- to 20-pound tackle busters. The fish are relatively easy to hook in the Lakes, if you can find them in shallow water. Practically any streamer that looks like a baitfish will work. It is not so common an occurrence, though, to find these conditions: they require very favorable weather. Usually in the summer and early fall the fish are deep. Only in early spring (when the average fish is only 2 to 3 pounds) and in the late fall, just before the run begins, are all conditions favorable for fly fishing for the big fish. The exception is surf casting for large browns and rainbows around the mouths of the rivers in the spring. Recently, some fish over 20 pounds have been caught in this manner.

When the run of salmon and steelhead begin in September, the big fish become concentrated in the lower sections of the large spawning rivers. The salmon run to spawn, and the steelies follow to feed, quite often on salmon eggs, though not exclusively.

The problem is spawning fish don't feed much, and are hard to get to take anything, let alone a fly. It took time to learn an effective technique and the right flies. A riffle to cast over, which does not look like a Manhattan subway entrance at rush hour, is one of the prime prerequisites. The Michigan Department of Natural Resources gave us the place. They designated eight miles of the Pere Marquette River in lower Western Michigan "flies only," and open twelve months of the year. This section is not deserted. Plenty of anglers take advantage of this ruling, but at least we don't have hoards of people bombarding quiet pools with 2 ounces of lead and 5/8 ounce spoons. The fish don't run away and hide. The steelies mainly hold in the lower river during fall and winter and come up in very early spring, January and February,

1. RESTING SPAWNERS
2. ACTIVE PAIRED SPAWNERS
2A. FRESH NEST
3. OVERHEAD SHADE COVER
   FOR HIDING FISH
4. FISH MOVING UPSTREAM

Resting and spawning lies for spring steelhead

to the gravel spawning areas. When the weather warms up just a little, the fish go on the beds: at this time they are most vulnerable. The salmon, however, come all the way up the river to these same areas in September to December, to spawn and die. ˙

The first big break for us came one fall on the Muskegon River, just forty-five minutes from Grand Rapids. Both the fall steelies and spawning salmon were in the river. We waded out to within casting distance of a large boulder situated deep in a run one mile below Croton Dam. Two bait fishermen in a boat were anchored just up from the hot spot. "Look at those dopes fly fishing," taunted one of the bait casters. "Don't they know they can't catch these fish on flies?" The other yelled over to us, "Do you guys ever catch fish on flies?"

"Not as frequently as a spawn sack does, but it's a lot more fun when we do hook one."

They looked at each other and snickered.

A moment later one of us felt a gentle tug. A hard strike with the rod, and a 16½-pound bright steelhead, fresh from the Big Lake, jumped not 15 feet from the hecklers' boat. The green fish jumped again, and one of us modestly replied to their previous question, "Yes, we do occasionally get a big fish on flies." It was the first really large steelie we had ever hooked.

The spring fishing is very different. Deserted then are the deep holes of the lower rivers and all the salmon are dead. The great redside fish are on the shallow gravel beds way up in the headwaters. Often streams normally thought of as brook trout creeks are black with spawning steelheads. The fish are darker, some half spent from their ordeal; they are not on the feed, but are *much more numerous*. You are fishing in relatively shallow water to visible giants, which can often be teased into striking. Sometimes they hit on the first cast. We have seen eight huge fish streak from cut banks or deep runs, all trying, as if in competition, to nail a large tan Whit nymph. Usually, however, you must tease these fish into striking. A baitfish imitation, such as the famous Blacknose Dace, dancing over the gravel bed for a long period of time, will often tease the fish into slashing at the fly.

We think that when fish get in the mood, almost anything will work. When the time is right the fish will hit a fly, and it does not need to be a large fly; a small

The Muskegon River at dawn

#12 often works well. This type of fishing remains a partial enigma, and in our opinion, always will. After all, the fish are spawning, not feeding, and therein lies the problem. You can't match the hatch because there isn't one, unless stray spawn can be considered a hatch.

Take a special situation. In the fall, the schools of big salmon in a pool will usually ignore all bait and artificials. But for one or two short periods during a day (or night) all the fish seem to decide to strike anything dragging in front of their noses. These periods come most often at dusk and dawn, but especially at night; they rarely occur in late morning or afternoon. At these "right times" practically everyone will have a fish on and it is almost like a carnival.

The culmination of our efforts to hook these great fish on flies came this spring when Dave Whitlock joined us in what is becoming his annual "Spring Steelhead Outing." We fished the Pere Marquette, the Little Manistee, and the Platte rivers. In two days we landed eight fly-caught steelheads, ranging from 2 to 12 pounds and averaging over 6.

We first tried the Pere Marquette but the run there was about over. It had been the mildest winter in a hundred years and the fish had spawned easily a month earlier. We found plenty of beds but few fish. Yet we did manage to land a 2-pounder and an 8-pounder before the morning was over.

After lunch, we hurried to the Little Manistee, where, although the run had been long in progress, the river was full of both spent and fresh fish. Here we landed six hens, all but one from the beds, and hooked and lost many more. Our tackle consisted of 8-foot rods, which balanced #7 lines. We used the new Hi-D sink-tips, and a 10-pound-test leader of about two feet. The short leader helps keep the fly down and doesn't seem to bother the fish. Sometimes we'd insert a braided-wire trolling line section between the line and the leader for deeper runs.

Egg Sack (old type)

The flies we found most successful were: an orange wool egg-sack imitation tied on #8 hooks, a black or yellow woolly worm, #6, and a light tan and dark grey Whit nymph, size 4, 3X long shank. All these flies are weighted. We also had some success with hair-wing salmon flies, tied halfway between low water and normal, as recommended by Ernie Schwiebert in *Art Flick's Master Fly-Tying Guide*.

The deadliest fly during the last season (possibly 80 percent of all steelheads fell to this imitation) is called the Spring Nymph or Wiggler Nymph. It is actually a simulation of the nymph of *Hexagenia limbata*, the naturals of which are relished by our fresh run steelies. Almost the only food found in the autopsies of these fish are *Hexagenia* nymphs. They are simple flies, and though many improvements come to mind, the original is so effective the big fish even seem to prefer it over the egg sack, the supreme favorite of the bait fishermen. One hesitates to tamper with such success. The tail and back are fox squirrel, the body is yellowish orange chenille or wool with a brown hackle-tied palmer.

Dark Caddis Pupa Nymph

Ernie Schwiebert, on a steelhead trip to Michigan last spring, tied the same fly but with a yellow spun-fur body over which orange spun-seal fur was wound and picked out to produce a halo effect when held to the sun. It proved to be a deadly improvement.

Marabou Streamer

FISH ON THE BEDS

When a pair of fish are found on the beds they usually can be teased into striking, or at least mouthing the fly, by repeated casts in front of the fish and allowing the fly to swim in front of it for as long as possible, and as deep as possible. This often takes a long time, as long as an hour, so don't get discouraged.

The real tough problem in fishing to either steelhead or salmon on a bed is getting the fly deep enough. It is easy for an experienced fly fisherman to drift an artificial past a pair of spawning fish but only the egg sack imitation works well fished in this manner. Most artificials must swim past or, better yet, swim back and forth, darting in and out and around the quarry's mouth. This is a tactic difficult to accomplish in the kind of flow found in a typical spawning riffle. Even a weighted streamer fished on a Hi-D sink tip line won't swim much under a foot while dragging directly against a moderately heavy current.

We have found the best solution to the problem to be a lead-core head. We buy a lead-core trolling line from our local sporting goods store and cut sections from it. We carry 3-, 5-, 10-, 15-, and 25-foot sections in a little plastic box. A loop is spliced in both ends of each line. The selected length of lead core is tied to the front end of your normal fly line (which should have a permanent monofilament butt) with a clinch knot. A short leader, 1 to 3 feet, is similarly attached to the other loop. In this manner you can change lengths of lead core rapidly. In these situations (casting to visible fish on beds) long casts are not necessary. Although lead-core shooting heads can be fabricated for distance casting, it would be pointless in this case.

The reason for the varying lengths of lead core is obvious. The speed and depth of desirable spawning riffles vary considerably. On a small stream such as the Upper Little Manistee, a 1-foot-deep, fairly gentle flow is common. On the big Pere Marquette, a 4-foot, very rapid stretch may be host to the steelhead.

When we find fish on a bed, we quietly pick a casting position up and slightly across stream. We observe the depth and flow (using polaroid glasses) and pick a length of lead core we think will get the fly down. Quickly it is attached to the normal fly line, then we cast up and across from the bed and swim the fly through the area. If the fly rides too high, we change to a longer length of lead-core head, experimenting until the correct combination is found. With a little experience the correct combination can be determined quickly.

Ernest Schwiebert watches spawning steelhead on the Little Manistee.

The proper position for handling a running fish. Note how the rod is pointed *at* the fish to reduce friction.

The strike, when it comes, is quite often very light; your reaction must be rapid and strong. These spawning fish (especially the salmon) have very hard mouths and you must set the hook well. After that, hang on and have at least a hundred yards of backing. These fish can run!

FISH IN RESTING POSITIONS

Fish in resting positions, especially when undisturbed, will often dart halfway across a pool or riffle to capture a swimming nymph. No action need be imparted to these nymphs. They are cast straight across stream and allowed to drift with the current. The fish often take a fly on the first cast and quite close to the surface.

We almost always spot the fish first in either situation. Blind fishing is practically useless.

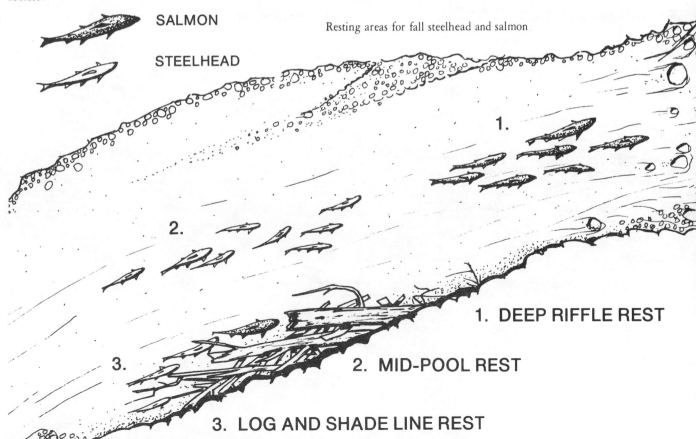

SALMON

STEELHEAD

Resting areas for fall steelhead and salmon

1.

2.

3.

1. DEEP RIFFLE REST

2. MID-POOL REST

3. LOG AND SHADE LINE REST

If the water is murky or no fish are visible, only experience and knowledge of the river can tell the angler where to fish. The neophyte on a strange river is all but helpless. A 15-mile stretch of the Pere Marquette is the prime spawning area on the hundred-mile-long river. Of the fifty or so good-looking riffles in the 15-mile stretch, only about twelve are heavily used. Any cover close to these twelve riffles makes good resting and taking lies to cast to when the fish are not visible on the beds. The newcomer casting to a beautiful piece of cover on the banks of a lovely, long, but unused riffle is wasting his time. Only intimate knowledge of the river will correct these wasted efforts.

ATLANTIC SALMON

The many streams in Michigan have miles and miles of clean white gravel riffles ideal for the spawning of anadromous fish; a few years ago the Department of Natural Resources stocked Atlantic salmon in some of these rivers. If these fish catch on as well as the steelhead and Pacific salmon have, the Great Lakes area could have a fly fishery equal to that of Norway, Iceland, and the Maritime Provinces of Canada.

The plan is to give Michigan streams a run of large fish during the summer months. This would fill the gap between the spring run of steelheads and the fall run of king and silver salmon. The Atlantics are at least the equal of the steelheads (although this can be argued in either direction) and are unquestionably a better game fish than the Pacific salmon.

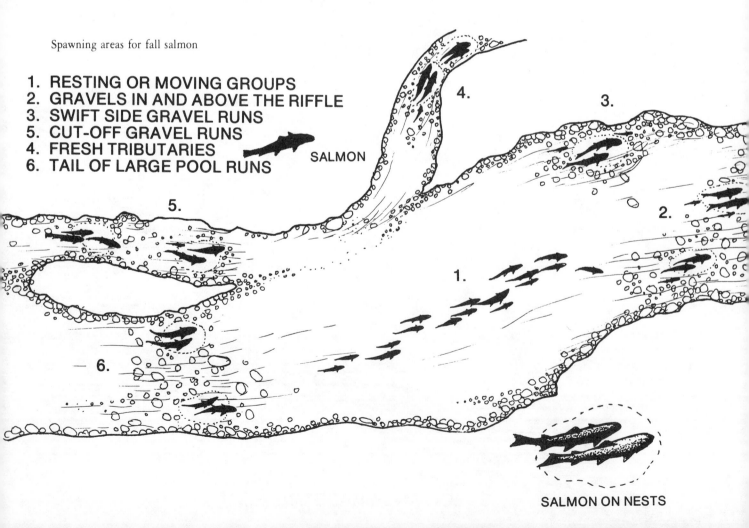

Spawning areas for fall salmon

1. RESTING OR MOVING GROUPS
2. GRAVELS IN AND ABOVE THE RIFFLE
3. SWIFT SIDE GRAVEL RUNS
5. CUT-OFF GRAVEL RUNS
4. FRESH TRIBUTARIES
6. TAIL OF LARGE POOL RUNS

SALMON

SALMON ON NESTS

A typical box of salmon flies for the new midwestern fishing

Since the Quebec strain ascends its native spawning rivers in June, July, and August, it was thought that the fish might run later in the warmer Michigan waters and the first run was almost ignored. One experienced fly fisherman fished to the Quebec strain during July and August of 1973 on the Boyne, which is a short stream. This sly devil kept the run a personal secret. Then, in late August, an official of the D.N.R. happened to run across our hero on the river and casually asked, "How you doing?"

"Pretty good," was the reply.

"What ya getting?"

"Oh, Atlantic salmon."

"Naw, couldn't be. What do they look like?" The D.N.R. man wouldn't believe the fly fisherman and he dismissed the incident with a request to bring in the next fish he landed to the local D.N.R. office.

Two hours later a bright silver, 27-inch fish was plopped down on the office desk and soon afterward a weir was hastily erected on the river. Only seven fish were taken by the fisheries people. The salmon had been in the stream at least two months before they were expected and one fisherman had a fine time for himself by keeping the great fishing to himself.

The mere thought of 50-pound Atlantic salmon barreling up Michigan streams staggers the imagination. Two strains have so far been introduced. One is from Canada (Grand-Cascapédia River), which is expected to run in May, June, and July; the other is a special landlocked strain from Sweden (Gullspang strain) which has been adapted to a fresh-water environment for four thousand years and has reached a size of more than 30 pounds.

Egg Sack (new type)

Spring Nymph

Woollyworm

Hexagenia Wiggle Nymph

Hairwing Salmon Fly

Two-egg Sperm Fly

Large Hexagenia Nymph

Alewife

Smolt

Tube Fly

When one thinks of the price one must pay to fish the Atlantic in their normal range and to have this, the ultimate fly fish in many streams running into the Great Lakes, the opportunities for the future seem bright indeed.

People from other states often regard this new fish area as a minor flash in the pan, unworthy of notice. Nothing could be further from the truth. Lake Michigan alone, as of this writing, is producing more king and silver salmon for anglers than all of the Pacific Coast states put together. This is a major fishing ground easily within striking distance of our major population centers. It is very important and is becoming more important. The potential is almost unlimited.

TIMING THE RUNS

Whether you are fishing for steelheads or salmon, timing is most important. You can't catch these fish if they are not there, no matter how good your technique or how effective your pattern.

ATLANTIC SALMON.   As of this writing, it appears these fish will run from late May through September. Twenty thousand smolts were planted in 1974, with forty thousand expected in 1975, one hundred thousand in 1976. By that time the egg supply should be good and the ultimate yearly stocking could be just about anything the Division of Natural Resources wishes it to be. Heavy rains and high water seem to trigger runs.

PACIFIC SALMON.   These fish start their run in Michigan rivers in late August and early September. The main run begins in late September and lasts through October, to the middle of November. In December, a good run of jacks is often encountered. When the main run of kings and silvers is in, they make so much commotion and are so large they leave wakes like submarines as they ascend the rivers. If they are not in evidence they are probably not there. Last fall the Muskegon had beds all over

CR with a bright steelhead taken on the Little Manistee

the spawning riffles with as many as 10 to 15 fish on every bed. One morning we had 34 fish on between seven and eleven thirty and landed 12, some up to 40 pounds.

Once during the height of the run we stood on the railroad bridge in the town of Newago and observed at least one thousand huge kings in a pool just above the bridge. The number of fish in the river was incredible.

STEELHEAD.   The big rainbows come into the rivers in three waves. The first begins in September and reaches its height in October and November. They are robust, bright silver, and perhaps the equal of Atlantic salmon. These fish are feeding and will hit the fly well.

The second wave usually ascends the rivers in January or February, during the midwinter thaw. It is triggered by high warm water and if you hit it just right (which is by no means easy) the fish will hit a fly even in very dark water. A dropper with two or three heavy split shot is used to get the fly close to the bottom. You must be able to feel the shot bouncing off the gravel or you are not getting deep enough. Most of these midwinter fish spawn during the frigid months of February and March. It is cold fly fishing, often with ice on the guides, but it is rewarding, especially on that rare sunny day. The best time is late afternoon when the river temperature is as high as it will get.

The third wave, and they may include two or three mini-waves, barrel up our spawning streams during the spring thaw. The main run seems to occur after the snow has melted and a real spring deluge occurs. When the river gets a warm rainstorm and rises two or three feet, it seems unfishable, but it is actually very productive. During high murky water, black squirrel-tail wing flies with red, orange, and green fluorescent butts and black fur bodies are highly effective. This is the time you will catch your highest average number of fish.

The best time is very elusive and lasts for only three or four days. As the water level drops after a late-April spate and the river becomes clear, the previously hidden fish become visible. Now everyone who didn't know where to fish during the high water suddenly discovers that not all good riffles hold fish. Naturally they concentrate on the hot spots so the fish are quickly caught or spooked. This is why the fishing time is so short. The spring nymph and medium low-water hair-wing salmon flies are the best patterns for the warm April clearing waters; sizes 4 to 8 are best. April is the month to anticipate the correct conditions, although early May can be good on some rivers, such as the lower Au Sable, in the shallow riffles below Foote Dam. The Little Manistee seems to be a good fall stream plus a fantastic early and late spring fishery.

A new fly brought to our attention this fall seems to work extremely well on both salmon and steelhead, especially when the fish are on the beds. It is called the Two-Egg Sperm fly and imitates a two-egg cluster; it's made with a little white marabou over the back and some silver mylar between the two eggs for a little flash. Spawning king salmon hit it consistently and it is even deadly on big browns holding behind redds.

CHAPTER 9

LAKE FLY FISHING

LAKE FISHING FOR TROUT presents problems not encountered in stream fishing. It is tougher to get strikes in still water, the fish are more selective, and a score of different aquatic insects inhabit still water. In a lake, trout will feed on extremely tiny insects, such as midges and microduns, because they can hover and sip without expending energy or fighting rapid currents. Their feeding style is similar to that of the quiet spring creeks. Since the fish have plenty of time to examine their food, good imitations are a must for consistent success. Also, in lake fishing for trout, as in saltwater fishing, you must be able to cast for distance and delicacy. The fish spook easily in clear calm water, and often don't feed in one place as a stream fish will. There is no current, so lines of drift do not exist. Since lake fish *almost always cruise* as they feed, you must be able to figure out at what speed and in what direction the fish are moving to be able to cast your imitation in the proper spot for a taking rise. If you guess wrong you will probably be casting over empty water.

Every lake has a somewhat different ecosystem from all others, so the trout's diet can vary drastically from one spot to another. Some lakes have huge mayfly hatches and others are wall-to-wall shrimp. Sometimes baitfish are the main food source, while many western lakes have large damselfly hatches. There is simply no easy way to approach strange water. It takes time to learn the waters and the areas that hold

124

food and feeding fish. It might take steady fishing for over two or three seasons to learn the insects of an area. Lake-born mayfly species are usually different from stream species, although the families and genus are familiar.

READING A LAKE

Fish feed where food is available. Insects and crustaceans can't live in extremely deep water where sunlight does not penetrate, so the shallow shoreline, up to fifteen feet or so (depending on water clarity) is the production area. Luckily for us, fly fishing is much easier in shallow waters. The very best spots are inlets where feeder streams drain into a lake. These areas usually abound with small fish and insects. Areas where large springs boil up in shallow water are also very good. If there are moss beds in these areas, they will probably hold shrimp. Fur nymphs worked over the beds are deadly. Sunken brush piles placed along the shoreline will attract insects, minnows, and large predator fish. Reefs are usually hot spots, and the spawning areas of many fish.

Since most trout lakes are clean, cool, and spring-fed (otherwise they'd be bass lakes) we need not worry too much about water clarity. If the shallow shoreline where the insects live is warm, the fish will feed there when the water is coolest, late evening and early morning. On a clear hot day, large trout, when not actively feeding, will lie below the depth where the sun rays strongly penetrate the water. This can be quite deep in very clear water. Much can be learned about lake fishing from expert bass anglers. They have found that if they lower a white plate into the water, the point at

Lake fishing for trout presents many unique challenges; fish often feed deep, although they prefer feeding on surface insects when they are available.

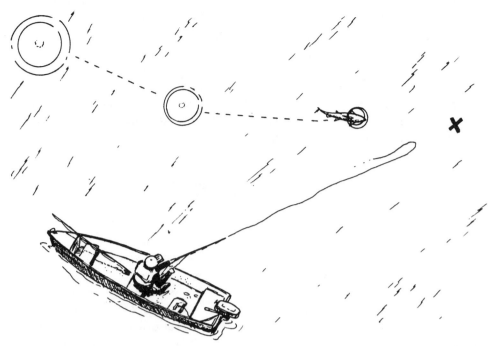

Since rising lake trout usually cruise as they feed, the angler must learn to correctly estimate the trout's feeding pattern, time his casts accordingly.

which it becomes lost to sight is one-half the depth where the fish are usually resting. It is only one-half the depth as the light must travel both down and back up through the water before the reflected rays are seen by the eye of the observer. Thus, approximately twice the depth is the correct level to fish. They say that light intensity is much more important than temperature levels. When the water is clear and the day is hot, a Hi-D sinking line and even weighted flies are necessary to reach the areas where fish are resting.

A. INLETS
B. OUTLETS
C. SHALLOW SPRINGS
D. BRUSH PILES AND DEAD FALLS
E. REEFS—DROPOFFS
F. ISLANDS
G. SHALLOW MOSS BEDS
H. LONG POINTS

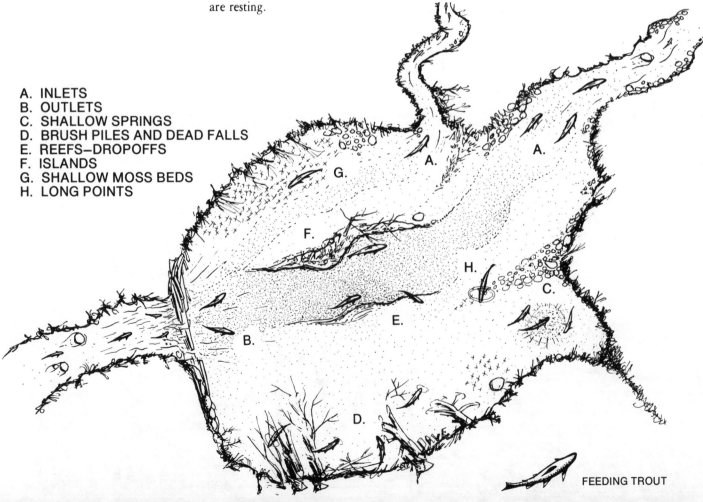

FEEDING TROUT

In the cool of the early morning and evening, the sun's rays are at an acute angle so they do not penetrate the surface as far; thus fish feed at these times not only because of cooler shallows, but also and perhaps primarily because of the diminished glare. Of course, the darker or murkier the water the more shallow trout will rest during the middle of the day. The white plate will tell you how deep to fish.

The harder or richer the water the more plants, plankton, nymphs, and fish a lake will support. Lakes are the same as rivers in this respect, so, if you have a choice, choose the hard-water lakes—that is, those lakes with the largest amount of lime content. The more lime, the more food and fish a lake or river will support. What this really means is the parts per million of bound carbon dioxide (ppm CO_2) it contains. If one is interested, a very simple kit can be put together for a nominal sum to determine the water's hardness. The kit and its use are well documented in that fine work by the late Sid Gordon, *How to Fish from Top to Bottom*. He also tells us that the richer the water the thicker and larger the *underwater* plant life (not the surface plants, such as the lily pads, which don't count). Thus, Henry's Lake in Idaho is wall-to-wall moss and also shrimp. Some people say that this lake has more shrimp than water. Henry's Fork of the Snake, which is partially fed by an outlet from the lake, also has rich aquatic vegetation and an exceptionally broad span of underwater insect life.

Probably many of the structures fished and techniques used in bass fishing could be applied to trout lakes. If you have ever seen a modern, fully equipped bass boat, you will understand the amount of sophisticated electronic gear used to locate fish, determine water temperature levels, light density, depth, underwater structures, and every other conceivable thing needed to help catch fish. (We shudder at the thought of the kind of tournaments held by bass fishermen being adapted to trout lakes. The results would be devastating.)

EQUIPMENT

The lake rod should be long enough and powerful enough for distance casts. Depending on your ability, probably the ideal stick is an 8-foot fiber glass rod that balances with a #7 line. Anything heavier will not be pleasant to use and the #7 outfit is large enough to fight almost any fish.

A shooting head or weight-forward line is ideal. The new sink tips are good for underwater nymph and streamer fishing. Leaders should be as long and as fine as possible in the still water (12 feet is good).

Good imitations are required, but for those you must know the water and be well prepared for specific hatches. In general, however, fur shrimp and damselfly nymphs are good as well as mayfly and midges. Midge hatches are almost universal on lakes, and large fish will often feed on them. During a rise, nymphs are usually more effective than duns, as the fish have plenty of time to get them on the way up, and the visibility from the fish's point of view is usually good with no current to interfere. Both nymph and emerger imitations are effective at this time, especially the stillborn type, which imitates a nymph struggling to escape from the nymphal shuck. During a spinner fall, half- and full-spent Hen or Partridge Spinners are effective.

When there is no rise to fish, subsurface flies are usually best; dry flies, even attractors, are not much good when no surface activity is in progress. Fur nymphs should resemble some type of insect or crustacean natural to the water. Wiggle nymphs really come into their own in still water, as the extra action seems more attractive and excites more strikes. Woolly worms are good, as are streamers that simulate the native minnows of the lake.

Shrimp Nymph

GIVING THE FLY ACTION

A floating fly may be cast in front of a cruising riser and allowed to sit, but better yet, it can be twitched a few times at the appropriate moment. This is a natural action, for the real fly often flutters on the water in both the dun and spinner stages.

During a rise to duns, artificial nymphs should be cast far in front of the cruising fish and permitted to sink. As the fish approach, the nymph is raised from deep water, imitating a natural that is swimming to the surface. This action can be slow or fast, smooth or with twitches, depending on the species of insect emerging. You may have to experiment if you're not familiar with the habits of a particular species.

Retrieves, used when no surface action is in progress, should simulate the natural swimming action of the imitation you are using. This also can vary from slow, steady retrieves, to slow with jerks, all the way up to stripping as fast as possible. The latter is often effective for streamers or very large nymphs. Again, experimentation may be necessary.

Other than the well-known hand-twist retrieve, the best method is to keep the line between the right forefinger and the rod handle, while stripping with the left hand. That way, some pressure is always on the line and you'll feel even a light strike. Also, by using this method the speed and the action can be varied according to conditions.

Dave's Shrimp

Damselfly Wiggle Nymph

THE INSECTS

Researchers have found that *lake trout will feed on surface insects when they are available. When they are not available trout will feed, as a preference, on insects which are not aquatic during their entire life cycle.* If neither choice is available they will feed on snails, shrimp, or minnows. *But they prefer adult mayflies, caddises and midges as the first choice, and as second choice, the nymphs or larval stage of the same insects.* This is a great discovery for fly fishermen, for it means our quarries prefer surface feeding primarily, with the immature forms of insects as a second choice.

There are many mayfly species that emerge from still water. Needless to say, they are usually different from fast-water types. Very small species, such as the *Caenis*, are common in lakes but rare in streams. Other genera we may expect to find are *Hexagenia*, *Ephemera*, a very few *Ephemerellas*, but many various *Callibaetis* types (speckled winged duns).

We often fish the *Hexagenia* hatch in Bear Lake, located in the upper part of the Lower Peninsula of Michigan. It is a late-evening emergence, which occurs in the latter part of July and in early August. The first time we encountered emergence we

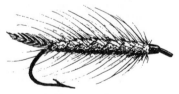

Dave's Fur Worm

Whitlock's Special Woollyworm

found that our dun imitations were practically useless during the hatch, and the fish were apparently not feeding much, at least not on the surface. Since the water is extremely clear, and the areas of emergence were about ten feet deep, we decided the big rainbows had plenty of chance to get all the nymphs they wanted long before they surfaced. Back at the cabin later that night, we brought out the tying kit and worked up a pattern that was a sort of cross between a nymph and a streamer, with a short marabou and peacock-sword wing, to imitate the swimming emerging fly.

Next evening when the hatch started, we positioned the boat near a spot where many naturals were hatching. It happened to be over a submerged, man-made brush pile. We cast the streamer-like imitations quite far and permitted them to sink to the bottom. Then, with a short, jerky retrieve, we raised them from the bottom to simulate the action of the natural on its ascent to the surface. The bows averaged about twenty inches long, and hit the flies savagely between 1 and 5 feet from the surface. This is a deadly technique on lakes during a hatch.

Later that same evening, a spinner fall occurred just at dark. The fish were cruising, and at first we had trouble getting strikes. We noticed that the naturals lying flush in the film were not still, but were fluttering somewhat as a moth or butterfly flutters when caught in the surface of a stream. The flies were so large they actually left rings on the water as they struggled. We began twitching our Hen Spinners to imitate this action, and had good fishing from then on.

Possibly the most common and important insects for lake fishing are midge species. They can range in size from #28, or smaller, all the way up to #16. They can be practically any color as literally hundreds of the species exist.

Stone flies are rare in lakes, but caddis and alder flies are common. They are fairly small flies, usually #16 to #18. Of course all the terrestrial types can be blown into the water and this presents the same kinds of problems it does on a trout stream.

On some western lakes, like Henry's, the damselfly is the most important hatch of the year. It is anticipated as much as the Green Drake is in Pennsylvania and the *Hexagenia* in Michigan. Very large fish can be caught on both nymphs and, in some lakes, dries during this hatch. A damselfly nymph tied wiggle style is very good. Freshwater shrimp, scuds, leeches, and back swimmers are common, and their imitations are often very effective.

If you can believe it, there is such a thing as a surface migration of snails during hot weather, and fish feed on them. It is difficult to recognize these migrations as they are hard to see in the water, but trout do feed avidly at these times, and an effective imitation can be constructed from cork.

A portable fly-tying kit is invaluable for the lake fisherman, for no one can possibly know what fly is going to emerge next from the hundreds of thousands of lakes over the entire continent. If you don't know, you can't prepare, so the best way is to have the means at hand to reproduce the existing hatch. It is a do-it-yourself deal, and to be consistently effective you must be able to tie your own flies or have a reliable local source available.

This is our opinion, but fly fishing lakes for trout is much more difficult than stream fishing for the reasons mentioned. We freely admit we prefer to fish moving water, especially water rich in aquatic insect life. It's more exciting and also more in-

Green's Leech

Mylar Threadfin Shad

Matuka Chub

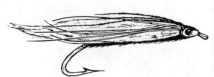

Mylar Marabou Minnow

A swimming damsel nymph, side and top view

Adult damselfly

Shrimp

Scud

Backswimmer

teresting. But the impression that still-water fishing is more difficult is not our idea alone. Will Godfrey, an Idaho fly-shop owner, guide, and part-time Professor of Economics in various western universities, lives (in the summer) on the banks of the North Fork of the Snake. He hosts many hotshot fly fishermen who come to the area with big reputations. He has a foolproof method of deflating egos. He'll arrange an overnight trip to the Centennial Mountains, where there is a group of truly beautiful lakes nestled in the lovely mountain basin. One lake runs into another by a series of small streams. Though actually they are no more than large ponds, the brook and rainbow trout there are really huge. Will tells of a great bow that rose, not to his dry fly, but to the airborne barn swallow that was swooping down to take his imitation. The fish ate the bird and ignored Will's fly. He didn't rise again, although Will cast over the area for the remainder of the evening.

These lakes have great *Ephemerella* hatches of the Pale Morning Dun types and blanket *Chirnomides*, plus fantastic numbers of freshwater shrimp. The water is marvelously clear and it is easy to humiliate the unknowing tourist who is not aware of the difficulties of still water and superselective cruising trout. One or two fish a day is considered pretty good, even by the initiate.

We were asked by this sly young guide-professor, to fish the Centennials. We luckily refused, being at the time preoccupied with the prolific hatches on the Snake River—though maybe we had an inkling he was trying to snooker us. Later we stole up to the area like thieves in the night to familiarize ourselves with the situation. It is tough fishing and, although the fish are very large and present in great numbers, not many anglers have ever caught a large number in one day.

Lake fishing is tough because of the still clear water, the cruising fish, the need for an exact imitation, and the fact that each lake has a different biosystem. Each single body of water needs study, at least over an entire year, to enable one to know what is occurring. But the fish are larger and heavier than stream-bred fish, so it is a challenge worthy of study and a successful day is one to remember proudly.

CHAPTER 10

SALTWATER FLY FISHING

FLY FISHING IN THE SALT for the first time can be a boring, frustrating experience, even though one may be an expert trout fisherman. It can also be extremely exciting. Almost everything is different from the usual trout techniques and this is especially true in a tournament. The flies, reels, rods, and even the knots used are unfamiliar, new equipment must be acquired and techniques relearned. There always seems to be some sort of tournament in progress and the guides are anxious for their clients to win, since this gives the guides publicity.

Guides can be very helpful but often are a disaster. Many saltwater fly-fishing guides are extremely autocratic and it is possible to wind up doing what the guide wants to do, which usually turns out to be sitting on a bank all day waiting for a tournament winner. Few really good fly-fishing guides exist, and they are always booked up for months, if not for years, in advance. It is quite difficult to convince them that you would be happier with many small fish on light tackle than with one giant world record. Personally we prefer to go merely for the fun, and that means plenty of action, not long periods of sitting in a boat.

One of the Florida Keys consistently produces the Miami Metropolitan Tournament winner for bonefish. If your ambition is to win this, the most famous tournament, popularly called "the Met," that is where you head. What the statistics don't

A small tarpon taken on a fly

tell you, however, is that there are few large bonefish and no small ones in this area. One expert saltwater fisherman, who lives on this key, fishes ninety days out of the year on the very best tides. He averages only seven to eight landed fish a year. This is not the place to spend a week's vacation if you want action. Another spot, not thirty minutes away by car, has all the fish you could wish for right off the beach. But they are not tournament winners so no one bothers them. On 6½- or 7-foot 2-ounce light trout tackle they are more fun than the larger bones on 9-ounce saltwater fly rods.

There are so many species to fish for that some aren't even named yet. All are good to fierce fighters, especially on light tackle. Long lightninglike runs are to be expected, with bulldog strength at the end. This fishing is not at all like matching the hatch trout angling. It's more of an athletic event in which the physical strength of the angler is of paramount importance.

This chapter makes no attempt to be all-inclusive; we merely want to share a few revealing experiences and insights on this growing brand of fly fishing.

TWO WAYS TO GO

If you don't mind spending a minimum of $90 a day, not counting food, travel, and lodging, hire a guide. Make sure that he knows something about fly fishing and that his boat is set up for it. Tell him what you want. If you wish lots of action and don't particularly care what species of fish you catch, make sure that the guide knows this and agrees to it ahead of time. If you are after a tournament or world record on a fly, that is possible, but be prepared to sit around a lot. In our experience, continuous action and Metropolitan winners do not go together—except by accident.

Once you have engaged your guide, start praying you have made a good choice. A typical example of the trouble you can run into happened to us a few years ago. We had two of the most sought-after guides in the state and we were after gigantic tarpon. We were fishing at the best time of the year, on the best bank, lying off the best flat anywhere in Florida. The first few days the moon was wrong, then the year was unusual and the fish had already gone. We sat on that famous bank for eight hours a day, for seven days, and landed three tarpon. That was not exactly a thrill a minute, even though the action, when it did come, could be conservatively described as worth waiting for. After the first few days we discreetly inquired about other types of fish in the area but our request fell on deaf ears. To these famous guides it was giant tarpon or nothing.

Impatient for a nonexistent run to materialize, we called a chap in Fort Lauderdale who had been recommended to us. His name is Jack "Bass" Allen. He is normally a bass guide in the Everglades area, but he understood what we wanted. "Bring your 2-ounce fly rods and be prepared to fight fish until your arms tire," he told us. "They'll be smaller snook, tarpon, and jack crevalle. They won't win the Met, but you'll have action." And he was right. A slow trip was transformed by the right guide into a vacation to remember.

Jack crevalle

We fished at night around lighted docks. This is where the snook and jacks feed like piranha. At dawn we fished the bays and hooked and landed many tarpon, from 20 to 60 pounds. A 50-pound tarpon on a 2-ounce #4 light fly rod is more fun than a 150-pounder on an #11 outfit. A 7-pound snook is like a 25-inch brown on a 7X tippet.

The most amazing part of this fishing is the area we fished. It was directly in front of canal and bayside homes in the center of a large city. Snook and jacks feed ravenously all night long on small baitfish and shrimp, which are attracted to lights around big yachts. We saw absolutely no one else fishing, and our flies were much better imitations of the natural feed than a spin fisherman could ever come up with. The feeding closely resembles trout rising to a great hatch of mayflies. The strikes are clearly seen by the angler as surface rises. The most effective patterns are small white and yellow marabou and small fur shrimp nymphs (really trout flies). The jacks and snook stopped feeding at dawn. That was when the real excitement began. In the bayou, surrounded by rich homes, even mansions, hundreds of tarpon began porpoising. They ranged in size from 10 to 70 pounds and were feeding on baitfish averaging one inch long. We were casting to visible fish for the next two hours, our flies were constantly in front of good tarpon, and we averaged one fish per hour, landed and released.

The incredible thing about this experience was that it took place in a fairly large town, and we were casting to feeding, rising fish with absolutely no competition. In seven days and nights of early-morning fly fishing, we never encountered another angler trying for these fish. The reason for this may have been that these fish feed on very small baitfish and crustaceans, so the spoons and plugs commonly used by spin anglers are not too effective. Here the fly rodders have the distinct advantage. They are the only ones who can consistently hook the surface feeders.

After four days with Jack Allen, we figured any other fishing we might encounter during this trip would be anticlimactic. We were pleasantly surprised, however, by Bob Marvin, another guide who had been recommended to us. We had three days of

Snook

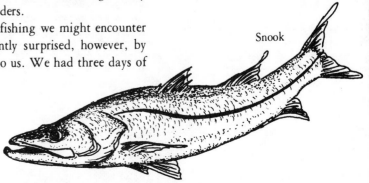

fishing left, so we drove down to Bob's home in Key West. He runs his guide service out of his house and his setup is the best we have ever seen. Bob's home is right on a canal so all of his boats and equipment are less than 50 feet out the back door. Best of all, his canal is in the most perfect location for fishing the finest water in the Keys. Less than fifteen minutes away are flats and channels loaded with bonefish, tarpon, barracudas, sharks, jacks, ladyfish, trout, snook, and many other hard-fighting species.

Fishing seems to run in the Marvin family. Bob's lovely wife, Kathy, is an enthusiastic fisherwoman who in fact presently holds the Women's World Record for Permit, 6# Spinning Division, of 38 pounds 6 ounces. Young Bobby has his own boat and spends most of his spare time in the back country. Bob is a strongly built, good-natured fellow who has just the right temperament for this type of guiding. Eight to ten hours in a small bonefish skiff are pure pleasure with this man, even if the fish are uncooperative. Bob is not only a great fly caster, but can pole over the flats and spot fish better than any guide we have ever been out with. And we have been out with a lot of guys with great reputations. What we really appreciate most about Bob, though, are his attitude and approach.

Kite fishing with Bob Marvin for billfish on a fly

During those first three days with him, he introduced us to more different types of saltwater fishing than we had encountered in all of our previous trips to the Keys. We poled and waded flats for bones, cudas, tarpon, and sharks. We fished the channels for tarpon, jacks, snappers, and groupers. We fished around wrecks and in large deep-water "glory holes" for jacks, snappers, ladyfish, and trout. We caught cudas, jacks, snappers, and even sharks on poppers. We had all this and a lot more, but mainly we had fun. We caught fourteen species of fish in those three days.

Here, then, were two guides who knew what we wanted but resisted our efforts to have them take us to it, and two others who gave us a great vacation the very first day we were with them. The first were famous but autocratic, the second, regular guys who became good friends in a few days. If you are able, get a guide. But you must put almost as much effort into the choosing as you would in choosing a wife; in either case, if you choose wrong, the results can be disastrous. Two weeks with the wrong guide are not quite as bad as twenty years with the wrong woman, but, if you have been dreaming about a saltwater fly fishing trip for years, it can be bad enough.

THE OTHER WAY

There is another method of fly fishing in the salt. It costs nothing, although a little time invested in research will pay big dividends. You may use your normal trout equipment, but should make sure that you have plenty of backing on your reel. Don waders or sneakers and use a normal trout streamer or nymph. Find a beach or a flat that is wadable and cast blindly. You will almost surely catch fish. The water along the highway that connects the keys is teeming with possibilities.

We stumbled onto this method a few years ago in Key West. It was March, and due to high winds, no boats would venture forth. Day after day, we arose early, arrived at the docks, and were told "Not today; it's too rough." After a long cold winter we had cabin fever and were eager to be out fishing. We scouted around and found a deserted area on Sutherland Key, north of Key West. Out of pure ignorance, we supposedly did just about everything wrong. We used 7-foot, 2½-ounce rods which took a #4 line. We had regular trout reels, though with lots of backing. Our lures were not saltwater flies but medium-size fur nymphs. We had no idea that, according to local tradition and local guides at least, we had no chance of catching bonefish. Well, we just wanted any fish. We weren't the least particular at that point. We were desperate. The sports shops told us we needed guides and boats, and that to be successful we'd have to get away from the Keys, even as far as the Marquesas Islands. But we were eager and the boats would not go out so we went ourselves.

Arriving at first light, we waded out as far as we could and cast blindly. We didn't stalk visible fish, we merely covered the water the same way we would on large trout streams when no hatch is in progress. With this simple method we caught bones, barracuda, jacks, sharks, and fish that looked like big bluegills with teeth like a piranha's.

A 25-inch cuda on a system 4 outfit is a real handful. A 5-pound bone is a thunderbolt. Later, we finally did get out to the back country as the wind and waves moderated, and caught much larger fish, but strangely it wasn't as much fun. It is the same phenomenon as we noticed in trout fishing. A 15-inch brown, in cool water water, on a 6- or 6½-foot 1¾ ounce rod with a 6X or 7X tippet is more fun than a 20- or 25-inch fish on a powerful 9-foot rod with a heavy 10-pound test leader. The same comparison is true in salt. A 30-inch cuda on a light trout outfit gives an incredible fight, 100-yard runs, and many salmonlike leaps. These fish are abundant, very close to shore and available to the casual wader.

The larger fish that are farther out are usually fought with 9- or 9½-foot #10,

A lemon shark rising for a popper; many sharks are spectacular fighters.

#11, or even #12 rods. They give a fierce fight, but the delicacy is missing. It's muscle against muscle, and with a strong leader the fish really has no chance. Often the tussle becomes boring after the initial jumps. Not so with the superlight outfit. Even a tired fish can escape a 4- or 6-pound-test leader. As in trout fishing, delivery and techniques are important and a feeling of intimacy between the fish and the angler is preserved. Also, the quarry has a damned good chance of winning. This is important, for to us—it is a great part of the challenge of fly fishing.

EQUIPMENT

One universal criterion for saltwater fly fishing is to have plenty of backing on your reel. Fish come in all sizes from small to gigantic. For the large fish, such as the giant tarpon, the traditional equipment consists of a 9- or 9½-foot glass fiber rod, using a 10 to 12 weight line, and a precision reel with a strong smooth drag. A good saltwater fly reel, unlike the freshwater type, is much more than a spool to hold line. These fish run far and fast and you must be able to put great pressure on them or they'll simply run out your backing and you'll never be able to tire them out. The Finnor is our current favorite. It is a beautiful precision instrument, and comes in three sizes; even the smallest holds plenty of backing for all but the largest of game fish. In fact, we often use it on your 8-foot rods when fishing larger trout rivers. Its drag is silky smooth and can be snubbed down to a complete stop if necessary.

For the angler who wants some real sport and prefers to use a single-action, manual reel, the New Berkley Specialist is the answer. You can control the drag with direct finger pressure, yet you don't burn your hand as happens with a palming reel. The Specialist has an activator lever that depresses two brake shoes into contact with the rotating spool. This is the most exciting way to fight a saltwater fish.

Small fiber glass rods, the very lightest, are ideal for all but the truly huge fish and will give the sportsman much more fun. The new carbon and boron rods are a very exciting development for salt water. They cast farther, more easily, and are much lighter than bamboo and conventional fiber glass rods. The solid and hollow-solid combination types are almost indestructible and should be great for fighting and pumping large fish to the boat.

The ability and equipment to cast for distance in salt water is mandatory. Anyone who can't cast 90 feet when a long cast is needed is greatly handicapped. One fact is much overlooked by many fishing writers. A 90-foot cast on a calm day, or a 100-

Whitlock's Blue Crab

Doug's Polyshrimp

foot cast with a wind, may be equal to only a 30- or 40-foot cast against a strong breeze. Saltwater fish seem to have an unreasonable habit of approaching, more often than not, from the upwind position, so one is actually casting into the wind. It is not really clear why these fish insist that you cast upwind, but for some unaccountable reason, they choose to approach at the most difficult angle possible.

Our favorite fly line for salt water is the new blunt tip style that has its center of gravity pushed farther forward and then tapers gradually from belly to running line. This profile gives the best and fastest possible shoot and eliminates the annoying "hinge effect" of standard saltwater tapers. We like blue, which provides good visibility to the angler yet does not flash brightly in the sun.

Shooting heads are a great help in distance casting. The first 30 feet of a normal double-tapered line is attached to a flat (oval) mono shooting line. It takes a little practice to handle and you may not like it at first, but once you get used to handling it, the ability to cast much farther is always at hand.

Sinking tips are unbeatable for fishing subsurface. They handle well, yet, when used with short sinking leaders, put the fly down quickly to depths of 4 to 8 feet. For greater depths and heavy tidal movements, we add twist-ons or mini leadheads.

Shock tippets are made out of either heavy mono- or nylon-coated steel leader material. If you prefer the nonmetallic variety, try the new commercial grade of monofilament put out by Berkley. It is a dream to work with and is the only heavy mono we've found that will relax and stay straight.

Poly-Mylar Hightie Streamer

THE FISH

There is an incredible variety of saltwater species. If you want a sail on a fly it is possible—for a price—as is a giant tarpon, a large bone, marlin, or tuna. Of course, each species is a story in itself, and an entire book would be required to cover the methods of enticing them all to the fly. Lefty Kreh has written such a book, *Fly Fishing in Salt Water*. The one new approach we would like to add to this much underused resource of saltwater fishing is the flies used in the various fishing found in the salt.

Some of the fly patterns that have been successful for us, other than the standard saltwater patterns, are: fur nymphs and shrimp imitations, yellow and white sparkling marabous, and a hair crab tied by Dave Whitlock. Large wiggle nymphs work extremely well, and on several occasions greatly outfished live bait used by people around us. The fur nymphs evidently resemble shrimp or small crayfish. Often even predators, such as barracuda, seem frightened by the gaudy, flashy streamers, especially on clear flats. After following and refusing traditional patterns they would take a more somber nymph unhesitantly. The best colors of furs are cream, tan, brown, pink, and light purple.

The white and yellow flashing marabous are especially deadly on snook at night, and on tarpon on the bays early in the morning. These are not very large, #12 to #16. Night fly fishing for snook near lighted docks is almost like dry-fly fishing to a rise for trout. You can see the snook and the jacks smashing into baitfish and small shrimp that are attracted to the low-hung lamps. The fly is cast into the lighted spot

Poly Bone and Permit Fly

Polywing Minnow

Poly-Mylar Shark and 'Cuda Fly

Poly Eel

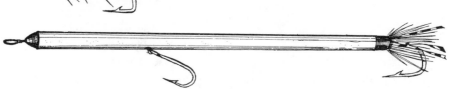

Whitlock's Eelworm Streamer

Dave's Straw-Streamer Fly

on the water and very slowly twitched across, almost on the surface.

The Blue Crab is an incredible concoction by Dave Whitlock, with hinged pinchers and even beaded eyes. It works well on the flats for bones and permit.

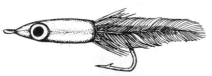

Darter

Straw Fly
Hooks: 1/0 short shank saltwater, connected by #20 steelon wire
Body: bright orange plastic drinking straw with small corks epoxied into each end
Tail: bright orange plastic skirt material, or silver Mylar strands

Dave's Doll Eye Silver

Tube Fly
Hooks: 1/0 saltwater, connected by #20 steelon wire
Body: flexible vinyl tubing dyed fluorescent orange, pink, or chartreuse, approximately 8 inches long
Tail: silver Mylar strands
Hackle: fluorescent to match body

Tarosik's Pencil Popper

Bob Marvin's Rubber Hackle Fly
Hook: 1/0 to 5/0 saltwater medium shank
Body: gold Mylar piping
Tail: 8 to 10 strands of yellow rubber hackle
Wing: 18 to 20 strands of yellow rubber hackle
Hackle: grizzly
Thread: black

Popper

Here are some tips on saltwater techniques:

1) Fast retrieve. You must develop a superfast retrieve for salt water. There are two ways of doing this. You can pump your rod as you strip or put the rod under your arm or between your legs and strip with both hands.

2) Spotting fish. This takes practice. Polaroids are a must; it is best to have the type with side shields and top shield. Focus your eyes at the depth where fish should

Poly-Mylar Skipper

Bonefish often "tail," offering a ready casting target.

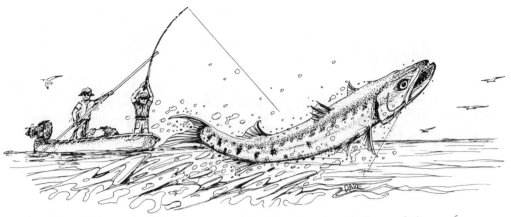

Saltwater fly fishing offers an incredible array of sporting fish; the barracuda is one of the gamest of all.

be, near the bottom, not at the surface. Practice by looking at one area only; focus; look for movement and color.

3) Attracting fish. Slap your fly on the surface of the water as hard as possible to attract fish. We have used this many times, using both poppers and streamers, to bring fish to the surface. This works great on jacks. We have even made it work on sharks.

4) Fishing topwater. Too few fly fishermen go into the salt with poppers, when in reality they are deadly and lots of fun. Sharks go for poppers, and we have also caught cudas, jacks, barjacks, snappers, tarpon, ladyfish, and snook. Bob Marvin once caught a bonefish on a popper.

5) Tides. Tides are like the current in a trout stream, except they are continually changing in velocity and direction. Once you learn to read them, you can figure out where the fish will be, since tides move their food around. Of course, they change from day to day, season to season, and location to location, so you should make a careful study of tides in the area you plan to fish.

The famous tarpon is a great game fish that takes a fly readily.

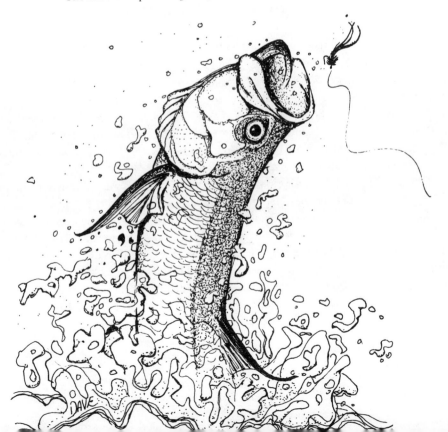

CHAPTER 11

SOME NEW DEVELOPMENTS IN TYING TECHNIQUES AND MATERIALS

THE NO-WINGED SPINNER

LAST SUMMER WHILE FISHING the morning *Tricorythodes* spinner fall we noticed an interesting occurrence. Though the fish were ignoring our Number 26 white/black hen spinners, they were rising very well to the *blood knots* in our leaders. The next morning we were well supplied with "knot flies" (just nylon wrapped around a Number 26 hook) and they worked. We couldn't figure out exactly why, but they did. We really didn't think about the event deeply, but did carry "knot flies" the rest of the season and used them when the hen spinner was unproductive (about 20 percent of the time).

This past May, while loafing on the banks of Michigan's Au Sable River and discussing the previous evening's Hendrickson spinner fall, we had the same observation. At first, for a short time, while the naturals had their wings in the upright position, full-hackle patterns or half-spent hen spinners were taken fairly well. Then for thirty minutes, at the height of the fall, all patterns failed. Toward the end, as the naturals thinned out, the full-spent hen spinner worked well.

Why didn't the trout take our imitations confidently during the feeding frenzy that occurs during the height of the fall? We started to explore the matter seriously. We had often thought that if someone could breed a chicken with clear feathers, we'd do fine, since most natural imagos have clear (hyaline) wings. In fact, in low-intensity light situations (such as dusk), the wings of the naturals are virtually invisible. In these circumstances, the clear wings lie in clear water with grey blue sky as the background; and the fish looking up from the stream bottom see nothing but the tails, legs, and most of all, the opaque body.

two types of No-Wing Spinners

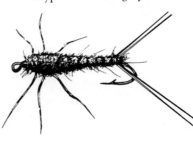

How to imitate invisible wings? The answer was so simple we felt foolish we'd never thought of it before. *Why on earth even try to imitate something invisible? Merely eliminate it from the pattern.* My God, if the fish can't see it, why put it on in the first place? And so the No-Winged Spinner was born.

This fly pattern is not a panacea. There are times when light striking upright or half-spent wings at an angle renders the wings quite visible. At these times a hen spinner half-spent or a full-hackle pattern are effective. These conditions occur (especially on our western rivers) during daylight falls and occasionally on eastern and midwestern streams. However, for the height of the fall at dusk, or on full-spent species such as *Tricorythodes* in full daylight, the No-Winged Spinner is deadly.

On very small patterns such as *Baetis, Pseudocloeon, Caenis,* and *Tricorythodes*, we tie long, widespread tails, thin abdomens with a slightly thicker thorax, and that's it. For larger species such as Hendricksons, we sometimes add legs for looks and balance. The legs can be imitated by hackle fibers, deer hair, or feather fibers tied short and split as natural legs—three fibers only on each side.

These patterns are tied on 3X fine-wire hooks, treated with a silicone spray, then dabbed with silicone line dressing so the imitations float as high as possible. They seem to be much more effective when fished not half awash but barely resting on the surface film. Of course, they are usually not too visible to the angler, but then neither are the naturals. When fishing these patterns, one must learn to make an accurate cast, follow the area of flow where the fly is thought to be, and strike when a fish rises in the general vicinity.

TYING THE NO-WING SPINNER

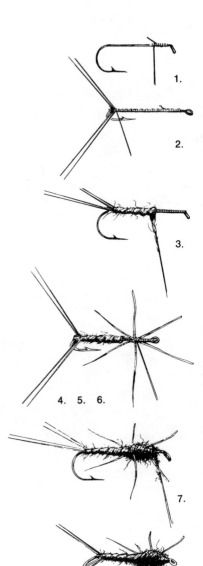

1) Place a 3X fine wire, turned-down-eye hook, in the vise and attach the fly-tying thread to the hook just behind the eye.

2) Take thread back to bend and tie in only 2 or 3 widespread fibers, longer than the body.

3) Spin fur or poly of appropriate shade on tying thread and wrap a fairly thin abdomen (very thin for small patterns).

4) Take one deer-hair fiber lying parallel to hook and tie in at the middle of fiber so the one fiber represents the foreleg and the rear leg on one side.

5) Do the same for the other side.

6) Tie in one hair fiber crosswise to represent the middle legs on both sides.

7) Spin fur or poly on tying thread (usually one shade darker than abdomen) and wind on thorax, working fur behind and in front of legs.

8) Tie in head and whip-finish.

NO-WINGED SPINNER PATTERNS

Brown No-Wing Spinner

The Brown No-Wing Spinner is almost a universal pattern. Tied in sizes #6 through #22, it simulates 75 percent of all *Subimago* species.

Tails: 3 tan hackle fibers tied twice as long as the body and widely split
Abdomen: medium reddish brown spun fur or Poly II (larger sizes can be ribbed with gold wire or yellow nymo)
Thorax: slightly darker red brown spun fur or Poly II
Legs: 3 fibers on each side of the body of deer body hair or pheasant tail fibers, tannish

Cream No-Wing Spinner #10-#16

The Cream No-Wing Spinner simulates various cream spinners such as the *Stenonema* species

Tails: 3 cream hackle fibers—twice as long as the body
Abdomen: cream ribbed with gold wire
Thorax: tannish cream spun fur or Poly II
Legs: cream hair or fibers. Three on each side

Black No-Wing Spinner #22-#28

This pattern imitates the various *Tricorythodes* species. On some species, the abdomen is whitish instead of black.

Tails: 3 long cream hackle fibers
Abdomen: dark brownish black spun fur or Poly II
Legs: none

Olive No-Wing Spinner #16-#24

Some *Baetis* species, a few *Ephemerella subimagos* such as *E. inermis* and *E. infrequens*, *Pseudocloeon anoka* and *edmunsi*, exhibit olive bodies

Tails: two or three (depending on species to be imitated (#16-#18 generally three, #20-#24 generally two) light olive hackle fibers
Abdomen: medium olive tan spun fur or Poly II
Thorax: medium olive tan spun fur or Poly II
Legs: none (optional)

These four patterns in the suggested sizes should imitate practically any species of natural spinner the angler could conceivably run into either in the East or West.

MICRODUNS AND MICROSPINNERS

Tying realistic patterns for the tiny microduns of such species as *Pseudocloeon anoka* and the microspinners of *Tricorythodes* has always been an exasperating ordeal. No matter what we did, they always looked a little too big and too fat; hackle on these minute mayflies often makes them appear to be grotesque caricatures of the naturals. Even the standard methods of tying the No-Hackles make much too fat a body, except for the duns of the genus *Caenidae* (family *Caenis*, *Brachycercus*, *Tricorythodes*), and even on these, the slim-bodied spinners are the important stage. With the new body materials, Poly II and Fly-Rite's extrafine Poly, and the use of the tip of a center quill feather (hen hackle is best) a delicate, realistic imitation can be fabricated quite easily.

These microduns and microspinners are at least as important as the larger ephemerids and often, after June, the most important, if not the only aquatic insect on the water. They are not only important on limestone streams and spring creeks, but fish also rise well to the minute mayflies in the quiet pools of freestone streams of both the East and West. Many anglers shun these hatches simply because they could never get patterns that were effective.

The duns and the spinners of *Baetis*, *Cloeon*, *Neocloeon*, *Pseudocloeon*, *Centroptilium*, and some small *Ephemerella*s all have very slim bodies and wide but delicate wings; the duns of the family Caenidae, genera *Brachycercus*, *Caenis*, and *Tricorythodes* have rather fat, robust bodies. The duns, however, are not the important stages of these flies. The spinners of this family create much more surface feeding, and after the expulsion of the eggs, the bodies are extremely thin while the thorax remains robust. These peculiarities of our tiny mayflies must be taken into account when tying effective patterns.

The ubiquitous microduns are found on virtually every trout stream that has any mayflies whatsoever. They are often present in great numbers and produce fine rises on rivers that have few or no large ephemerids.

The microduns are almost universal, from east to west, and from north to south. Although approximately forty different species of these genera are known, only five dun patterns and six spinner patterns, in various sizes, are needed to be well prepared to meet these challenging hatches.

The first name is the color of the wing, the second the color of the body. Tails should be the same shade as the wings.

DUNS
1) Cream/Yellow #18 through #24
2) Dun/Olive #18 through #24
3) Dun/Tan #18 through #22
4) Slate/Brown #22 through #26
5) White/Grey #22 through #26

SPINNERS
1) White/Black #22 through #28
2) Dun/Olive #18 through #26
3) Dun/White #20 through #28
4) Dun/Orange #22 through #26
5) Dun/Brown #18 through #26
6) Dun/Yellow #18 through #24

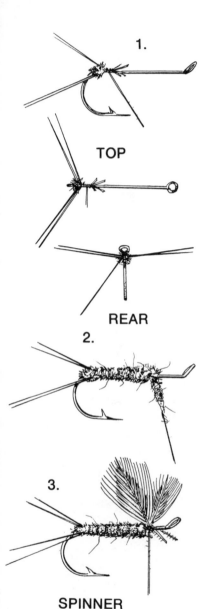

1.

TOP

REAR

2.

3.

SPINNER

DUN

4.

Dun is light grey, slate is dark grey, grey is medium grey, olive is medium olive, and brown is medium-dark brown.

These are prototypical patterns and colors are not exact for every single species, but are close enough to be effective. Size and shape are much more critical than accurate shades, which vary among individual insects during the same hatch.

The bodies of all these flies must be very slim with only a slight thickening at the abdomen. The wings should be either hen-hackle tips, shoulder or body feathers dyed the correct shade. The feathers used should be the tips of the largest feathers on the neck, not the smallest; the large feathers have wide tips and provide a more realistic outline when wet. Cock hackle tips are too narrow. Wings, such as duck-quill sections, while providing a good outline, produce a much thicker body and are not acceptable on the slim microduns.

The exceptions are the White/Black hen spinners #22 through #28 for *Tricorythodes* spinners, which while possessing very slim abdomens (black tying thread 6/0 only), have a very robust thorax. This is built up with either black Poly II or Fly-Rite dubbing material. All dun patterns are tied with upright divided wings, while spinner imitations are tied spent. The tying thread should be the same color as the body.

TYING THE MICRODUNS AND THE MICROSPINNERS PROTOTYPICAL PATTERN

1) Tie in two or three tail fibers of correct shade, short for duns and long for spinners. These should be widespread. Cement in place with vinyl cement, if desired.

2) Spin a tiny amount of Fly-Rite dubbing material, a mere wisp, on the tying thread and wrap abdomen.

3) Tie in wings from the very tips of two large hen hackle feathers, upright for duns, spent for spinners.

4) Spin a tiny amount of Fly-Rite dubbing on tying thread and wrap thorax off head.

Nymphs and emergers can be more realistic, well-balanced, and durable, and will retain their delicate outlines, if you adhere meticulously to certain easy procedures. For instance, we all know that it is easier and quicker to tie a bunch of tail fibers in one clump, at the hook bend, for a typical nymph imitation. Unfortunately, natural nymphs do not carry their tails in a clump. They are positioned like a wide fan, both

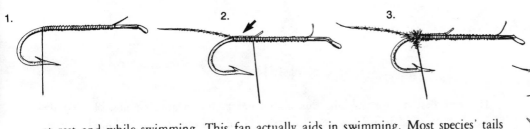

1.   2.   3.   4. 5.

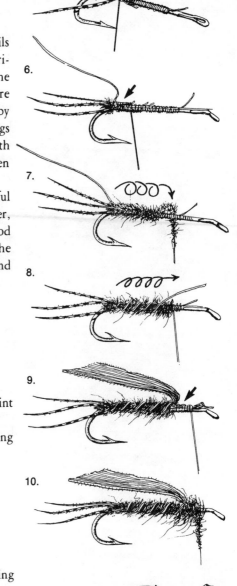

6.

7.

8.

9.

10.

11.

12.

13.

at rest and while swimming. This fan actually aids in swimming. Most species' tails are fringed to some extent, and the undulating up-and-down motion acts like the horizontal tail of a porpoise. How much nicer, more realistic and pleasing to the eye the fly is if the correct number of tail fibers (two or three, depending on the species) are tied widespread, and lashed permanently into place, so when mauled by casting and by fighting fish, they spring back to their original position. The same care for the legs will result in a fly that looks professional in the best sense of the word. Legs on both nymphs and emergers look better and "work" in the water if tied DeFeo style. Even among professionals, few take the little extra time required.

The low price commercial tiers usually get for a dozen flies does not permit careful craftsmanship. They must cut corners to make a living. The gifted amateur, however, may dress the patterns in the recommended way. And, if you are friendly with a good pro and offer to pay the price that flies tied the way we recommend are worth, he probably will be happy to oblige. The end result is well worth the extra effort and price, both to your eye and the supercritical eye of a selective trout.

TYING A REALISTIC NYMPH

1) Place hook in vise and, starting at eye, wrap tying thread back to bend.

2) Tie in one tail fiber at bend.

3) Spin a tiny amount of fur on tying thread, and wrap a small bump over point where first tail was lashed down.

4) Tie in one fiber on each side of fur bump, and crimp into fur with tying thread.

5) Cement with vinyl cement. (Optional.)

6) Tie in some fine gold wire.

7) Spin more fur on tying thread, and wrap body to thorax position.

8) Wrap ribbing of fine gold wire to end of thorax.

9) Tie in one end of duck or goose wing feather section at end of thorax.

10) Spin more fur on tying thread, and wrap thorax more thickly than body.

11) Bring feather section over top of thorax, and tie in behind head, leaving enough room for legs and head.

12) Tie in legs DeFeo style.

13) Wrap head, whip-finish, then varnish.

FUR

The very best fur for dubbing dun bodies has as fine a grain as possible. Young beaver is great, and it has few guard hairs to be picked out. It can be bleached with Lady Clairol hair bleach, then dyed to the desired color. German fitch is also very good, and it has the advantage of getting somewhat more reliable colors when dying.

Domestic white rabbit is good if you get a prime pelt with lots of underfur. Some of these skins have nothing but guard hairs and are very difficult to use. Muskrat is good, but it comes in only two colors, light and dark grey. For rough fuzzy nymphs, the southern fox squirrel is excellent, and our friend Dave Whitlock uses it on many of his suggestive patterns. He spins on underfur and guard hairs together, producing a very fuzzy and effective nymph.

DURABLE WINGS

Vinyl cement and polyurethane resin are clear, thin plastic liquids which, when placed on duck-wing sections, will make them very durable. You need not spread it on the entire wing; one-third up from the base is good enough.

POLYPROPYLENE YARN AND FLOSS

This is one of several new synthetic materials that is very good for bodies. It is impervious to fish slime and water. It is actually lighter than water, having a specific gravity of approximately 0.91. It is shiny, translucent, and gives a very lifelike appearance when wrapped as a floss, but must be cast delicately or the smooth body will break the surface film—causing the iron of the hook to carry the fly down. When spun (although this is very difficult) it floats much better than fur. A very tacky wax is a great help in spinning the cut-up fibers. Polypropylene can also be blended with fur in a blender, which also makes it easier to dub.

POLY II AND FLY RITE MATERIAL

These materials are a vast improvement over the original polypropylene yarn, which is coarse and difficult to spin, especially for bodies smaller than size #18. Poly yarn has a kinky texture and displays a "memory" characteristic that seems to contribute to this difficulty. Poly II and Fly-Rite have not only solved this problem but also have some other outstanding advantages. The individual fibers are straighter, finer, and have been "relaxed." These features make it easy for even the beginning flytier to spin slim, delicate bodies down to size #28. Poly II comes in a unique "mat" form with its randomly laid fibers bonded loosely into a flat sheet. Rather than cutting fur from the skin or working from bulky skeins of yarn, the tyer merely pulls the proper amount of material from the sheet and spins it directly onto the tying thread.

Blending is easily accomplished by "stacking" the fibers from various sheets between your thumb and forefinger. Since it is flat, like a piece of paper, Poly II is not bulky and is easily stored in a small area, making it a natural for the streamside tying kit. Its floating characteristics, durability, and lifelike appearance are unmatched by even the best natural furs, and there are no guard hairs to contend with. Poly II can be obtained from the Orvis Company and the Fly Fisherman's Bookcase. The Fly-Rite extrafine Poly dubbing material not only has all of the advantages of Poly II but it comes in loose form, ready to use. It is undoubtedly the hottest new fly-tying material to come along in the past few years.

The inventor of both Poly II and Fly-Rite, Dave McCann of Bridgeport, Michigan, has done a meticulous job of matching all the important colors, especially for our Super-Hatch patterns. His olives, tans, browns, and yellows are the best shades we've seen.

Poly II yarn can also be used as wing material for both duns and spinners. It has the right amount of translucence, is unbelievably durable, and makes wing construction a simple task.

SOFT STRAW

This is a synthetic material available to the fly tyer in ribbon form and many colors. It can be used for bodies, ribbing, and wing cases, but is used most effectively as a wing material on both dun and spinner imitations. The texture and translucence of Soft Straw make it a most realistic and impressive-looking wing material. Some of the subtle shades of grey, tan, and cream convey great illusions of authenticity. One of the good features of this material, at least for the fly tyer, is that it can be easily split to the proper width and will tear in a straight line. Wings are best formed with scissors after mounting. Durability seems to be superior to other film-type wing materials and can be improved with the addition of lacquer or urethane resin.

MARKING PENS AND LIQUIDS

A good way to obtain light bellies and dark tops on nymph bodies is to wrap the body with a spun fur the color of the underside, then mark the top with a Magic Marker, or one of the new felt-tip pens in brown or black. This is probably the easiest way to fabricate a two-toned nymph. The pens can also be used to put the markings on wings, and on the dun and spinner bodies.

Also on the market are waterproofing liquids, available in spray cans, that come in a variety of colors. We find that some of the colors, mainly the greys, tans, and olives, are quite handy as field expedients in darkening or changing the color of a "wrong color" imitation. Patterns with wings that are too light are a frequent streamside problem that can easily be solved with this technique.

TUFFILM

This is a plastic spray used by artists on pencil and charcoal drawings to prevent smudging. Dave Whitlock uses it to spray flight feathers of ducks and geese, before cutting sections for tying the wings of no-hackle duns and standard wet and dry flies. It keeps the fibers together, and makes it much easier to tie primary and secondary wings. He also uses it on the feathers of such smaller birds as starlings, meadowlarks, and pigeons. These little delicate feathers are very difficult to use unless sprayed with this product. After spraying, they become extremely easy to handle.

DOUBLE-WING NO-HACKLE SIDEWINDER

Several years ago, at our request, René Harrop of St. Anthony, Idaho, developed a No-Hackle with two sets of wings. The idea was to create a wing system that would maintain a realistic silhouette, even after hours of casting and many landed fish. The result of René's efforts is a double-wing sidewinder that greatly increases the life of the No-Hackle Dun. These imitations retain the natural look no matter how much they are abused, and eliminate the need to put resin or cement on the wings. René also worked out a technique of marrying various colors of quill segments together. This produces a striking effect that is not only very realistic in appearance but very deadly, especially on the Pale Morning Dun hatch.

Dave Whitlock also devised a method of tying double wings on medium-sized No-Hackle Duns. They look very natural, since both the large fore wing and the small hind wing are incorporated in the artificial. Also, the added weight at the center of the hook lowers the fly's center of gravity and adds two extra outriggers to help balance the fly, which will now land upright a great percentage of the time. He sprays the entire feather with Tuffilm, and ties on two feathers, one short and one long, *one side at a time.*

TYING THE FOUR-WING SIDEWINDER

1) Start with tails and body tied in usual manner.

2) Cut two feather sections from a duck, starling, or any other appropriate bird's primary wing, which has been sprayed with Tuffilm, and hold on backside of hook in position.

3) Wrap tying thread around base with two or three turns.

4) Cut matching feather sections from opposite wings, and tie in on near side. Feathers must be held firmly between thumb and forefinger while tying down.

5) Spin fur on tying thread, wrap thorax and head, and finish.

Dave shapes the wing with scissors, but this is optional.

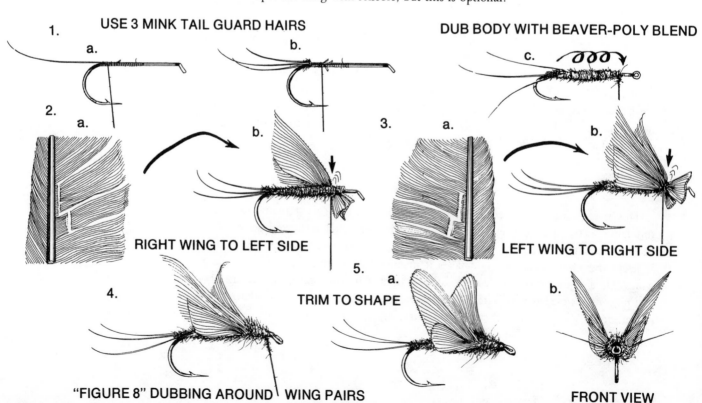

USE 3 MINK TAIL GUARD HAIRS — DUB BODY WITH BEAVER-POLY BLEND

RIGHT WING TO LEFT SIDE — LEFT WING TO RIGHT SIDE

TRIM TO SHAPE

"FIGURE 8" DUBBING AROUND WING PAIRS — FRONT VIEW

FINE MYLAR THREAD

This flashy material is now available in fine ribbon or thread. These new forms permit the construction of streamer and bucktail wings that not only display maximum flashing qualities, but also "work" and "breathe" in the water, much like soft hackle tips and marabou. Increased effectiveness, especially in slower water situations, results when this material is used singly or in combination with feathers and hair. Experimentation with other pattern types, such as spinners, emergers, and pupas, looks promising.

CLUMPERS

Many of our No-Hackle Dun patterns are constructed with quill segment wings, usually from duck or goose primaries. These quill sections are relatively fragile, and the individual fibers tend to dishevel and come apart after usage from casting and/or fighting fish. Once the wing fractures, and the wide, fat outline is broken up, the No-Hackle loses some of its effectiveness, unless a realistic silhouette can be maintained. This all-important silhouette is best maintained by utilizing very wide quill segments in the tying process. Unfortunately, it is extremely difficult, even for some expert tyers, to mount such wide wings symmetrically and without damaging or breaking up some of the fibers.

A solution to this problem of maintaining a proper wing outline (without having to master a difficult tying technique) is to tie what we call a "Clumper" No-Hackle. Even the best-tied No-Hackle wing is going to end up in a clump unless the wing is painted with vinyl cement, so why not start with a clump of fibers in the first place? Then you don't have to worry about messing up the quill segments. Just take two clumps, straddle the hook, and proceed in the regular manner of tying a No-Hackle.

TYING THE CLUMPER-SIDEWINDER

CHAPTER 12

FLY RODS

WHICH MATERIAL is superior for the construction of a fly rod—bamboo or glass? Had this manuscript been written four or five years ago, the answer to this question would have been quite different. And a year from now, the reply might not even include these two materials. This gives us some idea of how quickly improvements and new discoveries are being made in the rod-making industry. The rapid advancement of plastics and plastics technology has triggered a similar trend in fly-rod development. Every time a new material, a new formulation, or a new process is brought to light, new and improved products are possible.

Several years ago, the contest between good bamboo and good glass had to be rated a toss-up. At that time, bamboo deserved the edge in craftsmanship while glass took the honors in casting ability. Nothing could possibly have been more beautiful or more cherished than an expensive, handcrafted cane rod. For aesthetics and quality, there was no comparison. The feel, supposedly, was also superior—smooth, unique, traditional. Top-notch glass, on the other hand, was a better casting tool. Casting was easier because of improved loop control and a higher strength-to-weight ratio.

Today, the balance between bamboo and glass has changed. It is our strong belief that *modern, top-grade glass rods are superior to top-grade cane rods of any era*. The unbalance was brought about by two factors—better design and better materials. Rod makers have finally learned how to utilize the outstanding properties of glass, mainly its high modulus of elasticity and strength-to-weight ratio. In the beginning, glass rods were ill-designed. Many were too heavy and clubby. These "clubs" were usually the result of excessive diameters and coarse-grained cloth. Present-day rods are rolled with fine-weave glass on much smaller diameter mandrels, some tapering to .030. Blanks are made from patterns that are far more sophisticated than their ancestors. Originally, attempts at obtaining light, delicate action resulted in the well-known but much disliked tip-action rods. Some of these "tippy" rods are still on the market but their numbers have been greatly reduced.

Today, patterns used to make the high-quality, better-action blanks can be quite complicated. Special shapes are skillfully engineered into each pattern to produce the desired rod action. No longer is rod-making strictly a trial-and-error process. Aerodynamics, force equations, stiffness profiles, high-speed photography, wind tunnels, stress-strain gages, and even computers are vital to the design of top-notch blanks.

The materials used in rod construction have also come a long way. Woven glass cloth is the base constituent of all quality glass rods. The strength of both the individual glass fibers and of the final weave has steadily increased over the years. Finer cloths that produce greater flexural strength in conjunction with thinner wall sections have also been developed. The major resin systems used to impregnate the glass cloth are phenolic, epoxy, and polyester. Phenolic is used in most of the highest quality rods, partially because of its better physical properties but even more importantly, because of its superior bond strength. The product resulting from the marriage of glass and resin is called a matrix, thus, the better the resin bonds to the glass the stronger the matrix. Phenolic has a great ability to impregnate thoroughly and bond completely, so the blend of phenolic and glass results in a strong, tightly knit, void-free matrix. After all, matrix strength, not resin strength, determines the quality of the blank. Epoxy has better physical properties than phenolic but does not form such a well-bonded matrix. Rods of good to very good quality are normally made with epoxy systems while the very best glass blanks come from phenolic resins. Polyester has mediocre physical properties and is less expensive than the other resins, making it the choice for most of the cheap, poor-action rods.

Over the years, advocates of bamboo have claimed that glass simply does not have the feel of good cane rods, implying that bamboo has the right feel and glass has the wrong, or undesirable, feel. It is certainly true that glass does not have the same feel as cane. Just because the feel is different does not mean that it is undesirable or inferior. Good glass has a unique feel of its own that is just as natural, just as correct as bamboo. And well-designed glass definitely casts better than expensive cane. This is due mainly to the high modulus of elasticity and the design versatility of glass. High modulus promotes quick recovery from deformation which, to the fly caster, means better loop control. What this characteristic really means to the angler is that the rod stops vibrating more quickly and returns to an unbent position sooner, resulting in smaller and fewer shock waves rolling down the line. Wind resistance can double or triple in a loop that has excessive "wrinkles." Slow, sloppy recovery is the single biggest fault we have found in many of the high-cost bamboo rods that continually show up at our schools and clinics. Typically, the owner of such a rod is, at best, a mediocre caster who is attempting to reach out for greater distance on the casting field. These efforts usually result in knotted leaders, piles of unstraightened fly line, and much cursing.

Just as glass is finally being perfected, at least by a few manufacturers, two new and exotic fibers, graphite and boron, are entering the rod-building scene. Both are high-strength, high-modulus materials that have found extensive use in the automotive and aerospace fields. Graphite is produced by subjecting rayon fibers to extremely high temperatures, from 1800 to 2000° F. Slightly lower temperatures, 1200 to 1400° F, produce carbon fibers that exhibit lower physical properties than graphite. Two basic types of graphite can be produced by this process, one having high flexural strength and the other displaying high modulus. At present, the high flexural is best for rod building. The high modulus variety has very low flexural strength, causing it to fracture easily when stressed under load. Individual graphite fibers, approximately .0003 inches in diameter, can be used in a variety of ways for building fly rods. The most common method consists of weaving the tiny strands into a cloth that can then be used conventionally on a tapered mandrel. Yarn, tape, or bundles can also be made from these individual fibers and used in a variety of manufacturing techniques. Other fibers, such as glass, Dacron, or boron, can be woven or blended with the graphite to achieve a combination of properties. The addition of glass, for example, slightly smooths and slows down the action, resulting in a more traditional feel.

The stiffest, highest modulus fiber of all, boron, is made by depositing natural borax on a fine tungsten wire. Boron fibers are manufactured in two basic diameters, 4.0 and 5.6 mils. The tungsten wire is approximately .0005 inches in diameter, comprising a very small percentage of the total cross section of each fiber. Due to its superior modulus, boron is used extensively in critical aerospace and aircraft applications. The modulus of elasticity of boron is actually higher than steel yet it is only one-sixth as heavy. This unique combination of properties permits the fabrication of rod blanks with extremely slim profiles—which result in high tip speed and greater line control.

Unlike graphite, boron cannot be woven into a cloth to be wrapped on a mandrel. As mentioned, the finest boron fibers presently being manufactured have a diameter of 4.0 mils. This size, compared to graphite at .0003, is far too stiff for creating a flexible woven material. These rigid strands are suitable for the longitudinal direction of the weave but are totally unusable for the circumferential fibers. Attempts at wrapping such stiff fibers around a small-diameter mandrel result in fractures. An alternate method that appears to show promise is utilization of boron fibers longitudinally with the more flexible fibers, such as graphite or glass, used for the cross weave. To date, most of the better boron blanks have been produced by a solid-core technique. In this process, narrow strips of epoxy-boron tape are laid up by hand on a core of steel wire or balsa wood.

This solid-core process, if it can be adapted to mass production, bears tremendous potential for the future. Solid construction, of course, permits the slimmest of profiles, which, in turn, produces minimum wind resistance during the casting stroke. The resulting increase in tip speed allows the fly caster greater control of his loop over longer distances. Perfection of the manufacturing technique should result in a high-quality, homogeneous matrix and excellent reproductability characteristics.

For most anglers choosing a rod length is governed by personal preference—which

Pale Morning Dun, Floating Nymph

Grey/Olive Micro-Dun

Turkey Quill Hen Spinner (Hexagenia)

Grey/Yellow Double-Wing No-Hackle

Great Golden Stonefly Wiggle Nymph

Dun/Olive No-Hackle with Poly II wings

Slate/Tan Stillborn Caddis

Humpy Midge

Slate/Olive Stillborn No-Hackle Dun

Yellow Stillborn Stonefly

Grey/Olive Stillborn No-Hackle Dun

Slate/Olive Stillborn Dun

The Streaker

Hen Matuka

Pink Saltwater Wiggle Nymph

Bob Marvin's Rubber Hackle Fly

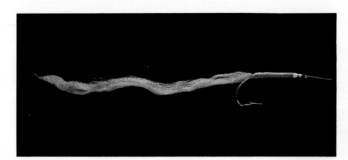

Poly Saltwater Worm

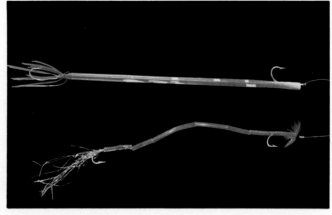

The Straw and Tube Flies

was probably formed from past experience, the recommendation of a friend, traditional beliefs, and/or advertising. At first glance, such reasoning seems to be quite satisfactory for determining this relatively minor aspect of equipment selection. In reality, however, picking the "length of the lever" is an important decision and should be based on critical data, such as a person's casting ability and strength, type of fishing to be done, how much fun and satisfaction one wants to derive from the sport, and how accomplished one wants to become.

An angler's casting talent and strength have significant bearing on the rod length selection. Poor casters need all the help they can get so they should not penalize themselves even more by using a rod length unsuited to their ability. An expert caster can easily handle any rod length, but the neophyte may experience difficulty with a lever that is excessively long or one that is extremely short. We disagree with the traditional belief that long rods make casting easier. It's a mechanical fact that, for the same casting stroke, a short rod automatically throws a tighter loop than a long rod. On the other hand, the shorter the rod the tougher it is to keep that fly out of your ears. A practical length range for most anglers for most trout-fishing situations is 6½ to 7½ feet. These shorter, lighter rods are also a boon to those who are able to spend only a few hours on a trout stream each week. As in any other sport, a steady diet of practice is required to keep the proper wrist and arm muscles in shape.

The type of fishing one does is another important factor in determining the rod length. Probably the most significant aspect to consider is, "How close will your casting hand be to the water?" The general rule of thumb, unless, of course, you're an expert caster, is the closer your casting hand must be to the water the longer the rod should be. For typical, shallow-water trout situations, where most runs and riffles are only knee-deep, even the shortest of rods should not get you into trouble. As you wade deeper and deeper into the water, however, and your casting hand drops closer to the water's surface, it is highly advantageous to have a longer lever. When fishing the deep runs of Henry's Fork and the Yellowstone, for example, rods 7½ to 8½ feet are most helpful in keeping the back loop from striking the water.

Small streams, such as the upper Au Sable in Michigan and the spring creeks of the West, are best friends with the small rods. Rods 5½ to 6½ feet long are much more efficient than the cumbersome variety. This type of angling requires short, accurate, delicate casting with a light line and is almost impossible to accomplish with a big rod. First of all, both the height and angle of the plane of casting are adversely affected with the long stick. Individuals who try to conquer small streams with monstrous equipment quickly encounter problems because their loops are so high in the air. Constant tangling and frequent loss of flies usually develop from such an elevated casting plane. Contrary to popular opinion, you'll experience far fewer backcast difficulties if you keep your loops low over the water. Practice throwing your loop *under* problem areas rather than always over them. Reduced wind resistance is another reason for keeping your casting plane low. The breeze is much stronger 10 feet up than it is at head height. Knowledge of this fact can greatly diminish your casting problems on a windy, blustery day, no matter what type of water you are on. Throwing a tight, bullet-shaped loop as low as possible over the water will help you master most wind situations.

The short rod will not only keep your casting plane low, resulting in less tangling and more control in the wind, but it will also help keep the angle of your casting plane in the proper perspective. Ideally, for most fishing situations, your casting plane should be parallel to the water. This is true for both your false casts and the final delivery. With the short rod, you can let your candy cane straighten a few feet above the surface and gently parachute to the water. Unfortunately, the long rod advocate does one of two things, neither of which is conducive to the small-stream angler. Most will tilt the casting plane forward so they can aim their forecast more directly at the target. This causes the delivery to be drilled into the water, scaring every fish in sight, and backcasting at such a high angle that every tree near the stream is snagged. Some slightly more sophisticated anglers cast their candy canes on a nearly level plane but, with the long rod, they are elevated so high that they splash down rather sloppily on the water. Control and accuracy are also sacrificed when a high casting plane is used.

Situations where gravity is a major factor dictate the use of longer rods. In other words, the total weight extending beyond the rod tip is critical to length determination. In salmon, steelhead, and saltwater fishing, for example, heavy lines, large flies, and long casts all contribute greatly to the amount of weight that must be held in the air. To keep all this bulk from slapping the water while false casting and the fly high enough to keep from snagging one's ear, a long rod—normally 8 to 9½ feet—is best. Moreover, a 5- to 6-foot rod is more than adequate to handle short casts with a #4 floating line, fine tippets, and miniature dry flies. The relatively small amount of weight represented by such an outfit as this is buoyed up by the air resistance of the casting stroke, making gravity a minimal factor.

As the trend toward smaller flies, lighter lines, and improved material technology continues, so will the trend toward shorter rods. This tendency is already quite strong among fly-rodders for trout and should grow in such other areas as bass, panfish, and certain types of salmon and saltwater fishing. We feel that most panfish and bass fishermen use rods that are much longer and heavier than necessary. This type of fly fishing rarely requires long casts and, except for the larger poppers, the flies, hair bugs, and popping bugs, are not too heavy. Most of this type of angling is done from a boat where the elevation from the water is good, so why use a typical 8½- to 9-foot rod? Such long rods simply aren't necessary. We find 7- to 7½-footers quite adequate.

There are also some saltwater and salmon situations where the shorter rod is supreme. Fishing for baby tarpon and snook in Florida's canals and backwaters can often be best accomplished with 7-foot rods. On occasion, we've even gone to 6½-footers, which were adequate for throwing streamers and small poppers and well suited for snag-free casts around the ever-present overhanging growth. On Michigan's small salmon-filled streams, such as the Pere Marquette and the Little Manistee, we rarely use rods longer than 7½ feet to battle kings and cohos up to 30 pounds.

The final, and perhaps most important, consideration for rod length selection is "How much *fun* and *satisfaction* do you want to derive from the sport?" The main reason most of us get so involved in fly fishing is because it gives us pleasure. Anything we can do to make our sport more fun, more enjoyable, and more satisfying is therefore all to the good. We feel that the use of lighter, finer, more delicate equipment contributes immeasurably toward this end. The most important tool of our trade is the fly rod, making it the logical starting point for increased enjoyment.

Many fishermen demand that their equipment do all the work, hence their preference for large, heavy rods. Obviously, if one wants to throw a long distance, say 90 feet, the job can be done more easily and with less effort from the caster by using a long lever and a hefty line. We agree that efficient, well-balanced equipment is important, but feel that it is much more important for the caster to have good technique and to use equipment that makes fishing fun. The long rod advocate usually looks down his nose at the short rod, exclaiming that it is just a toy and requires too much effort. Well, it may take a little more effort, but who says more effort can't be fun?

An expert can make almost any rod and line combination work reasonably well, but most casters need a balanced outfit to be successful. A balanced outfit *does not* mean one that has a magical fulcrum, or balanced point, somewhere in the fore portion of the grip that creates a teeter-totter effect. It means a rod and line combination that works effortlessly and efficiently to accomplish the angler's purpose.

A fly rod is a flexible lever. Each rod has its own flexibility characteristics or stiffness profile. Application of a load, in this case a fly line, to the tip end of the rod causes it to bend, the amount depending upon the load. Each rod has an optimum load, or range of loads, that makes it bend efficiently. If this range is exceeded, as in trying to cast a chain with a buggy whip, the overloading causes the rod action to break down. This condition is very unpleasant for the angler; loops sag, presentation is sloppy, and accuracy is destroyed. These problems develop because the excessive weight of a too-heavy fly line completely overwhelms the upper third, or tip section, of the rod, which, in turn, causes the rod tip to travel in a wiggly, wavy path.

On the other hand, a line that is too light for a given rod will have the opposite effect—that is, fail to bring out the rod's full action. This could be likened to casting a string with an ordinary wooden yardstick. Without rod action, the caster must do all the work and have a good knowledge of technique.

Almost all fly rods coming off today's assembly lines are marked with the line weight that the manufacturer feels is the best. By and large, these designations are fairly accurate, at least the ones from the companies with the good reputations in fly fishing. If possible, however, we recommend that you actually cast a rod and line combination before you buy. Any shop worth its salt will let you do this, in fact, will *want* you to do so. If you encounter any resistance, take your business elsewhere.

Start with the manufacturer's recommended line weight and be sure to try at least one weight heavier and one weight lighter. Always test until you find a line weight that you know is too heavy and one that you know is too light. Throw both long and short casts, but test mainly at the distance where most of your casting is done. Remember, line weight designations are based on 30 feet of fly line past the tip-top, so if you normally fish with 15 to 20 feet of line, a heavier weight might be more practical. Casting ability, type of presentation required, distance of casts, and type of fly must all be considered when selecting a line weight for a certain rod. Basically, delicate presentation, small flies, and good casting ability allow lighter lines, while long-distance, large flies and lesser casting ability mean heavier lines.

We've noticed that the top-quality glass rods on the market have what we call a flat-line weight curve. By this we mean that their optimum load range is very great. Most of the cheap glass rods, and bamboo rods in general, can handle only one line weight: a size higher or lower and they simply are not suitable for casting. Several of the best glass sticks and most of the new exotic fibers we've tested can handle three line weights very well. This feature has come about because of improved materials and design technology.

Correct rod action for any given person should "feel right," cast efficiently, and accomplish the angler's purpose. For complete enjoyment of the sport, each person must be happy with the way his rod feels in his hand as he makes the casting stroke. If the most important tool of fly fishing is unwieldy, or unpleasant to use, much of the fun is lost. Casting with a smooth-action fly rod is an enjoyable and satisfying experience in itself. Far too often, in our schools and clinics, we encounter people with rods that have such bad action that there is no way they can be enjoying themselves, either on the casting field or in the stream.

Rod action must not only feel good to the angler but must also throw the line in an efficient manner and accomplish the intended purpose. Some rods, for example, are so soft and floppy that their action breaks down when more than 30 feet of line are extended. Such sticks are inadequate for proper loop control and are completely unsuitable for many types of fishing. An overly stiff rod may form neat precise loops, but would be worthless for delicate short-range nymphing.

Ultimate rod action, as of now, is produced by one of two methods, or a combination of both. The first, and most common, consists of varying the wall thickness through the use of very intricately designed blanks. Russ Peak, of course, is the unchallenged master of this technique. His ability to create any desired action is un-

Russ Peak, the Stradivarius of glass.
(Photo by Herman V. Wall)

canny and his rods are works of art. Ownership of a Peak rod is a most prestigious sign among the more sophisticated angling clan. We have tested dozens of Russ's blanks and have yet to find one that was not a pure joy to cast. It is amazing that with only a phone call, Russ can evaluate you and your fishing ability, then build a rod that not only has great action and fishes well, but seems to have your personality blended into the final product. Unfortunately for the angling world, production is limited due to the fact that each rod is personally crafted by the master himself.

Other rod makers have tried to produce superior action by using this method with varying degrees of success. Large companies find it very difficult, if not impossible, to adapt this technique to volume production.

CHAPTER 13

MODERN EQUIPMENT

MANUFACTURERS OF FLY-FISHING EQUIPMENT have made tremendous strides in developing tackle that is truly functional and efficient. Many of these achievements have directly paralleled the growth and discoveries made in the plastics industries. As technology grows, so does the quantity and quality of fly-fishing products.

Rods have become stronger, lighter, and more durable, due mainly to the development of better resins, higher modulus glass, and systems that produce a tighter and more uniform matrix material. Fly lines shoot farther, float higher, and last longer due to improved coating formulations and innovative methods of application. New nylon copolymers, combined with extra forming and conditioning operations, have resulted in leaders and tippets that turn over better, lay out straighter, and land larger fish than ever before. Fly reels and their drag systems are lighter and smoother because they employ new low-density synthetics that are wear resistant under frictional and shock loads. Even the material used for backing has tailor-made properties—it is high-strength, low-stretch and nonrotting. The list of products goes on and on. Fly boxes, waders, vest closures, fly spray, Qwik-sink solution, magnifiers, bug nets, leader wheels, zinger chains, patch kits, rod cases, wading staffs, night-lights, and even flies are either all or partly constructed of plastic.

This is just the beginning. Only the surface has been scratched. New synthetics and plastics are being discovered every day. With the advances that are taking place in the automotive and aerospace industries, the pace will accelerate even more in the future. Exotic new fibers, such as carbon and boron, have recently entered the rod-making scene and may soon revolutionize the art of fly casting.

Modern materials and manufacturing techniques are responsible for a large portion of the new and improved products, but another factor is equally important. Common sense and logic have finally begun to triumph over traditionalism and old-fashioned ideas. Short, lightweight rods are rapidly replacing the long, cumbersome "clubs" that were so common a few years back. Fly lines come in a variety of weights, tapers, and shapes, each perfectly suited for specific situations. No longer do knowledgeable anglers look down their noses at quality glass rods and say, "It just doesn't have the feel of bamboo." Brightly colored fly lines really don't scare the fish after all, but instead have become a "must" for their high visibility value. Stiff butted leaders, popular with everyone a few years ago, have been replaced by the new, more efficient flat butt variety. Fly casting problems are now being solved utilizing air resistance principles rather than by "mass and stiffness" concepts. Stiffness profiles are used by better rod manufacturers as criteria for design instead of cut-and-fit, or trial and error methods. These are only a few of the nontraditional, but more logical, ideas that have evolved from a better-educated, more informed tackle industry over the past few years.

FLY REELS

In selecting basic fly fishing equipment, the fly line is of prime importance, and therefore becomes the starting point. Most anglers in the past purchased a rod, using length and possibly weight as their criteria, and then attempted to match a line with the rod. In many cases, this procedure resulted in equipment grossly mismatched for the type of fishing the individual had in mind. Today, knowledgeable fly fishermen start with the fly line, using it as a building block for adding other basic components.

Actual fly line weights are measured in grains and refer to the weight of the first 30 feet, which is considered to be the optimum amount of line for most casting situations. It makes no difference what the taper or density, the weight of the first 30 feet determines the line weight designation. The following is a list of AFTMA fly line weight standards.

Species & Size	Water Type & Size	Fly Type & Size	Distance	Delivery	Wind	Line Weight Range
Trout—Small	Small Stream	Small Flies	Short	Accurate Slow	Light	3-4
Trout—Small to Medium	Small to Medium Stream or Pond	Small Flies Small Streamers	Short to Medium	Accurate Slow	Light to Medium	4-5

Species & Size	Water Type & Size	Fly Type & Size	Distance	Delivery	Wind	Line Weight Range
Panfish— Small	Stream or Pond	Small Flies	Short	Slow	Light	5-6
Trout— Medium to Large	Medium to Large River or Pond	Flies and Streamers	Short to Long	Slow	Steady	5-6
Trout—Large	Large River	Streamers and Bucktails	Long	Slow	Windy	7
Bass—Medium to Large	Medium to Large Lakes	Large Flies and Poppers	Medium to Long	Medium	Steady	7-8
Steelhead— Large	Large Rivers	Large Streamers	Long	Slow	Steady	8-9
Saltwater— Very Large	Open	Very Large Streamers	Long	Accurate Fast	Windy	10-11

Fly lines come in a variety of shapes, each having advantages and disadvantages. Basically, there are leveled and tapered lines. The level types have constant diameter from one end to the other and are adequate for certain types of fishing, mainly for panfish and bass. Due to their simple construction, they are inexpensive; but their heavy, blunt tips slap down rather heavily on the water. This feature makes the level line impractical for most trout fishing where delicate delivery is paramount.

There are two basic types of tapered fly line, double taper and weight forward. For most trout, salmon, steelhead, saltwater, and bass situations, these lines are more efficient and practical than the level variety. Delivery and distance are the main reasons why lines are manufactured in these special shapes. By progressively reducing, or tapering down, the tip section, a much softer, or delicate, delivery is possible. This is the theory behind the double-taper fly line, which is constant diameter in the middle, or belly, and tapered down at each end.

Line Weight #	Actual Weight (Grains)	Tolerance
# 1	60	± 6 grains
# 2	80	± 6 grains
# 3	100	± 6 grains
# 4	120	± 6 grains
# 5	140	± 6 grains
# 6	160	± 8 grains
# 7	185	± 8 grains
# 8	210	± 8 grains
# 9	240	± 10 grains
#10	280	± 10 grains
#11	330	± 12 grains
#12	380	± 12 grains

Weight-forward lines are designed to achieve greater distance and are characterized by a heavy belly section and a small-diameter running line. In effect, they are much like a "chestnut on a string." The tapering process produces a large-diameter "head" near the front of the line, thus moving the center of gravity forward. It also creates a fine-diameter running line, which results in greatly reduced friction in the guides. With the heavy head out past the tip-top, it is quite easy to make long casts with minimum effort.

Whether you select a double-taper or weight-forward line depends on the type of fishing you want to do and how well you can cast. For small streams and short casts, double-tapers are fine, but if most your casting is done to targets more than 35 feet away, then weight-forward would probably be better. This, of course, is only a general rule of thumb. Good casters, provided they have plenty of backcast room, can throw a double-taper just as far as they can throw a weight-forward. Double-tapers provide better loop control and greater accuracy, so a person with superior casting ability might want this type of line. On the other hand, anglers unable to control 40- or 50-foot loops must rely on weight-forward lines to make long casts. Most fly fishermen don't realize that both double-tapered and weight-forward of the same weight have the same taper for the first 30 feet. So for this distance, both types should cast, control, and deliver in a like manner.

Standard fly lines come not only in various shapes—level, double-taper, and weight-forward—but also are available in both sinking and floating models. Floaters are by far the most popular type, outselling the sinkers by a wide margin. This is undoubtedly due to the fact that most fly fishing is done in shallow water. The ease of picking a line *off* the water rather than *out* of it is also a major factor.

Most floating lines are comprised of a core material, usually braided nylon, which is coated with low-density thermoplastic formulation. This lightweight coating is varied in thickness to form the tips, bellies, and running portions of the tapered lines. The final specific gravity ends up being less than that of water, normally about .95, resulting in a line that will float high on the surface all day long.

The same general type of construction, care, and coating is used for sinking lines, the only difference being the coating density. Obviously, to sink, a line must have a specific gravity greater than water, or more than 1.0. To accomplish this, heavy components are formulated into the coating material. The ratio of these dense materials is proportional to the sink rate desired—slow, medium, or fast. Because of their increased density, sinking lines are characterized by much smaller diameters than their floating counterparts of the same line weight. Since this means far less air resistance, longer casts can be made. In our experience, slow and medium sinkers have very little value. Especially in stream fishing, we find floating lines and long, sinking leaders to be just as effective and far more enjoyable to use. When you really want to go down deep and go down fast, use the fast sinker, either full length or in a floating-sinking combination.

Specialty lines and features have added new dimensions to the fly fisherman's world. No longer do we just fish on top. No longer do we have to ignore the big riser just out of range. And no longer must we continually strain our eyes trying to locate that camouflaged fly line. These problems have been pretty much alleviated through commonsense approaches.

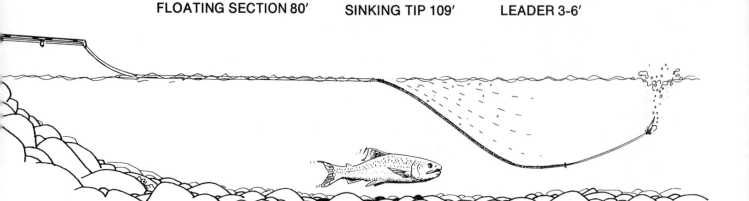

FLOATING SECTION 80'   SINKING TIP 109'   LEADER 3-6'

The sink-tip flyline in action.

The floating-sinking fly lines that have appeared on the market recently are a real boon to the angler who wants to fish wet without a great sacrifice in line handling qualities. The tip, or front portion of these lines, normally 10 to 30 feet, is fast-sinking, and the balance is floating. This combination has two distinct advantages. The fast-sinking tip quickly drops the fly to the proper depth while the floating line provides easy pickup and good line handling. With the conventional full-length sinker, it is almost impossible to pick more than 20 feet out of the water cleanly.

For large streams and rivers that have heavy currents and deep runs, the 10-foot quick-sink tip is unbeatable for effectively scouring the lower levels. On the Upper Yellowstone, for example, this line is deadly for presenting large wiggle nymphs and streamers to those wild, native cutthroats. During cold-water nonfeeding periods especially, it can turn an otherwise "dead" day into a spectacular one. We've also used the floater-sinker effectively in many lakes, ponds, and backwaters. It has worked well when fishing for those fat rainbows in the small, fertile lakes around Spokane, and has saved the day in northern Maine when the smallmouth were completely turned off at the sight of top-water bugs. It has also scored big for us in many saltwater encounters. Remember, when using full-length or partial sinking lines, keep your leaders short. An unweighted fly on a long leader will often stay near the surface, even though the line is lying right on the bottom. Three to 4 feet is normally long enough.

Specialty lines with extreme forward tapers are designed for bass bugging and saltwater fishing. The center of gravity is pushed forward, even closer to the tip than on a standard weight-forward line. This really amplifies the "chestnut on a string effect" and gives the caster a better mechanical advantage. For the bass fisherman, the extra momentum of the bug-taper allows better turnover of large, wind-resistant hair bugs and popping bugs. For the saltwater angler, the heavy head handles the wind better and permits extremely fast deliveries, both of which are critical to successful saltwater technique. For both, more distance can be obtained with very little effort.

For maximum distance with minimum effort, the shooting head is supreme. This specialty line consists of a fly line head attached to a running or shooting line. The head portion is normally, but not always, tapered, and is typically 30 feet long, al-

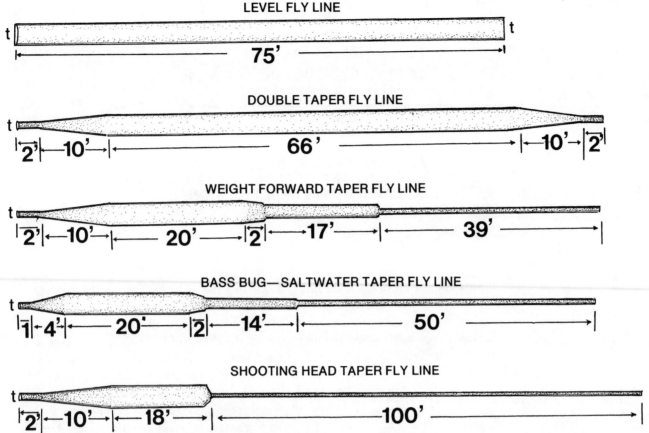

LEVEL FLY LINE

t   t

75'

DOUBLE TAPER FLY LINE

t

2' — 10' — 66' — 10' — 2'

WEIGHT FORWARD TAPER FLY LINE

t

2' — 10' — 20' — 2' — 17' — 39'

BASS BUG—SALTWATER TAPER FLY LINE

t

1' — 4' — 20' — 2' — 14' — 50'

SHOOTING HEAD TAPER FLY LINE

t

2' — 10' — 18' — 100'

Basic fly line shapes

though other lengths can be used. We have heads as long as 50 feet and as short as 8 feet. Twelve- to 20-footers have worked quite well for various small-stream, tight-backcast situations. Thirty feet, however, is the most common length and the one manufactured by most fly-line companies. It resembles the head section of a weight-forward line and has a dacron attachment loop at the rear end. Monofilament line, either flat or round, is tied into the Dacron loop. Twenty-pound flat mono is the most popular because it has minimal friction in the guides and superior nonkinking properties.

Shooting tapers come in both floating and sinking types. Floaters perform well in many shallow-water situations, in lakes, large rivers, and open saltwater flats. Qwik-sink heads are extremely productive for steelheaders in the deep, heavy runs of western rivers. They are also effective for dredging the bottom of trout and bass lakes.

It's important to understand that shooting heads also have several disadvantages. Presentation is anything but delicate, accuracy is usually poor and inconsistent, and line handling can be a nightmare. Rocketing a shooting head into orbit in the practice field looks like, and can be, great fun. But using this technique in combat can be frustrating. Proper use requires know-how and practice. Equipment balance, fundamental loop control, and lots of line-handling ability are all required for a polished technique.

A unique version of the shooting head is called the nymph head, designed and popularized by Dave Whitlock. This rig is basically a shooting head that has been streamlined so the average angler can quickly become proficient at a kind of fly fishing once considered very difficult. Two of the basic problems connected with nymph-

20 FT. SPECIAL WEIGHT FORWARD LEADER

A.   B.

C.

The special weight forward
leader

A. 12 TO 15 FT. OF 15-LB. FLAT MONO
B. FRONT 4 FT. OF FLAT BUTT LEADER
C. 18 TO 24 INCH TIPPET (OPTIONAL)

ing are keeping the drag off the line and detecting the strike. By keeping the drag off the line, of course, drag is also kept off the fly, allowing it to float naturally in the current. The monofilament behind the 30-foot head is practically weightless, so after the cast and mending procedure are completed, the chance of building up more drag is greatly minimized. The head can float far downstream as the featherweight mono is stripped from the reel and wiggled out through the guides. Dave's nymphing outfit is made up of a 30-foot head backed by 100 feet of 20-pound-test flat monofilament. Both fly line and mono are bright yellow and are joined by an epoxy connection, also created by Dave. The flat nylon is razored to a point, drawn up into the center of the fly line, and epoxied into place. This type of connection has numerous advantages. First and foremost, it is smooth and therefore nonfouling in the guides, with no knots or bumps to catch and cause snapped tippets. Hinging and line wear, common with most knotted connections, are greatly reduced due to the gradual taper of the portion of the backing that is inserted into the fly line. Also, both the line and backing are geometrically centered with each other, thus reducing twist in the whole system.

The same epoxy connection is used to attach a knotless 9-foot flat-butt leader to the tip of the shooting head. A fluorescent orange marker, actually a short segment of fly line coating, is then slipped over the leader and up to the epoxy connection. This acts as an indicator for detecting strikes.

Another advantage of the flat-butt leader, besides its turnover characteristics, is that you can easily slide the indicator anywhere on the ribbonlike butt section and it will stay exactly where you put it. This butt portion is about six feet in length, on a 9-foot leader, so for shallow water nymphing, you can place the indicator within 3 feet of your fly. This is a great aid when fishing nymphs and wet flies; the closer your visual

A shooting head setup with flat
mono

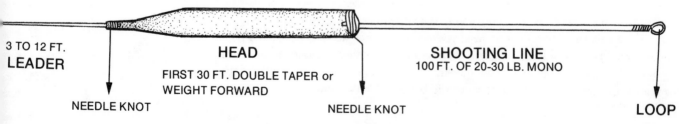

3 TO 12 FT.
LEADER

HEAD
FIRST 30 FT. DOUBLE TAPER or
WEIGHT FORWARD

SHOOTING LINE
100 FT. OF 20-30 LB. MONO

NEEDLE KNOT

NEEDLE KNOT

LOOP

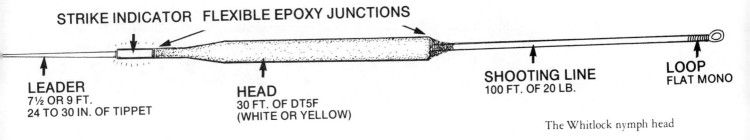

STRIKE INDICATOR   FLEXIBLE EPOXY JUNCTIONS

LEADER
7½ OR 9 FT.
24 TO 30 IN. OF TIPPET

HEAD
30 FT. OF DT5F
(WHITE OR YELLOW)

SHOOTING LINE
100 FT. OF 20 LB.

LOOP
FLAT MONO

The Whitlock nymph head

contact with the fly, the more quickly you can detect a strike and make your move. In fact, one of the most important qualities you must develop to be a good nymph fisherman is confidence, and the greatest aid in building confidence is maintaining visual contact all the way from the "business" end of your leader to the line coming out of your reel. With Dave Whitlock's nymph head, you have this visual contact; everything from the reel to the tip of the fly line is bright yellow and the indicator on the leader is bright orange.

This high visibility is an important feature for floating and floating-sinking lines. It is always a distinct advantage to be able to see the line as it drifts down through the currents. By maintaining close visual contact, you can keep better track of your artificial, and thus set the hook better. In this era of small flies, sizes #18 to #24 seem to be the rule rather than the exception; it can be and often is impossible to pick out your imitation as it floats among the naturals. Knowledgeable anglers have finally come to realize that oversized, overdressed, and gaudy flies just can't work consistently during selective feeding periods. Large Royal Coachmen and bivisibles are easy to see 30 feet out but at crucial times trout are not normally impressed. The effective fly must be just as small, just as subtly colored, and just as hard to see as the naturals. There are *more* of these small species, their hatching periods are *longer*, and they are *more prolific* during individual hatch periods. These are known facts. So the serious hatch matcher, in order to be effective, must comply by using microscopic imitations. Quite often, these minute flies are impossible to see, especially in ruffled water or when the sun is at the wrong angle. Under such conditions, the angler must establish visual contact with something that will indicate the approximate location of his fly. The tip of the fly line can be used as this indicator, if it has sufficient visibility.

For some illogical reason, fishermen over the years have felt that brown and green provided a sort of camouflaging effect, making the line less visible to the fish. Actually, it makes the line less visible to themselves, thus creating an extra hardship in following the fly on the water. The trout couldn't care less what color the line is. With the typical 9 or more feet of leader that most of us use, he shouldn't even know that the line exists, much less what color it is. And if the fly line does float through his window, the light-colored type is far less noticeable than a dark one. We noticed this many times during our underwater observations and photography sessions.

The *angler*, then, is the most important factor of fly line color, not the fish. To help solve his visual problems, he should select a line that has the highest visibility for most fishing situations. The two best colors are yellow and orange, with yellow having a slight edge. Both colors show up at about equal intensity in bright sunlight; however, during the best fishing periods, early morning and evening, and on cloudy days the yellow shows up better and is easier to follow. Also, for the aesthetically minded, yellow lines look super with the brown and dark brown rods that are so popular today. Let's be honest, the present-day angler is concerned about his or her appearance on the stream. This includes clothing and equipment. Another, and just as important, reason for selecting a high-visibility fly line is its value in the casting field. How can you expect to improve your loop control if you can't see your loop? If you can't see it, you can't adjust and improve it. In our schools and clinics, many people show up with old dark brown and dark green fly lines, which are almost impossible to see in the air. This makes instruction very difficult because you can't advise the student properly until you can see what he's doing wrong. With the bright yellow line, loops become very visual and alive. Whether you're curve casting on the stream or practicing loop control on the casting field, you'll be more effective and a whole lot happier with a high-visibility line.

Finish and flexibility are two important features that should be considered in selecting a fly line. Most anglers are at least aware of the finish and examine it closely, rubbing their fingers back and forth over the coating. Unfortunately, many individuals misinterpret what they see and feel. They think that an ultrasmooth finish means highest quality in fly line. This is not the case. Real premium fly lines, the ones that make casting enjoyable, display a slight roughness or bumpiness. Less friction is produced by this pebblelike surface as only the tops of these tiny bumps make contact in the guides. Lines with a glassy smooth finish make more contact in the guides and this, of course, creates more friction. Also, water seems to cling to this type of line as it shoots out through the guides, causing a further reduction in distance. In the dealer's display case, the velvety smooth surface gives the appearance of top-notch quality and the "feel" test is even more convincing. Some line manufacturers go all out to achieve this effect and ballyhoo their sleek smooth finish. Just remember, point contact creates far less friction than surface friction.

Fly line flexibility normally goes hand in hand with fly line finish. If the finish is soft, the flexibility is soft, and if the finish is hard, the line is stiff and wiry. The ultimate line, of course, would be perfectly limp on the inside and hard on the outside. Limpness is required for proper loop formation; the hard coating enhances shootability. Until recently, manufacturers were unable to combine the best of two worlds. Their efforts to obtain maximum limpness resulted in soft, waxy finishes that hung up in the guides. Attempts at perfecting hard, pebbly low-friction surfaces resulted in stiff, rigid lines that were atrocious to cast. Fly lines have been introduced recently, however, that have a firm outer skin and feature an ever-so-slight roughness, yet the interior is soft and supple, producing a combined limpness that is perfect for loop control and line handling ability. This type of construction has produced an added bonus, excellent durability. As most anglers know, one of the biggest complaints over the years has been the short life-span of a line. We have actually worn the coating off the core of some lines in less than twenty hours of fishing. At present-day costs, this boils down to about a dollar an hour for line usage.

In the future, improved plastics technology and man's ingenuity will undoubtedly create lines that float higher, shoot farther, and last longer. Many of these advancements are either on the drawing boards or being experimented with already. One of these is what we call the "moment arm principle." Presently, line weight is the only criterion used for determining what line will work on a certain rod. Actually, the force that bends the rod is the product of line weight and moment arm, which is the distance from the rod tip to the line's center of gravity. Weight-forward lines are designed on this principle—and they work fine for long-distance casting. Unfortunately, for casts up to 30 feet, the range of most fishing, the principle is negated with present line tapers. For close-in fishing, you need the "moment arm" just as much as you need it for long distance, maybe even more so. Think of the difficulty required when working with long leaders and only a few feet of fly line out at the tip. This problem could be greatly alleviated by pushing the center of gravity well forward in the first 30 feet of fly line.

FLY LINES

The fly reel does not play an important role in most trout-fishing situations; its main function is line storage, so for the typical 8- to 12-inch fish, you could just as well stuff the line in your pocket. For fighting larger fish, however, and possibly for reasons of personal pride, it is much more convenient to have a reel that operates smoothly and efficiently, yet is lightweight and durable. Many reels on the market ranging from 15 to 50 dollars fit this bill.

Manual fly reels are the most popular and the most practical. More importantly, they are the most fun. One of the most exciting parts of angling is fighting a good fish on a light single-action reel. The crisp sound of quality click drag is a status symbol on any trout stream. Without the excessive mechanical drag systems, this is a real "one-to-one" situation, man against fish.

Palming for drag

Automatics are impractical for all but a few trout fishing situations. Because of their weight and bulkiness, they are completely out of "sync" when combined with modern lightweight rods. Unintentional triggering and variable tension are other features that detract from their popularity. Anglers in boats, such as guides who must pole a riverboat with one hand and fish with the other, can make the most practical use of the automatic. But generally speaking they are simply not very pleasant to use.

True fly fishermen stick to the manual, single-action reel, although a good strong, smooth brake is necessary for large saltwater gamefish. Some anglers prefer the heavy-duty variety with elaborate drag systems much like those found on spinning reels. This greatly reduces the skill required to subdue big, acrobatic fish. Just set the drag and keep cranking. These reels are quite expensive, $100 to $150, and are extremely heavy. This weight is partly due to the complicated drag system and partly to the built-in capacity for backing. A good guideline for buying a reel is to select a well-known brand. Get the lightest-weight model of the right capacity you need, and spend as much as your pocketbook will allow. Hardy, the Scientific Anglers reels, and the Orvis CFO are all excellent.

LEADERS

Tradition tells us that leaders must be constructed of hard mono in the butt section. This, of course, is based on the premise that stiffness guarantees good turnover. If we fished in a vacuum this would certainly be true, but of course, we can't: air resistance plays an important role in our whole casting system. It affects the fly, the leader, the line, and even the rod. We are constantly trying to fight drag, as evidenced by the development of "skinny" graphite rods and the effort put forth by fly casters to master the tight loop.

We struggled along with the stiff-butted leaders for many years, and after countless frustrations, finally decided there had to be a better way. High-speed photography gave us our first clue to the problem. In studying the close-up photographs of fly lines and loop formations, we noticed that the leader always had a much wider and more open shape than the line. Even when a beautifully shaped, extremely tight loop had been formed in the fly line, the leader would always roll along wide and sloppy. Sometimes the loop in the leader would be five or six times wider than the loop in the line. It was obvious that a drastic increase in air resistance developed as soon as the line straightened and the leader began to roll out. The problem then became one of figuring out a way of keeping the loop in the leader as tight as the loop in the fly line. The answer, as we saw it, had to be related to profile or stiffness. Considering that the diameter of the leader is smaller than that of the line, we worked with the stiffness factor. We eventually found that a piece of hard .020 mono is at least five times as stiff as the tip of the fly line.

What we needed, then, was a leader-butt material whose flexibility matched that of the fly line as closely as possible, yet whose mass was sufficient for good turnover. The limpest .020 round mono on the market was much too stiff, so we tried 20-pound flat mono and it worked beautifully. It naturally bends in the direction of the minor axis, which is about .012, and comes much closer to matching the flexibility of the fly line

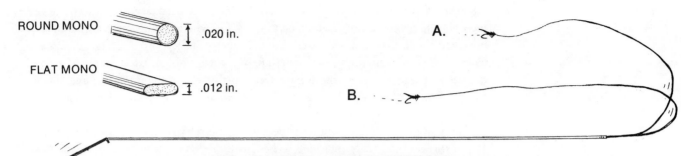

ROUND MONO ⊥ .020 in.

FLAT MONO ⊥ .012 in.

A.

B.

A. STIFF LEADER—OPENS UP LOOP
B. FLAT BUTT LEADER—KEEPS LOOP TIGHT

than anything else on the market. This more flexible material forms a much tighter loop, which has reduced air resistance and, therefore, has better turnover. There is a much smoother transfer of energy from line to leader to fly. Along with improved turnover, numerous other advantages evolved with the flat butt leader. Have you ever tried to stretch the coils and kinks out of a heavy piece of nylon, especially on a cold morning? With the flat butt, only one easy pull is necessary to make it as straight as an arrow. Line to leader connections are a dream with this ribbonlike material. Nail and needle knots are smoother, slimmer, stronger, and easier to tie.

Originally, we had to tie our own flat butts, using flat 20-pound mono for the butt section and then tapering down with regular round nylon. These turned over in fine fashion, but unfortunately had all of the normal problems of knotted leaders—poor transition, too many potential failure points, and, of course, a multitude of moss catchers. Joining flat and round mono was a bit tricky, too.

Now these problems have been solved by Berkley and Company, which manufactures a flat-butt knotless, tapered leader. The flat portion extends about two-thirds of the total length and then is smoothly contoured into a fast round taper and tippet. It turns over like a rocket and is the finest leader that we've ever used. This leader does have two slight problems, both of which can be solved with one quick operation. The tippets are a little weak and a little short, so merely snip off about 15 inches of the tip and replace it with 20 to 24 inches of your favorite tippet material.

For those who would rather tie their own leaders, use the following formula for a 4X. Use the same proportions for other sizes.

20-pound flat mono	64″
.015	6″
.013	6″
.011	6″
.009	6″
.007	20″

On some large, slow-moving rivers, such as Henry's Fork, where the big fish feed selectively along the shallow banks, we like extralong leaders. We carry spools of flat mono for this purpose. Just add as much 20-pound as necessary to make the leader meet your needs. Four or 5 feet added to the 9-foot knotless flat butt is a smooth casting combination that turns over well. For even longer leaders, up to 20 feet or more in length, we go to a slightly different set-up. We cut off about 5 feet from the butt of the flat-butt leader, leaving the front 4 feet, which includes the tip, taper, and about a foot of butt section. Then we add 12 or more feet of 15-pound flat mono. This creates a weight-forward leader that turns over like a bullet, even in a strong wind. The only drawback is that you must be able to control your loop shape with this rig. If you throw candy canes that tend to be closed or slightly tailing, the extreme flexibility of the 15-pound flat mono will cause tangling. This weight-forward concept can also be applied to regular 9- to 12-foot leaders. In addition to fighting the wind well, they facilitate curve casting, especially the positive variety. Remember, though, that these leaders are not for neophyte casters.

Along with the increased visibility of bright yellow fly lines, we have been experimenting with fluorescent leaders recently. The strict traditionalist will undoubtedly be turned off by this revolting idea, fearing that every trout within sight would swim for cover. This has not been the case. In fact, not once have we found a situation where the high-visibility leader has caused a drop-off in success, but there has been an advantage. Even with size #28 midge adults and pupas in clear, slow-moving water, the bright yellow or pink leader and tippets do not put fish down. We think that the trout is only concerned with the *fly* which, of course, represents his main diet, and ignores all of the other objects, of which there are many, that come drifting in and on the currents. Since high visibility leaders are not on the market, we dye our own with the common fluorescent dyes available from most fly-tying houses. Pink and yellow seem to show up the best.

The leader used in Whitlock's nymph head system is a good indicator that is effective not only for nymphs fished deep, but also for streamers, tiny dries, and anything fished in or just under the surface film. The indicator is a 1-inch section of bright yellow or orange fly line coating fitted over the butt of the leader. When used with the flat butt, which creates the square peg in a round hole situation, this high visibility sleeve can be positioned almost anywhere on the leader, even down to within 3 feet of the fly. Quite often, we grease the leader down to, and including, the indicator and put Qwik-sink solution on everything below that juncture, the fly included. This is a great setup for fishing nymphs, emergers, and pupas slightly subsurface.

The Qwik-sink leader is another type that has added greatly to our angling effectiveness. It truly sinks, not in a few seconds, but immediately after falling to the water. This characteristic, made possible by a unique manufacturing process, is invaluable any time you want to go wet. We like it particularly for fishing streamers near undercut banks and pocket water. To be effective in such situations the fly must sink immediately, otherwise, by the time the streamer is working properly, it will have drifted out of the strike zone. Any false casting at all dries the feathered wings of a streamer so that it will not float during the first part of the drift. Weighted flies partially solve the sinking problem but are not as pleasant to cast and, quite often, simply are not as effective as the unweighted type. The Qwik-sink leader is a much better solution; it sinks so quickly that the fly is immediately pulled under. Remember, though, that the instant sink mechanism begins to fade after a few hours. We carry lots of Qwik-sinks, and change after every three or four hours.

The Qwik-sink leader is also valuable when fishing emergers and pupas in the top layers of current. We find that greasing the butt section, normally the first 4 or 5 feet, allows just the right depth and angle of drift for much of our emerger fishing. For midge pupas, we will sometimes apply floatant to within a few inches of the fly. Another technique is to apply grease only at the tip end and on the fly. After a partial or complete float, usually with a nymph, bucktail, or streamer and, on occasion, with a dry fly, a stripping motion will make the artificial follow the path of the sunken butt section. This can be deadly during certain spinner falls.

Many anglers argue that the tippet section of a dry-fly leader should sink because they feel a floating tippet creates a shadow or disturbance that frightens the fish. We believe that it makes no difference to the fish whether the leader is above, in, or below the surface film; once in the window, it all looks the same. But whether it does or not doesn't really matter because the trout is looking for the fly, not the leader. For dries, we want a floating leader; for wets, we prefer a sinker.

Leaders for use with sinking and sink-tip lines should be very short. Three to 5 feet is usually plenty. Long leaders tend to buoy up the fly and defeat the purpose of the sinking line. We have not encountered any increase in selectivity with the short leader. Normally, with this type of rig, you are using large flies anyway. A typical 5-foot salmon or steelhead leader for use on sinking lines would be:

30" of 20-pound
18" of 15-pound
12" of 12-pound

Knots are important to the fly fisherman but not to the extent that we must learn them by the dozen. Only two knots are required for most fly-fishing situations—a knot for tying on the fly and a knot for joining monofilament. Most anglers use the clinch or some version of the clinch, which is all right, but we prefer a version of the turle knot. The knot itself is a turle but it is pulled up tight on the *front* of the eye rather than *behind* it. We like this knot for several reasons. It is much smaller than a clinch, so on size #20s and down it is less bulky. It is easier to tie, especially at dusk and after dark. Also, it has excellent knot strength.

FLAT MONO NAIL KNOT

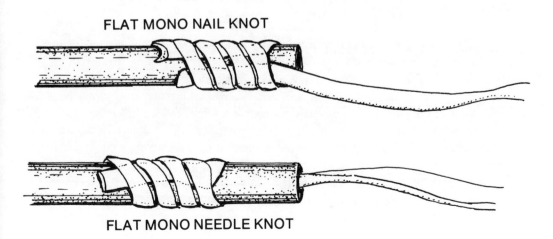

FLAT MONO NEEDLE KNOT

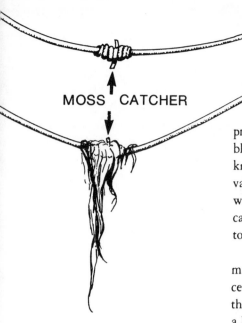

MOSS CATCHER

The blood knot is the standard connection for joining monofilament but the improved surgeon's knot may be more practical. About the only real advantage of the blood knot is that you can leave both pieces of mono attached to their spool while the knot is being tied. With the improved surgeon's, one must be precut. A distinct disadvantage of the blood knot is that both strands must be quite similar in diameter, within two or three thousandths of each other. Variances of ten thousandths or more can be joined with the improved surgeon's knot. In an emergency, it can even be used to connect the leader to the fly line.

The Whitlock epoxy knot makes a tremendous line-to-leader connection. It has one major advantage over any other method of attachment: the leader protrudes from the center of the fly line. The hinging effect is minimal and the entire connection slides through the guides in an almost undetectable fashion. The only drawback is that it is a little more difficult to assemble.

The needle knot has the advantage of being centered but is a bit more time-consuming to tie than the nail knot. All three make excellent line-to-leader connections, so pick the one you feel is most suited to your needs and ability.

A point to remember when tightening knots: always put saliva on the knot and tighten *slowly*. A quick pull on a dry knot creates a sudden frictional buildup and the resulting heat and pressure can cause instant failure. Similarly, when straightening leaders, or any monofilament, build up your hand pressure *slowly*, hold for a few seconds, and then *slowly* reduce the pressure.

The Whitlock epoxy connection

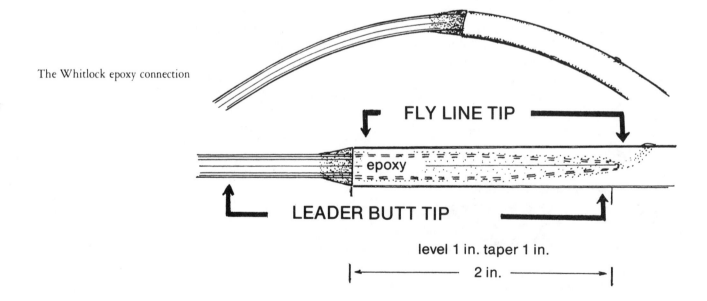

FLY LINE TIP

epoxy

LEADER BUTT TIP

level 1 in. taper 1 in.

|← 2 in. →|

CONTENTS OF YOUR VEST

A properly stocked vest is a must for the serious angler. Once you're out on the stream you want to have everything you need at your fingertips. Here are our suggestions:

1) Fly boxes—compartment and foam bottom type
2) Goldfish net for collecting specimens
3) Stomach pump
4) Leaders—flat butt and Qwik-sink
5) Tippets—regular and Qwik-sink
6) Line cleaner
7) Albolene and Silicone spray floatant
8) Zingers with clipper, tweezers, hemostat, magnifier, millimeter gage, hone, scissors
9) Twist-ons for weighting flies
10) Amadun-drying flies
11) Hatpin—for picking out eyes
12) Rain gear
13) Toilet paper
14) Light for night fishing
15) Bug repellent
16) First-aid kit and matches
17) Mini lead heads

A jeweler's loupe to wear on your glasses can be a great help for tying on small flies and examining naturals.

CHAPTER 14

MODERN REGULATIONS FOR TODAY'S TROUT STREAMS

OUR TROUT STREAMS are rapidly approaching a point where anglers and fisheries management people must make some tough decisions. Many of our blue-ribbon waters have long since reached this point. The question we must face is: are we going to continue to manage our best waters for the greatest harvest for the greatest number of people, or will we try to produce the best fishing experience in a natural setting for wild trout?

These last words are almost a quote from the words of Jack Anderson, the supervisor of Yellowstone National Park, from a speech he gave at the 1973 Federation of Fly Fishermen Conclave in Sun Valley, Idaho. If we chose the greatest harvest for the greatest number of people we would be able to kill a small number of small trout for a short while longer. These, of course, we could take home and eat or give away to friends to prove what great anglers we are, or even opt to use their carcasses for fertilizing our gardens.

But we have another choice. We may decide to allow our streams to become naturally filled with 2- to 4-pound trout. We may decide that we again wish to see large trout surface feeding to small insects during long periods of the day. Of course, to achieve this goal we must be prepared to give up something in return. We must be prepared to relinquish the killing—and we must develop strict regulations and have them enforced fearlessly.

174

The federal managers of Yellowstone Park have made their decision; it is for the greatest fishing experience, not the greatest harvest. The regulations imposed vary from "fly fishing only" and "no-kill," to fly fishing with a limit of only one or two small trout. You may keep a 12-incher but not a 16-incher. Though this may sound weird, many studies prove the usefulness of these regulations.

Such studies are published yearly by the federal government and are available to the public. They have proved that fly fishing is a much more successful method of catching trout than either bait or lure fishing. Also, when you set a high inch limit on a river, you get a large decrease in the number of big fish, and a decrease in the average length of mature male and female fish. But a river must have large trout for predation on rough species and for full utilization of spawning areas, not to mention good fishing.

In 1870, a writer described the size of trout in Yellowstone Lake as "enormous and averaging two to four pounds." The density was described as incredible. Fisheries biologists estimated the catch back then as 52 trout per angler hour as opposed to less than .08 trout per angler hour today. By 1920, large trout were available only in the most remote regions. Trout in Yellowstone Lake normally live eight years and don't spawn until the age of three. In the last thirty-seven years, three age groups have been extirpated as viable portions of the spawning populations. Eight-year-olds were gone in 1938, seven-year-olds were gone by 1956, and six-year-olds extinct by 1966. It is estimated that with the 1972 regulations, five-year-old fish will be gone between 1975 and 1980, and are rare now. In 1870, 90 percent of the fish caught by anglers were five years or older. In the past five years, only 10 percent of the fish caught were five-year-olds. When no large fish are present the exotic species, such as suckers, increase their population greatly.

It was found that the larger the trout the earlier they start their spawning runs, and *the farther up the tributaries they run.* So *with no six-, seven-, or eight-year-old fish present, approximately one-half of the spawning area available was not being used.* The fish participating were simply too small to reach these areas.

In 1972, the best part of the main streams of the Au Sable (3½ miles) was stocked in the fall. Only two fish 18 inches or over were counted. Twenty years ago we know there were 18-inch fish in every pool.

Some people will say that large trout do not hit flies well, so we might be defeating our purpose when we restore a river to its wild state. Not so. Large fish *are* fish eaters, but when you have a large population of large trout they quickly reduce the number of baitfish and all but the wariest of the small trout population. It then becomes increasingly difficult for them to feed easily on the smaller fish because there are very few left. Now the fish *must* feed on flies because there is nothing else available. *Of course, if a good fertile trout stream has only two 18-inch browns in 3½ miles of river, why in the world should they bother with a fly hatch?* In such conditions there are plenty of small trout to eat, and in such numbers that it takes very little effort to find a meal. It would be *unreasonable* to expect such fish to feed well on insect hatches.

In rivers where there are large populations of big trout, and there are a few left here and there, *large fish do rise well to the fly.* Seldom, if ever, is a 6- or 7-incher seen on some of the western spring creeks.

The biologists on the Au Sable finally decided that what fishermen had been complaining about for years was true. The river was being overharvested. We say that it is about time we eliminated the word harvest from our sport. We are not pig farmers trying to earn an income, we are fly fishermen—and, hopefully, sportsmen. So let's have good sport, not good killing. After all, it's the great advantage we have over hunting; we need not kill our quarry to enjoy our sport. In fact, the sport can only be increased over the years *if* we refrain from killing. Fortunately, the managers of Yellowstone recognized the problem in time, and now we have good laws in effect which are improving the lakes and streams of this most beautiful area now!

It often appears that, as individuals, it is a monumental if not hopeless task to convince local fisheries managers to impose decent regulations for our state waters. They try to please everyone and that is impossible. Many people are just too greedy to accept what is needed. Only through enlightened organizations, such as Trout Unlimited and The Federation of Fly Fishermen, can we obtain a loud enough voice to be heard. It behoves us all to join these and similar organizations and give them our full support.

In another vein, it seems ridiculous that 40 million fishermen, not just fly fishers but all fishermen, have no political clout what-so-ever. If we could band together into a lobbying organization, no representative, senator, or president would dare ignore us. Trout Unlimited and the Federation plus similar groups, as helpful as they are, cannot legally spend money to lobby for clean water and other such antipollution activities. However, a new group has been organized for the express purpose of joining together *all* fishermen, from the dry fly purist to the cane pole catfisherman. It is to be strictly a lobbying group, and is designed to give us a say in all matters affecting our sport. If it's successful, no legislator would dare tell us that some factory, dumping acid into a fishing stream, is more important than we are. Once he knows all fishermen in his area will be informed of his stand, and that they may vote against him at the polls, he would be more sympathetic to our cause. The organization is The American League of Anglers with headquarters at 810 18th Street N.W., Washington, D.C. 20006. Write them. Join them. Politicians are interested in votes, and if enough of us join they will become seriously interested in us—and in our precious rivers.

CHAPTER 15

STREAM COURTESY

THE WHINE OF THE BULLET, as it sped by our ears, startled and frightened us. It had been a soft fall morning and the big Muskegon River was low, clear, and filled with steelhead, king, and silver salmon. The stillness of the morning was broken by the crashing of pistol shots. Some fishermen camped about four hundred yards upstream were calmly tossing beer cans in the flow and target shooting at them. Soon a nice string of silver cans was floating by us. The vandal sportsmen seemed to have plenty of ammunition, for the shooting continued for fully three-quarters of an hour. Originally they had been aiming upstream away from us, but now they were shooting toward our position, and a few of the slugs were ricocheting from the surface and coming very close indeed. After the near miss, we finally yelled rather impolitely for them to stop. Luckily for us they did, so we are still around to write this chapter.

Now, we realize that no chapter on stream etiquette will ever stop idiots like these from desecrating beautiful trout streams, or from creating dangerous situations. People who do the type of thing we just described may be unteachable, and we will probably always have to put up with a certain amount of plain stupidity.

In the golden days of fly fishing, when our rivers were uncrowded and filled with 14-inch brookies and 18-inch browns, the few fishermen one did encounter on the streams were almost always a courteous group of knowledgeable people, often steeped in the tradition of the English chalk streams. They knew a wet-fly fisher working downstream must make way when approaching the more aristocratic dry-fly fisher, who always worked upstream. And they really seemed to follow these rules.

In those golden days of underpopulation it was much easier to be courteous. It was not at all difficult to elude the three or four anglers one met in a day's outing. Dodging our fellow sportsmen these days, however, is an ever-continuing, and often insurmountable problem.

Fly fishing for trout is, by its very nature, an introspective sport; it demands solitude. That is not to say that it does not produce great friendships and comrades, because it does. But when one is stalking a free-rising "good-un" with a perfect cast and a lovely float, the last thing anyone needs is some clownish dolt splashing up to you and booming, "How's the fishing?" A true answer would be, "Great until you ruined it."

Unlike those men shooting at cans, many neophyte fly fishermen are discourteous out of ignorance and inexperience, rather than pure maliciousness. In these times, when even our isolated western streams are becoming very crowded, and the fly fishing methods are much more varied, stream etiquette is not as clear-cut as it once was. Dry-fly men, more often than not, fish downstream rather than following the ancients blindly. Streamer fishermen, nymphers, and wet fly anglers often are found facing upstream, against the current, in defiance of all the old traditions. Now, who gets out of the way of whom?

The old rules then, must be rewritten in light of modern conditions. If, in fact, the enjoyment of fly fishing demands at least a certain amount of solitude, the prime rule must be: Conduct yourself so as to disturb your fellow angler as little as the prevailing conditions allow. Now these prevailing conditions will vary considerably over a season. There is no way anyone will find much solitude on most of our good trout streams on opening day. You will probably have to insert yourself between two other anglers, who are already much too close together. On most rivers, that will be the only way possible to get into the water at all during the early season. During the late season, say after late June or early July, many of our great rivers are almost deserted, so there is not much of a problem finding a good pool, or even long stretches of water undisturbed.

If you are wading, and overtake a slower angler fishing in the same direction, get out of the water and walk around him. Go as far past him as reasonably possible (around a bend so as to be out of sight would be ideal) before returning to the stream. Above all, do not wade right up and start a conversation; you may disturb a pod of rising trout, and no one will appreciate such conduct.

When meeting another fisherman approaching from an opposite direction, ease around the edge of the stream, or get out if possible, as you pass. It is perfectly all right to have a pleasant conversation, as long as you do not disturb any fish within his casting range. These rules are nothing more than common sense and common courtesy, but it is truly amazing how many anglers just do not stop and think before barging in.

Nowadays, more people are floating our rivers and streams in canoes and boats. This type of fly fishing requires a slightly different set of rules. The floater should be able to handle his canoe or boat properly, and have it under control at all times.

When approaching a wading angler, he should pass in back of that angler so as not to disturb the water he is working. The most discourteous act a floater can perform is to come between a wader and the fish he is casting to, and then cast out to that very same fish. It is especially annoying when the intruder actually takes the fish you have quietly stalked and are working on.

This actually happens daily on some of the rivers we fish. The people who perpetrate these maddening acts are mostly perfectly nice people when away from the stream. It seems that in their lust for catching fish, they leave their brains at home.

You will undoubtedly encounter many situations for which there may be no specific rule, but it all boils down to this: common courtesy and common sense in all situations, and treat the other fellow's water with the respect it deserves.

A word, also, about respecting landowners' property. If we are to have any public water left in this country, with the exception of public fishing sites, we must treat the streams we fish as we would treat our own property. Many people don't, and this creates problems for those of us who do. Many of us from the Midwest and Far West would love to travel to the eastern United States on a pilgrimage to fish those storied, half-legendary streams of Gordon and LaBranche. We'd love to pay homage to the rivers about which Flick and Schwiebert and many others have written so eloquently. But much of the best water is now private and posted. Litterbugs, fish hogs, vandals, and poachers reduced the banks to junkyards, and decimated the trout population to the point where either the public had to be excluded or the streams would not be worth fishing. Some of these rivers have returned to their old greatness. But the average angler will never tread the banks unless he has an "in."

Many western waters are owned by ranchers who love their land. They simply will not, and need not, tolerate the senseless acts that resulted in the closing of our eastern streams. Twenty years ago, you had only to ask to fish anywhere in the West you wished to fish. Today, more and more landowners are refusing permission to all but their friends. A few so-called anglers scaring cattle, leaving gates open, and littering these waters will ruin it for us all.

It is probably inevitable that someday all but a small amount of public water will be posted, and this "free" country will become similar to England and the rest of Europe; there, of course, the elite few control the fishing rights, and one must join a club or pay a day ticket, even for the chance to fish a reservoir.

Fishing waters that run through other people's land is a privilege. It is not, and probably never should have been considered a "right," in which anyone who bought a fishing license could indulge. Someday private water will almost certainly become the rule. But if we can conduct ourselves like gentlemen, perhaps we may hold off the darkness for just a little longer.

INDEX

Page numbers in italics indicate illustrations.